The New Idea Cookbook

by

Margaret Fulton

Printed in Japan by Dai Nippon Printing Co. Ltd.
Published and distributed by W. J. Morgans,
Southdown Press, 32 Walsh Street, Melbourne, Victoria, 3000.
*Recommended and maximum price only.
ISBN 0 908429 28 2

Introduction

Regular readers of my pages in New Idea will know that that I love food — every aspect of it.

For me, shopping for food is an adventure, the greengrocer's a veritable Aladdin's cave: bright red and green peppers piled high; rosy red tomatoes; golden oranges and sunny lemons; luscious berries, perfumed peaches and shiny red cherries; plump green peas, crisp beans and leafy lettuce. And it all changes with the seasons, adding to the fascination.

The fish markets are a joy, with fish of silver, gold and ruby gleaming on their beds of ice, and crabs, crays, prawns, mussels and oysters all fresh and smelling of the sea.

My local butcher is an ally — he provides meat the quality I want, cut the way I want it. Like the other local shopkeepers, we know each other and always have time for a chat. It's all part of the world of food.

Fresh, natural ingredients are only a beginning to good food. It helps if you are a good cook — some are born but most of us get that way with practice. A sound, reliable recipe is an enormous help, and that's where I come in. A great part of my life has been spent in the kitchen, where, with my family of dedicated cooks, we continually test and try new recipes for my weekly pages. Let me tell you it is fascinating and very rewarding — we get to taste so many great dishes.

A recent astrology article in New Idea pronounced: "The Libran is an excellent host and enjoys entertaining. You are a great socialiser and have many friends. Meals for you are times for social gatherings." How true! I know, for I am a Libran! Conversation, bright, spirited even, seems to go with food. Whether with your family or friends, what better way to display your skills than around a friendly table.

If you enjoy my weekly pages in New Idea, I hope you will like these selections — recipes to take you happily through the seasons, month by month.

MARGARET FULTON

Contents

January

February

March

April

May

June

July

August

September

October

November

December

January

Salad days

During the warm days of a relaxed Australian summer, nothing tempts the appetite like a beautiful salad. And preparing salads is almost as satisfying as eating them. Our wonderful fresh vegetables and fruits give so much scope for creating new combinations, and nothing could be healthier. Perhaps we should take a cue from the Americans, and serve a salad every day! I like the idea of a salad first course, for instance — so good for weight-watchers, because it takes the edge off the appetite. I also serve side salads frequently, in place of hot vegetables. They're a natural with grills, but good also with roasts, quick saute dishes, chicken, fish, kebabs, meat balls, pasta and pies. Side salads can be eaten from individual bowls or plates or enjoyed the French way, served straight on to the dinner plate, where they help to mop up any delicious juices or gravy. Main course salads are just naturally becoming more and more popular as we consider our health and our budget. And how lucky we are to have a climate which lets us enjoy them all year round.

Salad ingredients

A salad is built from a selection of the following:

- Green-leafed vegetables. Choose tender mignonette lettuce, brown-leafed or green; crisp iceberg lettuce; tart curly endive; glossy young spinach leaves; burgundy-colored radicchio; delicate belgian endive; watercress; crisp and curly savoy cabbage; cos (romaine) lettuce; celery leaves; nasturtium leaves; and mustard, twin of cress.
- Meats, poultry and fish. These add substance and are the base on which to build the 'meal-in-itself' salad.
- Tomatoes. Indispensable for their color and sweet-acid flavor.
- Crisp-textured vegetables. These include cauliflower florets; celery; fennel; green, red and yellow peppers; green beans (parboiled and refreshed under cold water); cucumber; radishes; and young zucchini.
- Other vegetables. Select artichoke hearts, asparagus, avocado or sweetcorn.
- Potatoes, rice, pasta or croutons rubbed with garlic. They provide a nice contrast to the crispness of vegetables and add substance to a salad.
- Eggs and cheese. They add richness and round out a salad.
- Onions, shallots, chives and garlic. Use for robustness.
- Olives and capers add piquancy.
- Lightly toasted nuts and seeds give texture and flavor.
- Fruits — especially tropical and citrus fruits. These combine well with poultry, ham and crustacea.
- Salad dressing. Most salads can be dressed with a simple french dressing, but the choice of the right dressing will make that subtle difference. Try wine vinegars flavored with herbs or shallots and combine them with different flavored oils; fruity olive oil, safflower or peanut oil for lighter dressings, and the full flavored walnut oil — excellent with mushrooms and red meats.

- *Dressing recipes on pages 12-13.*

Guacamole

1 large ripe avocado
1-2 tablespoons lemon juice
1 small tomato, peeled, seeded and finely chopped
2 tablespoons finely chopped green shallots
1 clove garlic, crushed
½ teaspoon ground cumin
Salt and freshly ground pepper
Dash Tabasco

Peel and stone the avocado, mash with 1 tablespoon lemon juice and stir in remaining ingredients. Taste and add more lemon juice if you wish. Serve over lettuce leaves or as a garnish for tacos, steak or poached chicken; or as a dip with corn chips.

Right: The authentic Caesar Salad is a delectable combination of flavors and textures.

Chef's salad

The ham, tongue, chicken and cheese for this salad are cut into small fingers, so when shopping ask for slices about 1.2cm thick.

1 thick slice cooked ham
3 thick slices cooked smoked tongue
1 chicken breast, cooked
125g gruyere or emmenthal cheese
4 tomatoes
125g small mushrooms
3 hard-boiled eggs
1 red pepper
1 tablespoon finely chopped parsley
Combinations of lettuce or other salad greens

DRESSING
1 tablespoon white wine vinegar
3 tablespoons olive oil
1 teaspoon chili sauce
¼ small onion, finely sliced
½ teaspoon french mustard
Salt and freshly ground black pepper

Slice ham, tongue and chicken into strips. Cut cheese into matchstick pieces. Cut tomatoes into quarters and slice mushrooms. Arrange all these ingredients in a salad bowl on a bed of lettuce. Toss lightly in dressing and garnish with quartered hard-boiled eggs, strips of red pepper and finely chopped parsley. Serves 4.

Combine dressing ingredients in a jar and shake well before using.

Onion and melon salad

1kg honey dew or watermelon cut into wedges
1 tablespoon chopped mint
1 red salad onion, thinly sliced
3 tablespoons lemon vinaigrette

Remove the seeds from the melon and discard. Slice the melon wedges diagonally. Place in a bowl and sprinkle with the mint.

Mix the onion and dressing together in another bowl and leave for 1 hour, stirring occasionally.

Mix in the melon and transfer to a serving bowl. Serves 4 to 6.

Celery and mushroom salad

Good as a first course salad or as part of a salad meal.

6 tender celery stalks, trimmed and sliced diagonally
250g mushrooms, finely sliced
1 large canned pimiento, drained and sliced
2 green shallots, sliced
2 tablespoons chopped parsley
¼ cup red wine vinegar
2 tablespoons dijon mustard
¼ cup olive oil
¼ cup vegetable oil
Juice 1 lemon
Salt and freshly ground black pepper
Chopped parsley to finish
1-2 button mushrooms, sliced

Combine celery and mushrooms in a salad bowl, cover and chill. Place pimiento in blender or food processor, add shallots, parsley, vinegar and mustard, and puree; or place in a small bowl and pound with a pestle or the end of a rolling pin. Gradually add olive and vegetable oils, then mix in lemon juice, salt and pepper. Pour over celery and mushrooms, toss well. Cover and chill for 2 hours. Serve sprinkled with chopped parsley and freshly sliced mushrooms. Serves 4-6.

Orange, avocado and prawn salad

This makes a luxury lunch or main course for a dinner party.

½ cup lemon vinaigrette
2 avocados, peeled, stoned and sliced lengthwise
2 large oranges
500g cooked prawns, shelled and deveined
4 stalks celery, chopped
1 tablespoon snipped chives
2 cos or 1 iceberg lettuce
8-10 walnut halves

top with the avocado cut in slices, the bacon which has been grilled and cut into small dice, the finely chopped chili, chicken breasts, sliced radish and pepper. Spoon over anchovy dressing.

Italian salad

2 cups pasta shells
250g cooked ham, cut thick and cubed
6-8 black olives, halved and stoned
1 cup cooked green peas
2 ribs celery, finely sliced
½ cup thick mayonnaise
2 teaspoons dijon mustard
2 tablespoons snipped chives or italian parsley

Cook pasta shells in boiling salted water for about 10 minutes or until 'al dente' — just tender. Drain and refresh under cold running water. Mix ham with olives, green peas, celery and pasta. Add mayonnaise to mustard and stir enough into salad to bind. Chill, covered, for 30 minutes, turn into serving dish, top with snipped chives or parsley. Serves 8.

Rice and pine nut salad

1 cup long grain rice
2 cups water
½ teaspoon salt
15g butter
6 radishes, sliced
8 canned water chestnuts, sliced (optional)
½ red or green pepper, chopped
¼ cup chopped parsley
½ cup pine nuts, toasted
3 hard-boiled eggs, quartered
2 small tomatoes, quartered
1 lettuce, washed and leaves crisped
DRESSING
3 tablespoons lime juice
3 tablespoons olive oil

Thoroughly wash long grain rice. In a heavy saucepan combine water, salt and butter and bring to the boil, gradually stir in the rice. Simmer the rice, covered, about 20 minutes or until tender and water has evaporated. Fluff the rice up with a fork, transfer to a bowl breaking it up lightly as it cools. Stir in the radish, water chestnuts, pepper, parsley and pine nuts.

In a bowl, combine the lime juice and salt to taste, add the olive oil in a stream, whisking until the mixture thickens slightly. Toss the rice mixture with the dressing.

Line a salad bowl with lettuce leaves and transfer rice mixture to the bowl, decorate with egg and tomato quarters. Serves 4.

Pour half vinaigrette over sliced avocados.

Peel oranges, removing outside membrane, and cut between membranes to remove skinless segments.

Combine prawns, oranges, celery and chives. Line a large bowl with lettuce leaves. Place prawn mixture in centre and arrange avocado slices and walnut halves over it. At the table, pour remaining dressing over salad and toss lightly to combine. Serves 4-6.

Eggplant salad

A super accompaniment for grills or barbecued food. Serve also as a first course with lightly grilled flat pita breads to use as scoops.

1 eggplant
Salt and pepper
3 tablespoons olive oil
1 onion, chopped
2 cloves garlic, finely chopped
3 tomatoes, skinned, seeded and chopped
2 tablespoons chopped parsley
1 tablespoon lemon juice
Few lettuce leaves

Cut the eggplant into cubes. Place in a colander, sprinkle with salt and leave for 30 minutes. Rinse and dry with kitchen paper.

Above left: The Chef's Salad is hearty enough to be a meal in itself.
Above: Pasta and olives enhance an Italian Salad.

Heat the oil in a frying pan, add the onion and eggplant and fry for 8-10 minutes, stirring occasionally, until golden. Add the garlic and tomatoes and fry for 2 to 3 minutes.

Leave to cool, then mix with the parsley, lemon juice, and pepper to taste. Arrange the lettuce leaves in a serving dish and spoon the salad into the centre. Serves 4.

Mexican salad

Young nasturtium leaves give a delicious piquant flavor.

½ head of savoy cabbage
1 bunch watercress washed and broken into sprigs
6-8 young nasturtium leaves or mustard and cress
2 avocados
4 rashers lean bacon
1 chili
3 chicken fillets (half breasts), poached and sliced
6 small radishes
1 red pepper
Anchovy dressing

Slice the cabbage very finely. Combine in a large bowl with the watercress and nasturtium leaves;

Saffron rice salad

This lovely golden Spanish salad, colored and flavored with the beautiful saffron so prized in Spain, is a special-occasion salad. Vary it by using different fresh or canned seafoods.

1½ cups long grain rice
1 teaspoon salt
1 sachet or good pinch saffron
500g cooked prawns, shelled and deveined
1 x 105g can mussels, drained
½ cup stuffed olives, halved
½ cup black olives, stoned
1 red or green pepper, chopped
Salt and freshly ground pepper
Lettuce
2 canned red pimientos cut into strips
2 tablespoons chopped parsley
½ cup lemon vinaigrette

Wash rice well in several lots of water. Bring 3 cups water to the boil in a heavy saucepan with 1 teaspoon salt, dribble in the rice, then saffron, stir once it has come to the boil, cover, reduce heat and cook over low heat 10-15 minutes. Remove from heat and fork up lightly. Allow to cool slightly.

Transfer to a large bowl. Fold into the rice the prawns, mussels, olives and chopped pepper. Season to taste with salt and pepper.

Lightly toss in the dressing while the rice is still warm. Cover and chill. Wash lettuce leaves and use them to line a large bowl, lightly pile salad into bowl and decorate with pimiento strips, top with parsley. Serves 6.

Caesar salad

Here is the recipe for the authentic Caesar Salad.

1 cos lettuce (sometimes called romaine)
4 anchovies
1 crushed clove garlic
8 slices french bread
1 egg
Freshly ground pepper and salt
Juice of 1 lemon
3 tablespoons olive oil
1 teaspoon worcestershire sauce
3 tablespoons grated parmesan cheese

Separate lettuce leaves, wash carefully and dry. Crisp in refrigerator. Mash anchovies and garlic then spread on french bread. (These are now called croutes.) Bake in a slow oven 150C (300F) until crisp and dry. Allow to cool. Place egg gently into boiling water for 50 seconds only.

Arrange lettuce in a large bowl, season with salt and pepper, add coddled egg. Combine lemon juice, oil and worcestershire sauce in a small bowl then beat with a fork. Add to salad with cheese and croutes.

Roll leaves in dressing until each leaf is glistening with dressing. Be gentle — do not bruise the leaves. Serve at once. Serves 2 as a meal, 4 as a side salad or first course.

American potato salad

The trick is to put the still-warm potatoes into the sharp dressing so the potatoes absorb the flavor.

6-8 smallish red potatoes
4 tablespoons oil
2 tablespoons vinegar
1 tablespoon chopped onion
2 tablespoons chopped parsley
Salt and freshly ground pepper
3 hard-boiled eggs, peeled and sliced
2 celery stalks, sliced
2 dill pickles, sliced
1 tablespoon capers
2 teaspoons horseradish
½ cup mayonnaise or sour cream
2 tablespoons snipped chives or chopped parsley

Cook potatoes in their skins in boiling salted water until just tender. Peel if liked and while still warm cut into thick slices or quarters. Combine oil, vinegar, chopped onion, parsley, salt and pepper in a bowl, whisking to thicken the dressing, add warm potatoes and toss lightly.

Allow to stand until ready to finish and serve salad.

Add boiled egg slices, celery, dill pickles, capers, mix horseradish with mayonnaise or sour cream and fold through the salad. Transfer to salad bowl and top with snipped chives or parsley. Serves 6.

Egg and herring salad

2 pickled herring fillets, soaked several hours in milk
4 hard-boiled eggs, finely chopped
250g ham, diced
2 beetroot, cooked, peeled and diced
2 large potatoes, cooked, peeled and diced
1 apple, peeled, cored and diced
1 sour pickle, finely chopped
Sour cream dressing
Extra hard-boiled eggs for garnish

Drain herring and cut into bite-sized pieces. Just before serving, gently combine herring, eggs, ham, beetroot, potatoes, apple, pickle and sour cream dressing. Place in a serving dish. Garnish with quartered hard-boiled eggs. Serves 4 to 6.

Quick mayonnaise

The electric blender and food processor make short work of mayonnaise.

1 egg
½ teaspoon salt
½ teaspoon pepper
½ teaspoon mustard powder
2 teaspoons wine vinegar
1 cup olive oil

Place the egg, seasonings and vinegar in electric blender or food processor and blend on medium speed for a few seconds. Still on medium speed, add the oil drop by drop to begin with, through the lid, then in a thin stream as the mixture thickens.

Store in an airtight container in the refrigerator for up to 10 days.

TRADITIONAL MAYONNAISE: Replace the 1 egg with 2 egg yolks. Beat the egg yolks and seasonings together in a bowl. Add the oil drop by drop, beating continually. As the mixture thickens, add the oil in a steady stream. Add the vinegar and mix thoroughly.

Vinaigrette

¾ cup olive oil
4 tablespoons cider vinegar
1 teaspoon clear honey (optional)
1 clove garlic, crushed
2 tablespoons chopped mixed herbs (mint, parsley, chives, thyme)
Salt and pepper

Put all the ingredients in a screw-topped jar, adding salt and pepper to taste. Shake well to blend before using. Makes 1 cup.

LEMON OR LIME VINAIGRETTE: Use 3 tablespoons fresh lemon or lime juice in place of the cider vinegar.

MUSTARD VINAIGRETTE: Combine 1 teaspoon french mustard, 3 tablespoons oil, 1 tablespoon vinegar, 1 tablespoon chopped parsley in screwtop jar, shake until thick and creamy.

Anchovy dressing

2 anchovies
Milk
1 tablespoon wine vinegar
3 tablespoons olive oil
1 clove garlic, crushed
Finely chopped oregano
Freshly ground pepper

Soak anchovies in milk for 10 minutes. Drain and pat dry. Mash them to a paste and blend in the wine vinegar and oil. Add the garlic and oregano and season with pepper only. Serves 4 to 6.

Bacon dressing

Very good on bitter or robust greens, such as spinach, curly endive or witloof.

3 tablespoons bacon fat
1 tablespoon plain flour
2 teaspoons grated onion
½ teaspoon freshly ground pepper
¼ teaspoon sugar
2 teaspoons prepared mustard
1 tablespoon vinegar
1 cup water
Salt

Melt the bacon fat in a frypan, slowly stir in the flour and onion and cook, stirring constantly, for 2 minutes. Add the pepper, sugar, mustard, and vinegar. Blend and stir, then slowly add 1 cup water. Continue to stir and cook over medium heat until thickened. Add salt to taste. Can be served hot or cold.

Sour cream dressing

For fruit salads and vegetable salads.

1 cup light sour cream
2 tablespoons vinegar
2 teaspoons sugar (for fruit salad), or 1 teaspoon sugar (for vegetable salad)
1 teaspoon dry mustard
1/8 teaspoon cayenne pepper
Salt to taste

Combine all ingredients in a bowl and whisk until well blended.

Yogurt dressing

1 cup plain yogurt
2 tablespoons white vinegar
1½ tablespoons lemon juice
2 tablespoons chives, finely chopped
2 tablespoons parsley, finely chopped
Freshly ground pepper
Salt to taste

Combine all ingredients in a bowl and blend until well mixed. Refrigerate and use as needed. Good with coleslaw, rice salads and shredded vegetables.
HONEY YOGURT DRESSING: Add 1 tablespoon honey and omit the chives and parsley.
YOGURT, GARLIC AND BLUE CHEESE DRESSING: Add 3 tablespoons crumbled blue cheese and 1 clove garlic, crushed.
YOGURT AND MAYONNAISE DRESSING: Add up to 1 cup mayonnaise and mix well.

Above: Vary the ingredients of Saffron Rice Salad to suit your taste and budget.

● *For more salad and dressing recipes, see index.*

Barbecue time

A barbecue always takes on the air of an outdoor party, with great-tasting food and all those great smells, enjoyed in a relaxed, happy atmosphere. Those of us who work indoors look forward to as much time spent out-of-doors as possible. Those who spend a lot of time in the kitchen particularly look forward to someone else doing the cooking. Eight out of every 10 men like to don the apron and develop their skills at cooking a 'mean' chop. There are lots of lovely ways to make a barbecue special. Keep the menu simple making full use of the cooking surface, and prepare additional foods in the comfort of your kitchen — an interesting assortment of salads and a lovely cake.

Building a fire

When using charcoal, make sure there is enough to last for the entire cooking process. More added during cooking causes smoke and flames. Judging the amount of fuel comes with experience, but a 375g pack of charcoal briquettes is usually sufficient for a meal for four.

The charcoal should be reduced to glowing coals with just a brush of white ash on top before any cooking is started. This will take up to one hour or more for a deep bed of coals, so get the fire going well before the meal starts. Wood takes longer to reduce to live coals.

Cooking know-how

All meats for grilling should be at room temperature. Sausages are better if first blanched (put into cold water and brought slowly to boiling point, simmered a few minutes then drained) before cooking on the barbecue. They will not split or spit and do not require pricking. All grill racks or rods should be greased with fat or oil to prevent food from sticking. Use a sturdy brush to grease frequently.

Grease aluminium foil well before wrapping food to cook over the fire.

Do not rush the cooking. Keep meats well above fire. They cook better and taste more delicious if they are cooked slowly and not charred by intense heat or a direct fire.

Marinades

Explore the use of marinades. These aromatic mixtures of oil, wine or vinegar, herbs and vegetables do wonders for barbecued foods and grills. They tenderise the meat as they penetrate. After soaking the meat, the marinade liquid is often used to brush over the grilling food.

RED WINE MARINADE: Combine 1 cup red wine, 1 sliced onion, 1 teaspoon peppercorns, 1 bay leaf, 4 sprigs parsley, ½ teaspoon dried thyme and 4 tablespoons oil. Marinate steak or lamb in this mixture for several hours or overnight. Sufficient for 1-1½kg steak.

WHITE WINE MARINADE: Use the same recipe replacing red wine with white wine. Marinate chicken or lamb several hours.

MINTED WINE MARINADE: A particularly good marinade for lamb. Follow the recipe for white wine marinade and add 1 tablespoon honey and 1 teaspoon chopped mint.

Barbecued meat

LAMB CHOPS: Rub 2.5cm-thick loin or chump chops with salt and pepper and, if liked, a little chopped rosemary. Cook over hot coals for 10-12 minutes, turning occasionally.

GLAZED CHICKEN: Brush chicken pieces (legs and thighs or whole chicken cut into portions) with barbecue sauce, or marinate chicken in white wine marinade for several hours. Cook over hot coals for 25-30 minutes, turning and brushing occasionally with the barbecue baste or marinade.

HAMBURGERS: Lightly but thoroughly combine 1kg lean minced steak with ¾ cup evaporated milk, 2 beaten eggs, 1 cup soft white breadcrumbs, 2 teaspoons salt, good pinch pepper, 1 teaspoon dry mustard, ½ cup grated onion and ½ finely chopped green pepper. Shape into 8 patties and cook on a greased hot plate or barbecue griddle for 12-15 minutes, until cooked. Serve on toasted, buttered hamburger buns.

Right: A well-made fire, good Australian meat and tasty marinades add up to a superb barbecue.

Steak seasoning

Flavor steaks or lamb chops in one of the following ways to give good flavor and appearance.

MUSTARD STEAKS: Beat 2 teaspoons dry mustard into 60g butter and spread on meat before cooking — enough for 4 steaks.

PEPPER STEAK: Press coarsely ground black or crushed green peppercorns into steak on both sides and allow to stand 30 minutes or more before cooking.

HERBED STEAK: Press fresh or dried rosemary, thyme or oregano into steaks, season with salt and pepper and cook.

ORIENTAL STEAK: Combine 1 teaspoon grated fresh ginger, 1 clove crushed garlic, ¼ cup soy sauce, 1 tablespoon mirin (sweet sake) or dry sherry, 2 teaspoons sugar and 2 teaspoons oil. Brush on thin steaks before and during cooking.

BARBECUE SAUCE: Finely chop 1 onion and put into small pan with 3 tablespoons oil, 1 tablespoon vinegar, 2 tablespoons worcestershire sauce and ¾ cup tomato sauce. Bring to the boil, cover, lower heat and simmer for 5 minutes, stirring occasionally. Cool and use to brush on meat while cooking. Serve remaining barbecue sauce with steaks.

Steaks on the grill

Allow 250-375g of rump, T-bone or sirloin steak per person, cut 2.5cm thick for individual steak, 4-5cm thick if barbecuing a big piece of meat. Trim off excess fat and score edges so that steak will not curl during cooking. Have the meat at room temperature.

Grease the rack and put rack with meat 8cm from the heat over a deep bed of glowing coals. For rare steaks allow 4-5 minutes on each side for meat 4-5cm thick. If too rare, cook a few minutes more on each side as required.

TO TEST FOR DONENESS: When tiny beads of pink juice appear and the steak is pliant to the touch, it is rare. When more heavily dewed with juice and springy to the touch it is medium-rare. If firm it is well-done.

GRILLET STEAKS: You can buy excellent ribbed pans for grilling steak. These give an attractive pattern to the steak, latticed if liked by changing the position of the meat. Heat the grillet, brush with oil and, when it is beginning to smoke, put in the meat. Keep the heat high and do not move the meat for 2 minutes after placing meat on the grill as it may stick at first but will release itself if you wait. Turn it halfway around after 2 minutes, cook another 2 minutes, then repeat on other side, lower heat and cook to your liking. See above to test for doneness.

Remove the meat to a hot dish and let it rest for a minute or two. This is particularly important if cooking a large, thick piece as it allows the juices to settle back in the meat. The meat can then be cut in slices and served.

Vegetable packages

Wrap vegetables loosely in double-thickness aluminium foil, sealing the edges tightly. Cook on the grill about 10cm from the coals, turning now and again. Make individual packages, so each diner receives one.

MINTED CARROTS: For each serving, allow 1 small carrot cut into sticks a bit thicker than a matchstick. Season with salt, pepper, a sprinkle of sugar and a squeeze of lemon juice. Scatter with chopped mint and add a dob of butter. Cook on the grill for about 20 minutes.

GINGERED ONIONS: For each serving, allow 4 tiny onions or 1 medium onion cut into quarters. Season with salt, pepper, a sprinkle of brown sugar and a pinch of powdered ginger. Add a good knob of butter. Cook on the grill about 40 minutes.

SWEETCORN: Allow one ear of young corn for each serving. Peel the husks back and remove the silk. Sprinkle corn with salt and pepper and spread with softened butter. Replace husks, then wrap individually in foil. Grill for 15 minutes, turning several times.

HERBED PEAS AND MUSHROOMS: For each serving, allow 3 to 4 button mushrooms and ⅓ cup frozen peas. Season with salt, pepper, a pinch of dried or fresh oregano or rosemary, a sprinkle of snipped chives and a squeeze of lemon juice. Add a dob of butter. Cook on the grill for 20 minutes.

Note: Vegetable packages can also be cooked directly on the coals, but will need to be turned often. Allow a little less time than for cooking on the grill.

Escabeche of chicken

2 x 1kg or 1.5kg chickens or 8-12 chicken legs
1 tablespoon paprika
1 teaspoon salt
1-2 fresh red chilis
2 tablespoons salad oil
½ cup lime juice (about 4 limes)
1 large spanish onion
2 red peppers, seeded and cut into rings
Sprigs fresh coriander

Cut the chickens in halves, or quarters if using larger chickens, chop off wing tips and trim off excess bone from back. Wipe chicken with paper towels. Combine paprika and salt, rub into chicken and place the chicken in a shallow ceramic or glass dish. Seed and finely chop chili and combine with salad oil and half the lime juice. Take care to wash your hands after handling the chopped chili. Pour the chili mixture over the chicken, cover and refrigerate overnight, turning once or twice.

Cook chicken over a charcoal barbecue or under a heated grill, basting with remaining marinade until the chicken is cooked. The halves and quarters will take about 30 minutes and the legs about 25.

Meanwhile, peel and slice the onions into rings and drop into boiling water for 30 seconds. Drain and toss in remaining lime juice. Serve chicken, garnished with onion and red pepper rings and sprigs of fresh coriander.

Pepperonata

2 tablespoons olive oil
2 tablespoons butter
2 large onions, peeled and chopped
6 red peppers, seeded
2 cloves garlic, crushed
Salt and freshly ground pepper
6 ripe tomatoes
Few leaves basil or oregano (optional)

Heat the oil and butter in a heavy saucepan, add the chopped onions, stir well and cook them till soft and golden. Cut the peppers into strips and add to the onions with the crushed garlic. Season with a little salt and pepper, cover and simmer for 15 minutes. Peel, quarter and add tomatoes to pan, stir well and cook gently without the lid for about 30 minutes. Add the basil leaves or oregano just before serving, or you may add a bay leaf with tomatoes.

Serve hot or cold.

It will keep in the refrigerator for two weeks.

Barbecued citrus chicken

2 x 1kg chickens
CITRUS SAUCE
2 teaspoons teryaki sauce
½ teaspoon salt
2 teaspoons crushed ginger
1 clove garlic, crushed
1 teaspoon paprika
¼ cup salad oil
1 teaspoon grated lime, lemon or orange rind
⅓ cup of lemon or lime juice
GARNISH
Thin slices of lemon, lime or orange

Quarter the chickens and remove backbones and wing tips, press flat and place in a shallow dish.

Combine sauce ingredients in a screw top jar and shake well. Pour over chicken and leave for at least 2 hours.

Drain chicken and grill either over glowing coals or under a heated grill brushing frequently with marinade. When the chicken is cooked, remove to a heated serving dish and serve with steamed rice and Fruit Kebabs. Serves 4.

Fruit kebabs

Use the remaining marinade from the citrus chicken or make sauce specially for these delicious morsels. If you are using thin bamboo skewers, be sure to soak them in cold water for 30 minutes before spearing the fruit otherwise they might catch fire and spoil the flavor.

1 kiwi fruit, peeled and quartered
2 bananas, peeled and quartered
1 slice pineapple, peeled, cored and cut into cubes

Put prepared fruit in a bowl and add remaining marinade. Toss well and push fruit on to skewers. Barbecue, turning and brushing frequently till fruit is golden and hot.

Zucchini and tomato kebabs

4 small zucchini
16 cherry or 4 small tomatoes
Melted butter
⅓ cup grated gruyere cheese
½ teaspoon chopped oregano
Salt and pepper to taste

Trim zucchini and cut into 4 pieces. Drop into boiling water and cook for 2 minutes. Drain and thread on to skewers alternately with tomatoes. Brush with melted butter and grill under a preheated grill or over glowing coals for about 5 minutes or until golden. Put the grated cheese and oregano on a plate and roll the kebabs in the mixture and season with salt and pepper. Serve immediately. Serves 4.

Spareribs with whisky

2kg pork spareribs
⅓ cup whisky
¼ cup soy sauce
2 tablespoons molasses
1 large onion, chopped
3 tablespoons french mustard
1 teaspoon worcestershire sauce

Trim excess fat from spareribs.

Combine remaining ingredients, pour over spareribs and chill, covered, in the refrigerator for at least 6 hours or overnight.

Drain spareribs, reserving the marinade. Grill under a preheated grill or over coals, basting meat with marinade, for about 25 minutes on each side until spareribs are crisp and brown.

Cut into serving portions and arrange on a heated platter. Serves 4.

Indonesian satays

500g lean pork cut into 2cm cubes
Juice of 1 lemon
1 clove garlic
2 tablespoons soy sauce
2 teaspoons ground coriander
SAUCE
1 clove garlic, crushed
1 small onion, finely chopped
1 tablespoon peanut oil
¾ cup crunchy style peanut butter
½ teaspoon chili powder
¾ cup water

Above: Tired of the usual steak, snags and chops? Try a spicy Escabeche Of Chicken at your next outdoor barbecue.

1 tablespoon soy sauce
2 teaspoons brown sugar

Combine lemon juice, garlic, soy sauce and ground coriander, beat well and pour over pork cubes. Marinate for 2-4 hours turning occasionally. Thread meat on to bamboo skewers, 4-6 cubes to each. Barbecue on a greased grill for 3-4 minutes each side, brushing with marinade. Serves 4.

SAUCE: Fry garlic and onion gently in oil in a small saucepan. When soft and golden, add remaining ingredients and simmer till thick. Just before serving stir in any remaining marinade.

This sauce will keep in the refrigerator for several weeks and is delicious in sandwiches or as a dip for vegetables.

Fruits and berries

At this time of the year, fresh fruits are in luscious abundance and most of us enjoy them in plenty. The stone fruits — apricots, nectarines, peaches and plums — are at their peak, along with pawpaws, melons, grapes and more. Australia in summer is a fruit lover's paradise! A favorite way to serve these beautiful fresh fruits is to arrange them just as they are on a bed of ice. Decorate with green leaves to contrast with the colors of the fruits. A mixed fresh fruit plate makes a perfect weekend breakfast to enjoy outside on the verandah or terrace — with croissants, fruit toast, or other hot breads if you wish. It can also be served for lunch or dessert. Cut pawpaw and melon into wedges, stone and halve apricots, plums and peaches, leave cherries and grapes on their stems. For lunch, you might like to add ham, chicken, cold roast pork or corned beef — meats that go so well with fruit. For dessert, eat the fruit plain or with a lovely semi-soft cheese such as port salut, bel paese or brie. Most berry fruits have a very short season, but fortunately we are seldom without strawberries. They make exquisite fillings for crepes, delicious ice creams and mousses, complement a fruit salad and are just made for meringues and strawberry tarts.

Summer fruit tartlets

Tiny tart shells are piled high with glazed fruits over a layer of lemony cream cheese.

1 quantity sweet flan pastry
500g fresh fruit (strawberries, cherries, grapes, apricots, peaches, plums)
FILLING
185g philadelphia or neufchatel cream cheese
1 tablespoon sugar
½ teaspoon grated lemon rind
1 to 2 tablespoons cream or milk
GLAZE
1 cup jam (use apricot for pale fruits and redcurrant for red fruits)
3 tablespoons water
1 tablespoon lemon juice

Roll out pastry and line 12 tartlet tins, or break pieces off and mould into tins. Chill. Prick the base of each tartlet with a fork and bake blind in a moderately hot oven 190C (375F) for 8 to 10 minutes, or until crisp and golden brown. (To bake blind: Line each tin with greaseproof paper, fill with dried beans and bake. Remove papers for last few minutes to dry out pastry.) Allow to cool.

FILLING: Allow the cream cheese to soften at room temperature, then cream well with remaining ingredients, adding enough cream to give a spreading consistency.

TO PREPARE FRUITS

Strawberries: Wash, dry carefully, and hull. Leave whole if small, slice or cut in halves if large.

Apricots: Poach apricots in a light syrup (½ cup sugar dissolved in 1 cup of water) until just tender. Drain and remove stones. Small fruits may be left whole, larger fruits sliced or halved.

Peaches and plums: Prepare in the same way as apricots.

Grapes: Wash grapes and remove pips with the pointed end of a small sharp knife. Halve if liked.

Cherries: Wash cherries and remove stones with a cherry stoner or small sharp knife. Dry before placing in tartlet case, whole or halved.

GLAZE: Stir all ingredients over a gentle heat until smooth, then strain through a sieve. Return to the saucepan and boil until it hangs in heavy drops from the spoon to form a glaze.

TO ASSEMBLE TARTLETS: Place a spoonful of cheese filling in each shell, then pile the fruit on top. Brush the fruit carefully with glaze until it glistens and allow to set.

SWEET FLAN PASTRY: Sift 1 cup plain flour and a pinch of salt on to a pastry board or marble slab. Make a well in the centre and add 60g softened butter, ⅓ cup castor sugar, 2 egg yolks and 2 drops vanilla. Work the ingredients together with the fingertips of one hand, then use a metal spatula to quickly draw in the flour.

Knead the pastry lightly until smooth, wrap in plastic film and chill for 1 hour before using.

Right: Jewel-like glazed fruits make elegant tartlets that will turn an ordinary meal into a banquet.

Macedoine of fruit in vermouth

Vermouth adds a light, refreshing taste to fruit. Vary your choice of fruits according to personal preference and to the seasons.

¼ cup sugar
½ cup water
½ cup sweet or dry vermouth
1 piece cinnamon bark
1 pineapple, peeled and cut in wedges
3 navel oranges, peeled and cut in sections
Large bunch grapes, seeded

Combine sugar, water, vermouth and cinnamon bark, bring to the boil, cover and let stand for 1 hour. Pour the liquid over the prepared fruit and marinate for at least an hour in the refrigerator before serving. Serves 6.

Fresh fruit sherbets

If you have one of the magic electric ice cream machines, it's easy to make beautiful and refreshing sherbets. The basic method is the same for all fruits.

1kg ripe, fresh fruit (strawberries, plums, peaches, nectarines, apricots)
Juice of 1 lemon and 1 orange
1¾ cups sugar
½ cup water

If using strawberries, wash and hull. Drop stone fruit into boiling water, leave for 5 minutes, then drain and remove stones. (Slip skins off peaches, but there is no need to peel plums, nectarines or apricots.)

Puree the fruit in a blender, or push through a sieve, and combine with fruit juices. Chill.

Place sugar and water in a saucepan, stir over low heat until sugar dissolves, then boil for 2 minutes. Cool and chill.

Combine fruit and syrup, spoon into container of ice cream machine and process as directed. Transfer to a mould or tray, cover with foil, and leave in the freezer for 2 hours to ripen. Sherbet will keep for 1 to 2 days, but is really at its best if eaten within 6 hours. Serves 6.

Note: If you do not have an ice cream machine, proceed as follows: Pour the mixture into ice-cube trays and freeze uncovered until mushy. Turn into a chilled mixing basin and beat until light and thick. Whip 2 egg whites to a stiff snow and combine lightly but thoroughly with the mixture. Return to the trays, cover with foil, and freeze for several hours until firm.

Above: A Macedoine Of Fruit In Vermouth is simple to make but sophisticated in flavor.

Strawberries romanoff

This is one of the simplest yet most delicious ways in the world of serving strawberries.

8 lumps loaf sugar
2 oranges
2 punnets strawberries
6 tablespoons orange liqueur (curacao or Grand Marnier)
CREME CHANTILLY
1¼ cups cream
Sugar to taste
Vanilla essence to taste

Rub lumps of sugar over the skins of oranges until they are well impregnated with the flavor of the fruit. Crush sugar. Wash and hull strawberries. Macerate them in orange liqueur and sugar in covered container in refrigerator until serving time. Put into a serving bowl or individual dessert dishes in a pyramid shape.

Put cream chantilly into a piping bag with a rose or star tube and decorate strawberries with rosettes of cream. Serve immediately. Serves 6-8.

CREME CHANTILLY: Whip the chilled cream with sugar and vanilla to taste.

Maxim's iced raspberry souffle

2 egg whites
1¼ cups sugar
6 tablespoons water
250g fresh or frozen raspberries
Lemon juice
2¼ cups cream
1 tablespoon icing sugar
Fresh raspberries to decorate (optional)

Whisk egg whites until very stiff. Stir sugar and water over heat until the sugar is dissolved. Boil syrup undisturbed for 5 minutes or until a little dropped into cold water forms a soft ball. Immediately pour hot syrup over egg whites, beating all the time to form a meringue mixture. Place over ice and cool.

Sieve raspberries or puree in a

blender (sieving gives the best results). Add a squeeze of lemon juice, and chill. Whip cream stiffly, adding the icing sugar; chill. Incorporate the meringue and the raspberry puree. Fold in the whipped cream. If the color is too pale add a very little red food coloring.

Tie an 8cm collar of buttered foil around a small (3-cup) souffle dish or small round cake tin. Pour in the souffle mixture and chill in the freezer for 4 hours. Remove collar before serving.

If you wish, decorate the souffle with fresh raspberries, powdering them with a little sifted icing sugar. Serves 6.

Note: If raspberries are unobtainable, you could use loganberries or strawberries.

Mango mousse

1 sachet of gelatine
2 tablespoons water
1½ cups fresh or canned mango pulp
3 tablespoons creme de cacao or marsala
300ml cream

Dissolve gelatine in the water over a low heat. Cool and stir in the mango pulp. Place over ice until the mixture starts to thicken. Stir in creme de cacao. Fold in whipped cream.

Pour into a chilled mould that has been rinsed out with cold water and allow to set. Unmould on to a serving dish and serve with a salad of sliced bananas and strawberries.

Serves 6 to 8.

Summer pudding

A delicious combination of dark summer fruits and white bread, summer pudding can also be made with a selection of canned fruits such as plums, raspberries and cherries and, if wished, perfumed with kirsch or another liqueur.

⅓ cup sugar
½ cup water
Piece of orange rind
250g dark cherries
250g raspberries (fresh or frozen)
250g loganberries, blackberries or youngberries
250g blackcurrants (fresh or frozen — if unavailable use 250g of any of the above berries)
Lemon juice
Slices of white bread (day-old)

Bring sugar and water to the boil. Add orange rind and cherries which have been stoned. Simmer until soft. Add the other fruits and cook very gently for a few minutes. Strain and reserve the juice. Add a squeeze of lemon juice.

Moisten a 3½-cup bowl. Trim crusts from bread and cut each slice in half lengthwise. Line the bowl with the bread slices dipping them into the juice as you go. Fill with fruit mixture. Cover with more bread slices and spoon over a few tablespoons of juice if any remains. Put a plate on top which fits exactly inside the bowl and weight it firmly. Stand bowl overnight in the refrigerator.

Invert on to a serving dish and serve accompanied with a bowl of lightly whipped cream. Serves 6 to 8.

Passionfruit cream mallow

It's rich, but irresistible!

250g plain white marshmallows
¼ cup water
¾ cup passionfruit pulp (6 to 8 passionfruit)
2 egg whites
2 tablepoons castor sugar
One carton sour cream
Extra passionfruit pulp and whipped cream to decorate

Snip marshmallows into quarters with scissors dipped in cold water. Place in a saucepan with the ¼ cup of water and stir over low heat until the marshmallows have melted. Remove from heat and stir in passionfruit pulp. Stand in a bowl of iced water to cool.

Beat the egg whites until stiff peaks form, then beat in the castor sugar. When passionfruit mixture begins to set, combine with the meringue, then fold in the sour cream. Spoon into a serving bowl and chill for one hour, or until firm.

Serve decorated with whipped cream and passionfruit. Serves 6 to 8.

Peach crumb pudding

8 fresh peaches
1 cup sugar
1 tablespoon lemon juice
1 teaspoon ground cinnamon
1½ cups flour
125g butter

Drop half the peaches into boiling water, leave for a minute, remove and skin. Repeat with remaining peaches. Reserve 1 peach for garnishing. Halve peaches and cut into quarters and drop into a mixture of ½ cup sugar, 1 tablespoon lemon juice, ½ teaspoon cinnamon and 4 tablespoons flour. Mix lightly and turn into an ovenproof baking dish.

Mix remaining sugar and flour and cinnamon, rub in the butter to a crumb consistency. Sprinkle crumbs over the peaches. Bake in a preheated moderate oven 180C (350F) for 1 hour or until peaches are tender and crumbs are brown.

Decorate with slices of remaining fresh peach. Serve with ice cream or lightly whipped cream. Serves 6-8.

Note: You can also use 12 to 16 apricots or plums instead of the peaches.

Brandied cherries

You can enjoy the cherry-flavored brandy as a liqueur, and eat the cherries separately — or use cherries and liqueur as a sauce for ice cream or sponge cake.

1 cup sugar
1 cup water
1 piece cinnamon stick
1 strip of lemon peel
1.5kg dark cherries, stoned
Brandy

Place sugar, water, cinnamon and lemon peel in a saucepan. Bring slowly to the boil, stirring until sugar has dissolved, then boil for 10 minutes. Add cherries and simmer for 5 minutes. Remove cherries with a slotted spoon and pack into warm, sterilised jars. Add enough brandy to come half-way up the cherries, then top up with syrup, covering cherries completely. Seal jars at once, and store in a cool, dark place for at least a month before using.

Note: You can get cherry stoners at specialty kitchen shops and department stores. They remove the stone neatly, leaving the cherries whole.

Fruit coolers

Fruit combines beautifully with wine or other beverages to make summer drinks that also do duty as desserts.

PEACH SURPRISE: Prick a ripe peach all over with a fork. Place in the bottom of a wide-mouthed, tall glass and fill up with chilled champagne, rose or white wine. Enjoy the peach-flavored wine, then eat the peach.

For a party, add a dash of brandy or fruit liqueur before topping up with champagne.

APRICOT DELIGHT: Slice two ripe apricots per person and place in the bottom of a tall glass. Half-fill with apricot nectar, or pureed fresh apricots, and top up with chilled soda water.

PLUM FIZZ: Prick a ripe plum all over with a fork and place in a tall glass. Add a good dash of white rum and fill up with rose wine.

February

Tomato treats

Indispensable as fresh tomatoes are for eating either raw or cooked, they are only the beginning of this great vegetable's usefulness. Tomatoes take so well to being canned, pureed and concentrated that these forms are considered equal to the fresh product — indeed, are sometimes the first choice for their rich color and deep flavor, especially when fresh tomatoes are a little out of season and lack flavor. Tomato juice, tomato sauce and tomato relish find a place in most kitchens and are used both to accompany food and as ingredients. Tomatoes come in a number of varieties, from the large ridged ones (which usually have especially good flavor), through smooth red globes to egg tomatoes, just right for lunch-boxes. There are also yellow varieties. Tiny cherry tomatoes are brilliant for garnishing or salads. Dipped first into gin then into coarse salt, they make a sensational nibble to have with drinks.

Preparing tomatoes

TO PEEL TOMATOES:
Tomatoes which are to be used in casseroles, soups or sauces, should be peeled before cooking. They are often peeled for salads, too. Cover tomatoes with boiling water, count to 10, then remove and run them under the cold tap.

Make a tiny slit in the skin and strip the skin off towards the stem end. If the skin does not come away easily, drop tomatoes back into boiling water for a few seconds more, then run under cold water again. After peeling, use the point of the knife to cut out the blossom at the stem end.

TO SEED TOMATOES: Cut tomatoes in half crosswise and squeeze them in the palm of your hand, giving a little shake as you do so, over a sieve set over a bowl. Scrape out any remaining seeds with a fingertip. Discard the seeds and use the liquid in the bowl for the dish you are making or add it to a stock or sauce.

SEASONING TOMATOES: The correct basic seasoning for tomatoes is salt, pepper and just a touch of sugar to bring out the flavor. A little sugar added to dressings for tomato salads or to dishes using cooked tomatoes will give the fullest flavor.

Basic tomato sauce

This is a good sauce to make in quantity and freeze — the recipe can be doubled. Use it as the basis of a superb homemade soup, so different from the canned variety; serve it with sausages or hamburgers, grilled meats, fish or chicken, heat it with mussels, prawns or canned fish and serve over rice or noodles; cover frankfurters with it, top with cheese and bake; stir into browned minced beef and serve on toast or with mashed potato.

In this recipe, grated carrot gives the same slight sweetening effect as sugar, to bring up the tomato flavor.

1 large onion, finely chopped
2 cloves, garlic, crushed
2 rashers streaky bacon, rinds removed and chopped
30g butter
1 large carrot, grated
1kg ripe red tomatoes, skinned, seeded and chopped or 1 x 820g can tomatoes
½ cup dry white or red wine or ¼ cup sherry
Bouquet garni
Salt
Freshly ground black pepper

Cook onion, garlic and bacon gently in butter until onion is soft. Add remaining ingredients, chopping canned tomatoes and removing as many seeds as possible. Simmer partly covered for 45 minutes, stirring frequently. Add a little more water if needed. Sauce should be thick, but can be thinned as you wish with beef or chicken stock when you use it. Remove bouquet garni, correct seasoning and store, covered, in refrigerator or freezer.

Right: Tomato And Shallot Salad and Tomatoes Stuffed With Fresh Corn are ideal at this time of year.

Tomato and shallot salad

Very simple, but truly superb.

3 large ripe tomatoes, chilled
½ cup chopped shallots
¼ cup parsley, finely chopped
½ cup olive oil
3 tablespoons wine or lemon vinegar
½ teaspoon salt, or to taste
Freshly ground black pepper to taste

Slice the tomatoes and arrange them symmetrically on a chilled serving dish. Sprinkle with shallots and parsley. Just before serving, pour the oil, vinegar, salt and pepper over the tomatoes. Serves 6.

Tomatoes stuffed with fresh corn

Use fresh corn on the cob, cooked in unsalted water for 10-12 minutes, or canned whole kernel corn.

4 ripe tomatoes
2 ears corn, cooked
1 tablespoon chopped onion
¼ to ½ green pepper, chopped
1 canned pimiento, chopped (optional)
½ teaspoon salt
⅓ cup vinaigrette
Dash of Tabasco
Lettuce
Mayonnaise

Core and peel the tomatoes. Remove the pulp, leaving the shell of the tomato as a cup. Turn the tomato cups upside down to drain. Chop the pulp and drain in a sieve.

Cut the corn from the cobs and add the tomato pulp, onion, pepper, pimiento and salt. Season the Vinaigrette with Tabasco to taste and add to the vegetables. Toss all ingredients together and use to fill the tomato cups. Chill well. Serve on lettuce with mayonnaise. Serves 4.

Fresh tomato soup

Homemade tomato soup is delicious, quick, easy to make and inexpensive for most months of the year.

750g tomatoes
1 clove garlic
2 tablespoons chopped parsley
½ tablespoon chopped basil or marjoram
2-3 tablespoons olive oil
4 cups chicken stock
Salt and pepper
Pinch of sugar

Peel tomatoes and chop roughly. Crush garlic and place in saucepan with tomatoes, herbs and olive oil. Cook gently for about 5 minutes. Add stock, salt, pepper and sugar and cook for a further 5 minutes.

This soup can be eaten hot, in autumn or winter, or chilled in summer. Serves 6.

Pissaladiere

This robust onion tart flavored with olives and anchovies is a specialty of the Mediterranean coast of France. Cut into small diamonds, it is a very good savory with drinks. For lunch, cut in wedges and add a green salad.

PASTRY
3 cups plain flour
Pinch salt
90g each chilled butter and lard, or all butter
About 6 tablespoons ice water
Good squeeze of lemon juice
FILLING
1kg onions
¼ cup olive oil
Salt and freshly ground pepper
3 large, ripe tomatoes, peeled
2 cans flat anchovy fillets
About 1 cup black olives, halved and stoned

PASTRY: Sift flour and salt into a bowl. Cut lard and butter into small pieces and rub into the flour until mixture looks like coarse breadcrumbs. Mix ice water and lemon juice and quickly stir in with a knife, using just enough liquid to form a dough. Turn on to a floured board, knead lightly until smooth, then wrap dough in plastic film and chill for 1 hour.

Meanwhile, peel onions and slice very thinly. Heat the oil in a large saucepan and cook onions very gently without browning until they are almost a puree — this will take about 40 minutes. Season lightly with salt and pepper and cool to room temperature.

Roll out the pastry on a floured board to a circle big enough to line a 30cm lightly greased pizza tray, or flan ring with a removable bottom. Prick all over with a fork, and bake in a preheated very hot oven, 220C (425F) for 10 minutes.

Remove from oven, and cover pastry with onions, pressing them down. Slice peeled tomatoes thinly and arrange in an overlapping row around the edge, pressing them into onions.

Drain anchovies, reserving oil, and cut each fillet in half lengthwise. Make a lattice of anchovy strips over filling, and decorate with halved olives.

Sprinkle tart with reserved anchovy oil, and grind black pepper over. Reduce heat to moderately hot, 190C (375F) and bake for another 15 minutes, or until pastry is crisp and golden. Remove from oven and cool for a few minutes before serving. Serves 10 as an appetiser, 4 to 6 for lunch.

Note: Leftovers are delicious cold.

Taiba

The original Algerian recipe has enough chili to make it quite fiery — suit yourself about the amount you use. Add slowly after the other vegetables and taste as you go.

6 ripe tomatoes
2 red peppers
1-2 red chilis, or to taste
4 tablespoons olive oil
4 cloves garlic, crushed
2 tablespoons tomato paste
3 x 200g cans tuna in oil
1 teaspoon ground coriander
Salt and freshly ground black pepper

Cut tomatoes in half crosswise and remove seeds. Cut red peppers and chilis in half and remove seeds and ribs (work under running water when handling chili, and wash your hands immediately afterwards).

Grill all vegetables, skin side up, under a preheated griller at high heat until skins blister and blacken, then peel tomatoes and rub skins off peppers and chilis under running water. Chop all vegetables fine.

Heat oil in saucepan and add vegetables, garlic and tomato paste. Stir over moderate heat for 5 minutes. Drain and coarsely flake tuna and add it with coriander and salt and pepper to taste.

Simmer on low heat, stirring gently once or twice, for 4 minutes or until liquid has evaporated. Let taiba cool, then chill, covered, for 2 hours or overnight. Serve with crusty bread. Serves 6.

Mushrooms lyonnaise

500g fresh mushroom cups or open cups
60g butter
1 clove garlic
1 bay leaf
2 whole cloves
2 tomatoes
Salt and freshly ground pepper
Pinch nutmeg
30g butter
1 tablespoon chopped fresh parsley or chervil
6 spring onions, chopped

Quarter mushrooms if large, using both caps and stems. Heat butter in a wide-based saucepan with peeled garlic, bay leaf and cloves. When butter is hot, remove the seasonings and add mushrooms. Cook over a high heat for 5 minutes, stirring

constantly. Add tomatoes which have been skinned, seeded and chopped.

Season to taste with salt, freshly ground pepper and nutmeg. Bring to the simmer, cook covered for a further 10 minutes. Heat butter, add chopped parsley and spring onions, toss lightly and add to mushrooms.

Serve with toast or in little dishes and accompany with crusty bread to mop up the juices. Serves 4.

Quick gazpacho

Just the look of gazpacho makes you feel cool. Here's an easy version of this famous Spanish soup

6 large ripe tomatoes, peeled and diced
½ Spanish onion or 3 spring onions, chopped
1 green pepper, seeded and diced
1 cucumber, thinly peeled and diced
2 cloves garlic, crushed
1 tablespoon wine vinegar
2 tablespoons olive oil
1 x 425 ml can tomato juice
1 x 425g can beef or chicken consomme
Salt and freshly ground pepper
Ice cubes
2 tablespoons chopped parsley

Place vegetables and garlic in a bowl, add vinegar and oil and toss very gently with 2 wooden spoons. Add tomato juice and consomme, then season to taste with salt and pepper. Put a few ice cubes into 8 individual bowls, ladle gazpacho over.

Sprinkle with parsley. Serve with fresh crusty bread or with a bowl of lightly salted garlic croutons, made by frying squares of bread in oil flavored with a clove or two of crushed garlic. Serves 8.

Tomatoes stuffed with basil

For those keen gardeners, or shoppers with a good greengrocer who keeps a regular supply of lovely summery herbs, a super summer salad. If basil is not available, use lots of chopped parsley with a little of another herb of your choice.

6 ripe tomatoes
Salt
1 cup fresh basil leaves, closely packed
1 clove garlic
⅓ cup olive oil
¾ cup pine nuts
½ cup freshly grated parmesan cheese

Core the tomatoes and cut a deep depression in the centre for stuffing.

Above: Combine mushrooms and tomatoes to make an elegant starter — Mushrooms Lyonnaise.

Squeeze the tomatoes gently to remove most of the seeds. Salt lightly, and turn upside down to drain. Meanwhile, combine the remaining ingredients in the container of an electric blender and blend on low or high speed until well pureed, or puree with a mortar and pestle.

Spoon equal portions of the basil mixture into the centre of each tomato. Chill and serve cold. Serves 6.

Stuffed tomato salad

Tomatoes have such good flavor it makes sense to use them in many different ways. Serve as a first course before a light main dish or for a light lunch.

6 medium tomatoes
3 hard-boiled eggs, chopped
1 cup diced ham
½ cup diced celery
12 stuffed olives, sliced
1 dill pickle, chopped
½ cup mayonnaise or sour cream
Salt and freshly ground pepper
6 lettuce leaves

Wash tomatoes, cut tops off and

scoop out flesh to leave a shell. Invert tomatoes on a plate to drain for 20 minutes. Combine eggs, ham, celery, olives and pickles and moisten with mayonnaise or sour cream, season with salt and freshly ground pepper.

Fill the hollows of the tomatoes with prepared salad. Serve on a lettuce leaf. Serves 6.

Note: If liked, the tomatoes may be first skinned.

Tomatoes with herbs

This most versatile yet simple dish adds a touch of color and robust flavor to roast chicken or a mixed grill. The amount of garlic used depends on your personal liking for this pungent little bulb.

4 ripe tomatoes
Salt and freshly ground pepper
1-2 cloves garlic, chopped
2 tablespoons chopped herbs (basil, parsley, thyme)
¾ cup fresh breadcrumbs (optional)
30g butter

Cut off the top of each tomato and season generously with salt and pepper. Sprinkle each with a little of the garlic and herbs and top with breadcrumbs (if using). Put a generous dot of butter on top of each tomato. Arrange in a buttered gratin dish and bake in a moderate oven, 180C (350F), for 10 minutes. Serve from the dish. Serves 4.

Tomatoes au gratin

4 ripe tomatoes
Salt and freshly ground pepper
1 cup fresh breadcrumbs
¼ cup grated parmesan cheese
4 tablespoons oil

Cut the tomatoes into thick slices and arrange them overlapping in a lightly oiled flameproof dish. Season generously with salt and pepper, sprinkle with the breadcrumbs, then the cheese and finally the oil. Place the dish under a medium grill for 5 to 6 minutes or until the tomatoes are tender and the surface is lightly browned. Serves 4.

TOMATOES AND EGGPLANT AU GRATIN: Before grilling, intersperse the overlapping slices of tomatoes in the dish with 8 slices of eggplant which have been dusted with flour and very quickly browned in a little oil in a frying pan over fairly high heat. Serves 4 as a light main course.

Herbed tomato quiche

For those who enjoy a savory quiche, this custard filling is fragrant with fresh chopped herbs. It is lovely for a light luncheon or supper.

1 quantity rich shortcrust pastry (see index)
1½ cups cream
2 eggs and 2 egg yolks
2 tablespoons tomato paste
Salt and freshly ground pepper
4 tablespoons grated swiss or gruyere cheese
2 tomatoes
2 tablespoons chopped parsley
1 tablespoon fresh mixed herbs (lemon thyme, oregano, basil, chives)
3 tablespoons grated parmesan cheese
2 teaspoons butter

It is best to use a large French, shallow, false-bottomed flan ring 28cm, across but a smaller, deeper flan ring may be used. Make rich shortcrust and roll it out on a floured board in a circle to fit the flan tin. If using the smaller tin you may not need all the pastry. Remember it should be rolled thin. Lift the dough over a rolling pin into the flan ring and press the dough firmly into place.

Cut off the excess dough with a floured rolling pin and reserve it for other use.

In a bowl combine cream, whole eggs, egg yolks, tomato paste, salt and pepper, and beat lightly. Add 2 tablespoons swiss cheese. Cut tomatoes into 1cm slices. Spoon custard into pastry shell. Arrange tomato slices on top, sprinkle with salt and pepper and herbs, top with remaining swiss and parmesan cheese, dot with small pieces of butter.

Bake the quiche on the top rack of a moderately hot oven, 190C (375F) for 25-30 minutes, or until the custard is set and the top is golden.

Remove the quiche from the pan and let it cool on the rack. Serves 6-8.

Creamy tomato soup

1 cup basic tomato sauce (page 22)
3 cups chicken stock
1 cup cream
Salt
Freshly ground pepper
Snipped chives, fresh basil cut into thin ribbons, or nutmeg, to serve.

Puree the sauce in a blender until it is very smooth, or rub it through a sieve. Combine with stock and, if soup is to be served cold, stir in cream. If soup is to be served hot, bring the cream to the boil and stir in soup gradually. Taste and correct seasoning. Chill the soup if it is to be served cold. Serve scattered with chives or basil, or grate a little nutmeg over each serving. Serves 4.

Tomato relish

Homemade tomato relish is lovely with cold meats, grilled chops or cheese, or on sandwiches.

1.5kg very ripe tomatoes
500g onions, chopped
2 cups sugar
2½ cups malt vinegar
1 tablespoon plain flour
1 tablespoon curry powder
Pinch cayenne pepper
1 tablespoon dry mustard
1 tablespoon salt

Peel tomatoes, cut into chunks and drain off ¾ cup of their juice. Put tomatoes, onions, sugar and vinegar into saucepan and simmer, uncovered, until mixture is thick. Blend remaining ingredients with the reserved tomato juice and stir in. Stir until boiling, then simmer 5 minutes. Bottle in clean, warm jars and seal when cool.

Tomatoes piperade

Piperade is scrambled egg with fried sliced onion and pepper and herbs. It may be served warm with a thick slice of grilled or pan-fried ham or used to fill tomato cases. A lovely luncheon or brunch dish.

6-8 ripe red tomatoes
1 onion, sliced
1 green or red pepper, cut in shreds
1 tablespoon olive oil
90g butter
4 large eggs, beaten
Salt
Freshly ground pepper
2 tablespoons chopped parsley
1 teaspoon chopped mixed herbs

Peel tomatoes (drop into boiling water, count to 10, remove then slip off skin). Slice the top off each tomato, scoop out pulp, reserve the tops and pulp for later use, leaving a tomato shell. Place shells cut side down on plate in refrigerator.

Fry sliced onion and shredded pepper in oil and a little of the butter until soft. Add reserved tomato pulp.

In a saucepan melt remaining butter, add beaten eggs, salt and pepper, stir until cooked (scrambled) but still very creamy. Fold in parsley and herbs. Add vegetable mixture, adjust the seasoning and allow to cool.

Fill each tomato with piperade mixture, placing tomato 'cap' on top. Serve chilled. Serves 6-8.

• *For more tomato recipes, see index.*

Right: Even rugged he-men love the robust flavor of Herbed Tomato Quiche.

Cool and creamy desserts

Here gathered together are some of the smooth and creamy desserts I like to make at this time of the year — some are not family affairs but more for entertaining. They are all absolutely delectable and as perfect an excuse as any for inviting friends to dinner!

Spanish cream

This pretty old-fashioned moulded gelatine dessert takes on a new dimension when served with lovely summer fruit.

4 eggs, separated
½ cup sugar
2 cups hot milk
1 envelope (3 teaspoons) gelatine
¼ cup water
½ teaspoon vanilla

Beat egg yolks, adding sugar gradually, until thick and pale. Stir in hot milk and cook the mixture over low heat, stirring constantly, until it coats the back of a spoon.

Soften gelatine in water for 5 minutes, dissolve over hot water and stir into custard mixture. Stir in vanilla. Beat egg whites until they hold soft peaks and fold in.

Pour the mixture into a 4-cup mould and chill until firm. Unmould on to a plate and serve plain or with cream and fresh or cooked fruit. Serves 6.

Vanilla bavarian cream

1½ cups milk
4 egg yolks
¾ cup castor sugar
Pinch salt
1 tablespoon gelatine, softened in ¼ cup cold water
2 teaspoons vanilla
1½ cups cream
DECORATION
Strawberries or other fruit, grated chocolate, toasted almonds
TO SERVE
Raspberry Sauce

Scald milk and cool. Beat egg yolks with sugar and salt until thick and lemon colored. Place in a heavy saucepan with milk and stir over low heat until mixture coats spoon. Add softened gelatine, stir until dissolved, then add vanilla. Cool, then chill until mixture is beginning to set. Whip cream until stiff and fold in. Pour into a 6-cup mould rinsed with cold water or 6 individual moulds and chill for at least 5 hours. Unmould carefully on to a chilled plate. Decorate as desired and serve with a fruit sauce. Serves 6.

CHOCOLATE BAVARIAN CREAM: Add 60g chocolate, roughly chopped, to the hot milk and stir until melted, then proceed with recipe.

ORANGE BAVARIAN CREAM: Add grated rind of 1 orange to the hot milk, then proceed with recipe.

GINGER BAVARIAN CREAM: Add 2 tablespoons finely chopped ginger in syrup to the hot milk, then proceed with recipe.

RASPBERRY SAUCE: Gently heat 250g raspberries — fresh or frozen — with ½ cup sugar and juice of half a lemon, lightly mashing the fruit, puree in a blender then push through a sieve. A strawberry sauce may be made the same way.

Almond creams

¼ cup ground rice
3 cups milk
Pinch salt
¼ cup sugar
¾ cup ground almonds
2 tablespoons rosewater
DECORATION
Toasted slivered almonds or sliced strawberries
Whipped cream

Make a thin paste from ground rice and ¼ cup milk. Place remaining milk in a saucepan and bring to the boil. Stir in ground rice paste, salt and sugar. Cook, stirring constantly, over medium heat until mixture begins to bubble. Lower heat and simmer for 5 minutes, stirring often. Stir in ground almonds, blending well. Remove from heat and allow to cool a little, stirring occasionally. Stir in rosewater and pour into 6 individual glass coupes or wine glasses. Chill at least 2 hours. Serve decorated with toasted slivered almonds and if liked a little whipped cream or a few sliced strawberries. Serves 6.

Right: Three old smoothies are: an old-fashioned moulded Spanish Cream; delicate Almond Creams; a meringue-topped Cloud Custard.

Cloud custard

Serve with sliced strawberries or other soft fruit in season.

½ cup cream
1 cup milk
2 teaspoons cornflour
2 large eggs, separated
Pinch salt
½ teaspoon vanilla
4 teaspoons sugar

Place cream and milk (reserving about 1 tablespoon) in a small saucepan and bring to the boil. Meanwhile, mix cornflour to a smooth paste with reserve milk, and blend in egg yolks, salt, vanilla and 2 teaspoons of the sugar. When milk boils, pour a little on to cornflour mixture, stir well and return to saucepan. Stir over low heat for 3-4 minutes until custard is smooth and thick.

Remove from heat and cool. Beat egg whites until stiff, then beat in remaining sugar. Spoon custard into bowl with meringue, and lightly fold together for a pretty yellow and white effect. Chill until serving time. Serves 4.

Mexican flan

A rich, creamy custard appears on Mexican and Spanish tables. It's not unlike our creme caramel, the difference being it is made with evaporated milk.

CARAMEL
½ cup water
1 cup sugar
CUSTARD
1 x 410g can evaporated milk
¾ cup milk
2.5cm piece vanilla pod
4 eggs
½ cup sugar
Pouring cream to serve

To make the caramel, put water and sugar into a small saucepan and stir over low heat until sugar dissolves. Bring to the boil and cook quickly until golden brown. Pour into an 18cm sandwich tin or 6 individual moulds. Hold with a cloth and quickly rotate the moulds until caramel coats bases and sides. Set aside.

Heat the evaporated milk and fresh milk with the vanilla pod, do not allow to boil. Remove from heat and let stand 5 minutes. Beat eggs and sugar until well blended, then pour in the milk mixture gradually, stirring constantly.

Strain through a fine sieve and pour into caramel-lined tin or moulds.

Set the custard in a pan of hot water to come halfway up the sides. Bake in the centre of a moderately warm oven 160C (325F) 25 minutes for individual moulds, 45 minutes for a tin, or until a knife inserted near the centre of the custard comes out clean.

Cool, then chill in the refrigerator for several hours or overnight. Unmould on to serving dish or individual plates. Serve with pouring cream. Serves 6.

Chestnut cream

Canned chestnut puree flavors a luxury dessert that is quick to make.

2 egg yolks
¼ cup castor sugar
1¼ cups milk, scalded
2 teaspoons gelatine
2 tablespoons water
185g unsweetened canned chestnut puree
1 tablespoon rum or brandy
⅔ cup cream
Extra cream to decorate

Beat egg yolks and sugar together until pale and thick. Slowly pour on hot scalded milk, stirring constantly. Pour mixture into the top of a double boiler and, stir over simmering water until thickened.

Soften gelatine in water and stand container in hot water until gelatine is dissolved. Stir into custard. Cool quickly over ice until the consistency of unbeaten egg white. Beat in chestnut puree and rum or brandy. Whip cream and fold in. Pour into a large glass bowl or individual dishes and chill until set. Decorate with swirls of whipped cream and serve with a crisp biscuit. Serves 4-6.

Persian cream

Rosewater is used in many Middle-Eastern dishes, even to flavor rice. It is available at health food shops and many chemists.

1 tablespoon gelatine
¼ cup cold water
1½ cups milk
⅓ cup sugar
2 eggs, separated
1 tablespoon rosewater

Sprinkle gelatine over cold water and allow to soften. Heat milk and sugar in a heavy saucepan or top of a double saucepan. Beat egg yolks and add to warm milk and sugar, off the heat. Stir over very low heat, or over hot water until custard begins to thicken. Add softened gelatine and stir until dissolved. Allow to cool, then stir in rosewater.

Beat egg whites until stiff and fold into custard mixture. Chill for at least 4 hours.

Serve with partially frozen or fresh berry fruits, and whipped cream flavored with rosewater. Serves 6.

Rum caramel mousse

Something light and sweet is the perfect way to finish a relaxed lunch or dinner. This mousse is also very good with sliced mangoes.

CARAMEL
½ cup sugar
¼ cup plus 1 tablespoon cold water and 3 tablespoons rum
MOUSSE
2 teaspoons gelatine
2 tablespoons water
5 eggs, separated
2 tablespoons castor sugar
1 teaspoon vanilla essence
1⅓ cups cream
DECORATION
Whipped cream
Strawberries

To make caramel, combine sugar and 1 tablespoon water in a small saucepan and stir until sugar dissolves. Increase heat and cook, rotating pan gently, until a rich brown caramel forms. Remove from heat and, protecting your hand with a cloth, gradually stir in remaining water and rum to dilute caramel. Cool 5 minutes..

MOUSSE: Sprinkle gelatine over water and allow to soften, then stir into rum caramel mixture until dissolved. Beat egg yolks, sugar and vanilla with an electric mixer until thick and lemon colored. With motor still running, add caramel mixture in a stream, and beat until mixture is thick and fluffy.

Whip cream just until it holds firm peaks and fold into caramel mixture. Beat egg whites until they hold soft peaks. Gently but thoroughly fold caramel mixture into whites. Turn mixture into a 6-8 cup serving dish or 6-8 individual dishes. Cover and chill until set. Serve decorated with whipped cream and strawberries. Serves 6-8.

Buttermilk date cream

The combination of buttermilk and orange juice always gives a marvellous flavor, and the addition of fresh dates puts this superb American dessert in the dinner-party class. You can get these dates now at health food stores, good groceries and delicatessens.

¾ cup sugar
½ cup water
1½ tablespoon gelatine
Extra ⅓ cup water
1 cup buttermilk
⅔ cup orange juice

Pinch of salt
1 cup cream
1½ cups fresh dates, stoned and cut into slivers
TO GARNISH
Orange segments and zest

Heat sugar with ½ cup water, stirring until sugar is dissolved; bring to the boil and remove from heat.

Soften gelatine in ⅓ cup cold water for 10 minutes, stir the gelatine mixture into the sugar syrup and combine with buttermilk, orange juice and salt.

Chill the mixture until it thickens to the consistency of unbeaten egg white, but do not let it set.

Whip the cream until it holds soft peaks and fold it, together with the slivered dates, into the buttermilk mixture. Pour into a serving bowl. Cover and chill until set. Serves 8.

TO GARNISH FOR SPECIAL OCCASIONS: Peel strips of zest from one whole orange, using a vegetable peeler (the zest is the orange area of the skin, not including white pith). Cut the zest into fine matchstick lengths and cook gently in ½ cup water and 1 tablespoon sugar, about 5 minutes or until the zest becomes clear. Peel white pith from the orange and cut between the dividing membranes to take out skinless segments.

Arrange the slices cartwheel fashion on the dessert and strew over the strips of zest.

Orange custard creams

This is richer than an old-fashioned baked custard and is lovely for a dinner party dessert or family meals.

2 cups milk
1 cup cream
½ cup sugar
Rind of 1 orange
4 egg yolks
3 whole eggs
¼ teaspoon salt
1½ tablespoons orange-flavored liqueur — Grand Marnier or Cointreau
½ cup cream, whipped

In a stainless steel or silverstone-lined saucepan combine milk, cream, sugar and orange rind and bring mixture slowly to the boiling point, stirring until the sugar is dissolved. In a bowl beat the egg yolks and whole eggs; strain the milk mixture over them, stirring until just combined, stir in the salt and liqueur and pour into a large jug.

Pour the custard into eight half-cup custard cups and arrange in a baking dish. Add enough hot water to the pan to reach halfway up the sides of the cups and bake the custards in a moderately slow oven for about 30 minutes. Remove cups from pan and let the creams cool.

Serve with a swirl of whipped cream. Serves 8.

Above: Buttermilk Date Cream is an American dessert with an intriguing flavor combination.

Let's have a picnic!

My family upbringing imbued me with a passion for picnics. We lived in a tiny Highland village surrounded by hills and streams that provided perfect settings for al fresco eating. Picnics may be carefree and impromptu affairs; they may be planned ahead with a group of family and friends; they may be ship-and-shore affairs, or an elegant little outing for two. Whatever the reasons for taking to the great outdoors, one thing never changes — that is the importance given to food. When it comes to planning a picnic, details matter. This is one of the times I make lists, which I stick on the refrigerator with one of those cute magnets, and tick items off as I go. It is no fun to arrive at your destination only to discover a major item like a corkscrew missing. Good plastic containers will carry salads, meats and cakes and light foam-insulated cooling boxes will keep food at its peak. Invest in a couple of those inexpensive ice-packs that freeze and go in with the food to keep it cool. One final word: Do the right thing! Each of us who enjoys nature must take an interest in its preservation. At clean-up time, take all the remains back home to be disposed of properly. Enjoy your picnic and enjoy the great Australian outdoors.

Italian salmon salad

Take this to the picnic in a covered container and serve with crusty italian bread or rolls.

250g pasta shells
2 x 220g cans salmon, drained and flaked
1 red pepper, cored, seeded and diced
1 cucumber, finely diced
3 hard-boiled eggs, quartered
10 black olives, stoned and halved
¾ cup vinaigrette dressing
2 tomatoes, quartered

Cook pasta in boiling water until 'al dente'. Drain thoroughly and leave to cool.

Mix flaked salmon with the pepper, cucumber, eggs, olives and pasta. Pour over the dressing, reserving 1 tablespoon, and toss lightly. Put into a covered container. Serve with quartered tomatoes which have been drizzled with the reserved dressing. Serves 6.

Gingered chicken wings

Grill these on the morning of the picnic and pack into a foil container. They're best eaten in your fingers so supply plenty of paper napkins.

1kg chicken wings
4 tablespoons soy sauce
2 tablespoons lemon juice
2 tablespoons grated fresh ginger or 1 teaspoon ground ginger
2 teaspoons honey
2 tablespoons tomato ketchup

Cut tips off wings and cut each wing in two. Mix remaining ingredients together, add wings and turn to coat. Leave to marinate, covered, for several hours in refrigerator.

Drain wings and arrange on a greased grill rack. Grill under preheated griller for about 10 minutes, then turn, brush with marinade and grill a further 10 minutes. Serves 6.

Sour cream coleslaw

½ medium cabbage, finely shredded
2 tablespoons oil
1 tablespoon vinegar
1 tablespoon french mustard
1 clove garlic crushed with 1 teaspoon salt
1 cup sliced celery
1 red or green pepper, cored, seeded and shredded
6 green shallots, shredded
1 cup sour light cream
3 tablespoons chopped parsley
2 tablespoons snipped chives

Put cabbage into a large bowl. Combine oil, vinegar, mustard and garlic and beat with a fork until thick. Add to cabbage and mix well. Top with celery, shredded peppers and shallots. Chill well.

Just before leaving for the picnic, toss salad with sour cream, parsley and chives, mixing lightly. Serves 6.

Right: A picnic feast could include Veal And Peppercorn Terrine, Sour Cream Coleslaw, Italian Salmon Salad and Gingered Chicken Wings.

Veal and peppercorn terrine

A terrine cut in thick slices is just the thing for a picnic. Have dill pickles, green shallots and crusty bread, a dish of butter and some chilled wine to make it all perfect.

3 slices white bread, torn into pieces
1kg minced veal
2 tablespoons green peppercorns
1 egg, lightly beaten
1 teaspoon salt
6-8 rashers bacon, rind removed
½ cup dry vermouth

Put bread in a blender or food processor and make fine crumbs. Place meat in a mixing bowl and add peppercorns, egg, breadcrumbs and salt. Mix well and, using a wooden spoon, beat in half the vermouth.

Line a 6-cup loaf tin or terrine with bacon rashers, leaving ends hanging over edge of tin. Pack meat mixture into tin and fold overhanging bacon over the top. Pour over the remaining vermouth. Cover with a lid or foil and bake at 160C (325F) for 1½ hours, adding more vermouth after 1 hour if there is space in the terrine.

Remove from oven, place a weight on top and allow to cool, then chill. Serves 6-8.

German potato salad

The secret of this salad is to marinate the potato slices in boiling stock, then fold in sour cream or mayonnaise before serving.

6 medium potatoes
1 onion, finely chopped
1¼ cups chicken stock
4 tablespoons white vinegar
5 tablespoons salad oil
2 teaspoons prepared mustard
White pepper and salt
½ cup sour cream
Parsley sprigs

Cook unpeeled potatoes in boiling, salted water. Do not overcook or they will not keep their shape in the salad. Peel the potatoes while still hot and cut into slices. Place in a bowl with the onion.

Bring the stock to the boil with the vinegar added, and while boiling pour over potatoes. Marinate until almost all the liquid is absorbed, about 20-30 minutes. Pour off any excess liquid and gently fold in the oil mixed with the mustard.

Taste, and season with white pepper and salt if necessary. Lastly, fold in the sour cream. Serve at room temperature, garnished with parsley or other fresh herbs. Serves 8-10.

Cinnamon picnic cake

A good cutting cake, perfect for picnics, this may also be served warm with whipped cream flavored with cinnamon.

1¼ cups sugar
½ cup mixed chopped nuts
2 teaspoons cinnamon
125g butter
2 eggs
1 teaspoon vanilla
1 tablespoon lemon juice
2 cups flour
½ teaspoon baking powder
½ teaspoon bicarbonate of soda
¼ teaspoon salt
1 cup sour cream

Combine ¼ cup sugar with the nuts and cinnamon and set aside. Cream butter with remaining sugar until light and fluffy. Add eggs, vanilla and lemon juice, beating well. Sift flour with baking powder, soda and salt and add alternately to butter mixture with sour cream. Pour the batter into a greased and bottom-lined 23cm square cake tin. Sprinkle with the cinnamon mixture. Bake in a preheated moderate oven 180C (350F) for 35-40 minutes or until a skewer inserted in centre comes out clean.

Scotch eggs

500g sausage mince
Few drops Tabasco sauce
Few drops worcestershire sauce
6 hard-boiled eggs
½ cup flour
Salt and freshly ground black pepper
1 egg, beaten
Dry breadcrumbs
Oil for deep-frying

Mix sausage mince with sauces. Divide into 6 equal portions. Dust eggs lightly with flour seasoned with salt and pepper, then cover each egg with sausage mixture, pressing and moulding on well. Brush with beaten egg and roll in breadcrumbs. Chill for at least 1 hour. Deep-fry eggs in hot oil until golden-brown and the sausage mince is cooked. Drain on paper towels. Cool and chill. Serve cold with salads. Makes 6.

If you are cooking Scotch Eggs for the first time take care to weigh the sausage mince, divide into six equal portions and press the mince round the eggs in an equal thickness so that

Right: In the bush or in the backyard, enjoy Cinnamon Picnic Cake, Scotch Eggs, Smoked Salmon Open Sandwiches and Stuffed Peppers.

they will cook evenly. Do not overheat the oil or the outside will brown too quickly before the mince is cooked.

Stuffed peppers

4 large red or green peppers
STUFFING
45g butter
1 onion, finely chopped
⅔ cup rice
60g mushrooms, chopped
2½ cups chicken stock
250g ham or minced cooked veal or chicken
Salt and freshly ground black pepper

Cut tops off peppers and scoop out seeds. Blanch in boiling water for 2-3 minutes. Pat dry with paper towels and set aside.

STUFFING: Melt 30g of the butter in a saucepan and fry onion until softened. Add rice, stir over medium heat for 1-2 minutes, then add mushrooms. Pour 1½ cups stock over, bring to the boil, cover and simmer for 20 minutes or until rice is tender and stock absorbed. Stir in remaining butter and chopped or minced ham, veal or chicken and season with salt and pepper. Put stuffing into peppers and pack them closely together in an ovenproof casserole. Heat remaining cup of stock and pour over and around peppers. Cover dish with greased foil and cook in a preheated moderate oven 180C (350F) for 30 minutes or until peppers are tender. Allow to cool in casserole then chill if liked or take warm to picnic. To serve, cut in two if liked. Serves 4 or 8 as part of picnic.

Croissants with ham and cheese

This seems to me the ultimate in easy but brilliant picnic food. I've served savory croissants on the beach, in the bush and beside the car at country races.

If you don't have a local cake shop baking croissants, look for the frozen ones at your supermarket or the packaged ones in bread shops and delicatessens.

Allow two croissants for each person, and unless they are freshly baked, crisp them for a few minutes in a moderate oven, 180C (350F).

Using a serrated knife, slice through each croissant from the outer curve — but don't cut right through. Fill them with layers of thinly sliced ham and gruyere, emmenthal or jarlsberg cheese. Wrap in a clean tea towel, then in several layers of newspaper. They should still be warm when you arrive at the picnic spot.

Note: The salty, smoky flavor of prosciutto (Italian-style raw hàm) also goes well with cheese. See which you prefer.

Pumpkin scones

Pumpkin scones are among the most famous and nicest of country baking and are great for picnics.

60g butter
2 tablespoons castor sugar
¾ cup cooked, mashed pumpkin (well drained)
1 egg, beaten
½ cup milk
2½ cups self-raising flour, sifted
Pinch salt
¼ teaspoon each cinnamon and nutmeg
A little milk for glazing

Cream butter and sugar, add pumpkin and mix well. Add egg, then stir in milk a little at a time. Add flour, salt and spices and mix to a soft dough. Turn out on to a floured board, knead lightly and roll out to about 2cm thickness. Cut into rounds with a floured scone cutter. Place rounds on a greased baking tray, brush tops with milk and bake in a preheated hot oven 200C (400F) for 15-20 minutes or until golden brown on top and cooked through. Wrap in tea towels to keep warm. Serve split and buttered. Makes about 12.

Smoked salmon open sandwiches

Sprigs fresh dill
Cress or lettuce leaves
6 slices rye or black bread, buttered
6-8 slices smoked salmon
6-8 thin lemon slices
½ cup sour cream

Place chilled dill and cress or lettuce on buttered rye or black bread. Fold slices smoked salmon and place on top. Garnish with lemon slices and top with sour cream. Serves 6.

Orange and onion salad

This salad is divine with cold roast duck — a lovely combination for a special picnic. Try to get the purple spanish onion. Maldon sea salt is the one to use if you can get it.

3 oranges
1 small Spanish onion
2 tablespoons olive oil
Juice ½ lemon
Sea salt to taste
½ cup black olives

Peel and slice oranges. Peel and finely slice onion and add to the sliced oranges. Sprinkle with olive oil, lemon juice and sea salt. Cut olives in two, discard the stones, dot salad with olives. Serves 4.

Finnish cardamom cake

I am known among my circle of friends for this cake — our picnics wouldn't be the same without it, so I'm told.

2 eggs, beaten
2 cups sour cream
2 cups castor sugar
3 drops almond essence
3 cups flour
1 teaspoon bicarbonate of soda
½ teaspoon salt
1 teaspoon cinnamon
1 teaspoon ground cardamom

Place eggs, sour cream, sugar and almond essence in a large bowl and mix until combined. Sift flour with bicarbonate of soda, salt and spices and add gradually to egg mixture, beating until batter is smooth.

Pour into a greased 23cm gugelhopf, bundt or ring tin that has been dusted with sugar. Bake in a moderate oven 180C (350F) for 1¼

hours or until a skewer inserted into the centre comes out clean. Leave in tin for 10 minutes before turning out to cool on a wire rack.

Crispy cheese pies

Miniature pies with a piquant filling, good hot or cold.

CRUST
1½ cups flour
½ teaspoon salt
Freshly ground pepper
90g butter or margarine
2 tablespoons crushed cornflakes
1 egg yolk
A little water, if needed

FILLING
3 hard-boiled eggs, chopped
½ cup grated hard cheese
2 gherkins, chopped
1 teaspoon capers, chopped
3 rashers bacon, cooked and crumbled

TO FINISH
Milk
Extra grated cheese

Sift flour, salt and pepper together and rub in butter. Mix in cornflakes, then stir in egg yolk and a little water, if necessary, to make a firm dough. Roll out on a floured surface and cut with a 6cm biscuit cutter.

Spoon filling on to the centres of half the rounds, brush edges with a little milk and top with remaining rounds, pressing edges well together. Brush tops with milk and sprinkle with a little extra grated cheese. Bake in a hot oven 200C (400F) 18-20 minutes. Makes about 12.

FILLING: Combine all ingredients and mix well.

Above: For a super-easy picnic, try these Croissants With Ham And Cheese.

March

Sandwiches, open and shut

When England's Earl of Sandwich put a slice of meat between two pieces of bread, he certainly began something! A good sandwich can be a great meal — a nourishing lunch, breakfast on the run, a picnic, a teatime delicacy, a cocktail treat. At one end of the scale are the Shooter's Sandwich and the Hero, whole crusty loaves bursting with filling, designed for rugged appetites; at the other extreme are the small tea sandwiches to be eaten with gloved fingers, as described by Mrs Beeton. In between there are hundreds of variations.

The open sandwich

Open sandwiches have been copied throughout the world as one of the great Danish inspirations. They are made with thin slices of any type of rye bread, crusty french bread, toasted or plain, or crispbreads. These are spread with butter or fat, such as Herbed Lard, right to the edge of the bread to prevent any moisture from the topping making the bread soggy. The fat helps to hold everything in place.

The generous toppings turn the sandwiches into a meal; they are eaten at lunch, and always with a knife and fork.

Toppings are generally made up from foods found in the household pantry or refrigerator: cold roast meats or poultry; canned or spiced fish; potato salad; cheese; mayonnaise; cold scrambled or hard-boiled eggs. The delicatessen supplies salami, smoked pork and beef, ham, liver sausage, smoked salmon or mackerel, along with capers, horseradish, gherkins and pickles.

Fresh vegetables play an important role — tomatoes, cucumber, lettuce, onions — and herbs, such as chives, dill, parsley and cress, are all used.

Try these combinations or make up your own.

SMOKED TURKEY WITH CRANBERRIES: Place young lettuce leaves on thickly buttered rye or french bread. Place thin furled slices of smoked turkey on top and finish with preserved cranberries and watercress sprigs.

DANISH BLUE WITH RAW EGG YOLK: Cover buttered rye bread with a very thin slice of danish blue cheese. Place an onion ring in the centre and put the egg yolk in centre of ring, to stop egg from running off. Omit egg yolk if preferred.

ROAST BEEF WITH ROQUEFORT CREAM CHEESE: Place thin, furled slices of roast beef on pumpernickel thickly spread with equal quantities of cream cheese and roquefort. Top with sprigs of watercress.

BACON AND AVOCADO WITH TOMATO: Fry rindless streaky bacon rashers until crisp, drain and cool. Place bacon on buttered rye bread and top with a slice of tomato. Place sliced avocado over tomato and garnish with cress or alfalfa.

SMOKED SALMON WITH CREAM CHEESE: Place a slice of smoked salmon on french or rye bread, thickly spread with cream cheese. Garnish with spring onion rings and capers.

RADISH, WATERCRESS AND ANCHOVY BUTTER: Butter black or rye bread with butter which has been softened and flavored with anchovy essence or two pounded anchovy fillets, a little lemon and a grinding of pepper. Pile high with thin slices of radishes and watercress and drizzle with a little dressing.

SPICED HERRING WITH ONION RINGS: Place herrings on buttered dark rye bread, top with overlapping raw onion rings and garnish with capers or cress.

PATE WITH MUSHROOMS: Spread half a french roll or rye bread with butter and top with a thin slice of

Right: A tray of mouthwatering Danish-style open sandwiches. Use your imagination to develop new flavor and texture combinations.

pate. Finish with button mushrooms first marinated in a thick mustard-flavored dressing. Garnish with watercress.

ROAST PORK AND ORANGE: Top buttered light rye bread with thinly sliced pork; garnish with an orange twist and a piece of crackling.

ROAST PORK AND BEETROOT: Place slices of roast pork on buttered light rye bread or crispbread; garnish with a slice of cooked beetroot and a strip of crisp crackling.

HAM WITH VEGETABLE SALAD: Make vegetable salad with equal quantities of chopped cooked beetroot and spring onion and a little chopped gherkin. Add some stiff mayonnaise to bind. Place ham slice on buttered dark or light rye bread or french bread. Mound salad neatly on top and garnish with watercress sprigs.

SALAMI WITH POTATO AND CHIVES: Spread rye or french bread or crispbread with herbed lard and place slices of salami on it; arrange slightly overlapping slices of boiled new potato and sprinkle with snipped chives.

HERBED LARD: Melt some pure lard, or gently fry some fat pork or fat bacon dice until the fat runs. Add a little finely chopped onion and a few leaves of thyme and fry until onion is softened. Allow fat to solidify before using on bread.

Beef tartare sandwiches

Beef tartare, the classic raw beef mixture that is popular in much of Europe, may be eaten as a first or main course but makes a sophisticated sandwich. Mound it on french bread to serve with drinks or on rounds of the larger italian bread for a sandwich meal. The traditional way to prepare Beef Tartare is to scrape the meat to get a very fine minced texture, but a food processor does the job in a flash.

Butter
French or italian bread
Extra chopped parsley
BEEF TARTARE
500g lean round steak
¼ onion, very finely chopped
1 tablespoon capers, finely chopped
2 tablespoons finely chopped parsley
Salt
Freshly ground black pepper
¼ teaspoon dry mustard
Dash worcestershire sauce
Few drops Tabasco
1 egg yolk

Scrape the meat with the edge of a metal spoon until it is all scraped to a fine mince, discarding any fat and gristle as you go. If you have a food processor, remove all fat and gristle first, cut the lean meat into pieces and process with the steel blade until almost smooth.

Lightly mix the steak with remaining ingredients, seasoning well with salt and pepper. Pile on to rounds of lightly buttered french or italian bread, patting gently to firm it on and round the top. Mark with the back of a knife to form a crisscross pattern if you wish. Sprinkle with chopped parsley. Makes about 20 small sandwiches; 8 large.

Club sandwich

When in New York I love to order a club sandwich. Served with a nice choice of salad vegetables and pickled cucumbers, it makes a meal.

3 slices white bread
Butter
Mayonnaise
4 thin slices cooked chicken breast
Salt and freshly ground black pepper
4 thin slices firm, ripe tomato
3 rashers bacon, rind removed and fried crisp
Stuffed olive to garnish
Dill pickles and salad vegetables

Toast bread on both sides. Spread one side of each slice with butter and mayonnaise. Cover one slice with chicken, season with salt and pepper and top with second slice of toast, buttered side up. Cover with tomato and bacon, season and place third slice of toast on top, buttered side down. Cut diagonally in half and garnish with an olive secured with a toothpick. Serve with a few dill pickles and carefully prepared salad vegetables. Serves 1.

Chicken and avocado triangles

The combination of chicken and avocado tastes luxurious. It's a good way of making one avocado and a little chicken feed a few people.

12 slices brown bread
Butter
1 ripe avocado, peeled and stoned
2 teaspoons lemon juice
Salt and freshly ground black pepper
1½ cups chopped, cooked chicken meat
2 tablespoons mayonnaise
Finely chopped parsley to garnish

Butter bread lightly. Mash avocado with lemon juice, and season with salt and pepper. Combine chicken and mayonnaise. Spread half the bread with a layer of avocado, then chicken. Top with remaining bread. Trim crusts and cut each sandwich into 4 triangles. Arrange on a platter and garnish with a little finely chopped parsley. Serves 4.

The reuben

The name tells us that we owe the reuben to the traditions of Jewish cookery. Anyone who knows New York's wonderful delicatessens will remember hot sandwiches like this.

1 thick slice from a large loaf of rye bread
Thousand island dressing (commercial or homemade)
Sauerkraut, rinsed in cold water and squeezed dry
2 thin slices corned beef
1 slice swiss cheese

Toast bread on one side and spread the other side with thousand island dressing. Cover with a generous layer of sauerkraut and top with corned beef then with cheese. Grill until

Above: The Poor Boy is definitely not poor eating this sandwich is a meal for two.

filling is heated through and cheese melts. Serves 1.

Poor boy sandwich

This sandwich made in a long french loaf with lots of filling is sometimes called a Submarine or Hero.

1 long loaf french bread
Butter for spreading
Lettuce leaves
125g thinly sliced salami, ham, or your favorite meat
8 slices swiss or cheddar cheese, cut to fit
1 large onion (preferably the mild spanish type) cut into rings
Optional: tomato slices, halved black olives, chopped pepper or pimento, chopped anchovies, slices of dill pickle

Split the loaf in half lengthwise and butter generously. Line both halves with lettuce leaves. Arrange layers of salami, cheese and onion rings on the bottom half, and any extras you fancy. Put the top half on to make a sandwich, then cut into 4 pieces. Serve at once, or wrap each piece in plastic wrap and then foil to take on a picnic. Cut across into pieces to serve. Serves 4.

Shooter's sandwich

Cut a long crusty loaf lengthwise and remove some of the crumb. Grill a thick piece of rump steak until medium rare, slice across thinly and pile while hot into the base of the loaf. Drizzle over any juices that have escaped while slicing. Season with salt, freshly ground pepper and mustard and add sliced dill pickle if desired. Put top on and tie with string. Wrap tightly in aluminium foil or plastic film and put a heavy weight on top for about six hours. Cut across into thick slices to serve.

The BLT

This great American favorite is, of course, bacon, lettuce and tomato.

3-4 rashers bacon, rind removed
2 slices white bread
2 tablespoons mayonnaise
4 slices tomato
Salt
1 crisp lettuce leaf

Fry bacon until crisp and drain on a paper towel. Toast bread and spread each slice with mayonnaise. Pile tomato on one slice, salt and top with bacon, lettuce and second slice of toast, mayonnaise side down. Serve immediately. Serves 1.

Easter lunch

Easter is a time for reflection and rejoicing — without doubt the most important date on the Christian calendar. In my home I always make Hot Cross Buns, and Pashka from the Balkans and Russia — not because these were traditional in our family home, but mainly because they are so delicious. Although the spring lambs have grown, lamb always seems the dish for an Easter lunch — either a leg of lamb or a pretty crown roast. Enjoy this pleasant break. A little planning on the food front will make it all the more pleasurable.

Pashka

The word 'pashka' means Easter in Russian, and this creamy sweet is one of the traditional delights of the Russian Easter table. When friends drop in, serve it thickly spread on slices of fruit bread — or enjoy it for dessert, with a cup of strong black coffee and a crisp biscuit.

125g unsalted butter, softened
½ cup castor sugar
500g ricotta cheese
3 hard-boiled egg yolks
Grated rind of 1 lemon
½ cup currants
½ cup finely chopped mixed peel
½ cup chopped blanched almonds
½ cup cream, whipped
TO DECORATE
Glace fruits and mixed peel

Cream butter, add sugar gradually and beat until light and fluffy. Push ricotta cheese and egg yolks through a fine sieve. Add to creamed mixture with lemon rind, beating until thoroughly combined. Add currants, mixed peel and almonds, and lastly fold in the whipped cream. If mixture is very soft, chill until firm enough to shape.

Pile mixture on a serving plate and shape into a pyramid, using a broad knife or spatula. Decorate with glace fruits and mixed peel, and chill until firm.

Note: In Russia, the letters 'XB' (meaning Christ is risen) are outlined in mixed peel on one side of the pashka, and a cross on the other.

Crown roast of lamb

This is indeed a dish for special occasions. A crown roast is simply two racks of lamb bent round and sewn together at each end with the bones on the outside and the meat on the inside. A rack consists of the 6-7 rib chops or cutlets which adjoin the short-loin chops on one end and the forequarter on the other. For a crown roast or other dish using rack of lamb, the joint is chined, the skin and some of the thick fat covering are trimmed off and the meat is cleaned away from around the bones for about 4cm from the ends. Your butcher will usually do all this for you if you give a little notice. Order your crown roast by the number of cutlets, according to how many people you plan to serve. It is usual to allow two cutlets per serving, although for small spring lamb you may wish to serve three.

1 crown roast of lamb
MUSHROOM STUFFING
60g butter
2 spring onions, finely chopped
375g mushrooms, finely chopped
1 tablespoon chopped fresh thyme or 1 teaspoon dried thyme
1 tablespoon finely chopped parsley
1 cup fresh white breadcrumbs
Salt
Freshly ground pepper
GRAVY
1 small onion, finely chopped
1 tablespoon plain flour
1 cup stock or vegetable water
Salt
Freshly ground pepper

Make the mushroom stuffing. Melt 30g of the butter and cook the spring onions gently for 1 minute, then add the mushrooms, thyme and parsley. Cook briskly for 5 to 6 minutes then remove from the heat and add the remaining butter and breadcrumbs. Season with salt and pepper to taste.

If liked, slice additional mushrooms. Keep aside and, when serving the crown roast, top with mushrooms browned in butter.

Wrap the ends of the bones of the crown roast in aluminium foil. Stand the lamb in a roasting pan and roast in a hot oven 200C (400F) for 30 minutes. Spoon the stuffing into centre and roast for a further 30 minutes or until the juices run pale pink when the meat is pricked with a skewer. Transfer to a heated platter and allow to stand in a warm place for

Right: Traditional Easter fare includes Pashka, Hot Cross Buns and a basket of colored eggs.

about 10 minutes while making the gravy. When ready to serve, the foil is removed and a cutlet frill may be placed on the end of each bone. Carve at the table straight down between two bones into double cutlets. Serves 6-8.
GRAVY: Pour all except 1 tablespoon of fat from the pan. Add the onion to the pan and stir over a moderate heat until browned. Add the flour and stir until a good brown color then add the stock or vegetable water. Stir until bubbling gently, season with salt and pepper and allow to cook for a few minutes. Strain and serve in a sauceboat with the lamb.

Hot cross buns

There is nothing to match the flavor of your own hot cross buns.

4 cups plain flour
1 teaspoon mixed spice
½ teaspoon ground cinnamon
1 teaspoon salt
60g butter
¾ cup currants or sultanas
¼ cup chopped mixed peel
30g compressed yeast
½ cup castor sugar
½ cup lukewarm water
½ cup lukewarm milk
1 egg, lightly beaten
PASTE FOR CROSS
4 tablespoons self-raising flour
2 tablespoons cold water
GLAZE
¼ teaspoon gelatine
2 tablespoons water
1 tablespoon sugar

Sift flour with spices and salt into a bowl. Rub in softened butter, then stir in fruit and peel. Make a well in centre.

Cream yeast with sugar, add a little warm water to yeast to dissolve in completely. Add remaining water and milk to yeast and add with beaten egg to well in flour. Mix to a soft dough. Turn on to a lightly floured surface and knead until smooth and elastic. Shape into a ball, place in a clean, greased bowl and turn over so that the top of the dough is greased. Cover with greased plastic film and a cloth, and leave to rise in a warm place until doubled in bulk, about 1-1½ hours.

Turn risen dough on to a lightly floured surface and gently press out to 1cm thickness. Divide dough into 12-14 pieces and shape each into a ball. Place buns in greased round cake tins. Cover and leave to rise in a warm place for a further 20-30 minutes.
PASTE FOR CROSS: Combine self-raising flour and water and beat to a smooth paste. Fill into a greaseproof paper funnel or small piping bag, and just before baking, pipe paste in a cross on buns.

Bake buns in a hot oven 200C (400F) for about 15 minutes. Remove from oven and brush with glaze while still hot. Stand near opened and turned-off oven, so that glaze will dry on buns. Makes 12-14.
GLAZE: Sprinkle gelatine over water in a small pan. When soft, dissolve over a low heat. Add sugar and stir until dissolved. Remove from heat and brush, warm, over hot buns.
Note: If liked, omit paste and decorate with an icing cross. Mix 1 cup sifted icing sugar with enough hot milk (about 2 teaspoons) to make a firm consistency. Fill an icing bag fitted with a small plain tube and pipe crosses on to warm glazed buns.

Oriental prawn and grapefruit salad

Cut the vegetables into thin matchstick lengths (julienne), chill in iced water for 10 minutes and drain well. These little details make a difference.

1kg prawns, cooked, shelled and deveined
Lettuce leaves
½ cup julienne strips celery
½ cup julienne strips red pepper
¼ cup julienne strips shallots
1 cup bean sprouts
2 tablespoons lime or lemon juice
2 teaspoons soy sauce
½ teaspoon Oriental sesame oil
Salt and freshly ground black pepper

Above: The Crown Roast Of Lamb, Gingered Carrots and Saffron Rice make a mouthwatering sight for family and friends.

¾ cup mayonnaise
2 tablespoons chopped parsley
2 grapefruit, segmented
18 cherry tomatoes, or small tomatoes, quartered

Chill prawns until ready to serve. Arrange lettuce leaves on 6 small serving plates and top with prawns. Sprinkle over celery, red pepper, shallots, and sprouts, reserving some for garnish.

Combine in a jar, lime or lemon juice, soy sauce, sesame oil, salt and pepper; cover and shake well. Spoon over salad. Thin mayonnaise carefully with a little boiling water to make a light coating consistency. Spoon over salad. Sprinkle with reserved vegetables and parsley, then arrange grapefruit segments and tomatoes around. Serves 6.

Saffron rice

Spiced and aromatic, this rice is a perfect accompaniment to Easter lamb.

60g ghee
1 teaspoon cumin seeds
1 cinnamon stick
5 cloves
4-5 cardamom pods
1 small onion, finely chopped
2 cups long grain rice
Salt and freshly ground pepper
4 cups chicken stock
½ teaspoon saffron

Melt ghee in a heavy saucepan and add cumin seeds, cinnamon stick, cloves and cardamom pods and cook gently about 3 minutes, add the onion. Allow to cook gently in the ghee until soft and golden. Stir in the rice and season with salt and pepper.

Heat the stock with the saffron and pour on to the rice. Stir the rice and allow it to come to a boil. Cover the saucepan tightly and lower the heat.

Cook the rice gently for about 18-20 minutes or until all the liquid is absorbed and the rice tender. Remove lid and allow the rice to cook for a few minutes to release the steam.

Gingered carrots

375g baby carrots, scraped and trimmed
⅓ cup fresh orange juice
¼ cup honey
30g butter
1 teaspoon ground ginger
Salt
2 tablespoons chopped crystallised or preserved ginger

In a saucepan combine the carrots, orange juice, honey, butter, ginger and salt and enough water to cover the carrots and bring to the boil. Simmer, covered, for 8 minutes or until carrots are just tender. Add the crystallised ginger and cook uncovered over moderately high heat until the liquid is reduced, continue to cook shaking the pan until a glaze forms on the carrots. Serves 6.

Garlic-lamb provencal

Gigot Aillade is a French specialty from Provence. It is traditionally served at Easter with a green salad garnished with hard-boiled eggs.

1 leg of lamb, about 2kg
18 cloves garlic, 12 whole and 6 slivered
12 anchovy fillets, chopped
3 tablespoons olive oil
1 teaspoon chopped fresh rosemary
1 teaspoon chopped fresh thyme
Salt and freshly ground black pepper
½ cup dry white wine
2 tablespoons chopped parsley or mint

Make slits in lamb and insert a sliver of garlic and a piece of anchovy in each incision. Rub lamb with 2 tablespoons of the olive oil, the rosemary, thyme, salt and pepper. Let it stand for 1-2 hours. Place meat on rack in a roasting tin and roast in a preheated hot oven 200C (400F) for 20 minutes. Reduce heat to moderate 180C (350F) and cook for a further 1-1¼ hours.

Heat remaining tablespoon of oil in a frying pan and fry the 12 whole cloves of garlic slowly for about 10 minutes until they are soft. Set aside in a small bowl. Remove lamb from pan and pour off excess fat. Pour wine into pan, scrape off brown bits and with high heat reduce juices and wine by half. Add this liquid to garlic cloves and crush them with a fork. Stir in parsley or mint. Serve lamb sliced and pass the garlic sauce. Serves 6-8.

Simnel cake

'Simnel' probably came from the name of a fine wheat flour used by the Romans, while the 11 marzipan balls represent all the apostles except Judas.

2 x 200g packets marzipan
2 cups flour
¼ cup rice flour
Large pinch salt
¼ teaspoon baking powder
1½ cups raisins
½ cup currants
2 tablespoons chopped candied peel
250g butter
2 teaspoons grated lemon peel
1 cup castor sugar
4 eggs, separated
Sieved, warmed jam
Beaten egg, to finish
ICING (optional)
1 cup sifted icing sugar
Vanilla essence
Hot water

Grease and line a deep 20 cm round cake tin. Set the oven at moderate 180C (350F).

Roll one piece marzipan out and cut to a round to fit the inside of the cake tin. Repeat with second piece of marzipan. Set circles and trimmings aside.

Sift the flours, salt and baking powder together and mix in the fruits and peel.

Cream the butter with the lemon

rind until soft and add the sugar gradually, beating until light and fluffy. Beat in the egg yolks.

Whip the egg whites until stiff, then fold the flour mixture and egg whites alternately into the butter mixture.

Put half the cake mixture into the prepared tin, level it out and cover with a circle of marzipan, then put in the rest of the cake mixture. Bake in the centre of the oven for 2 hours, then reduce to 150C (300F); cover the tin with a double thickness of greased foil or greaseproof paper and cook for about 30 minutes more, or until a skewer inserted in the centre comes out clean. Allow the cake to cool a little in the tin, then turn out, slide it on to a baking sheet and cool the cake completely.

When quite cold, brush the top of the cake with a little warmed jam and place the second circle of marzipan on top, pressing it down well. Roll the reserved marzipan into 11 balls and arrange round the edge, securing each with a dab of beaten egg, and tie a band of foil round the sides of the cake to hold them in position. Place the cake in a hot oven 200C (400F), or under the grill for a few minutes, to brown the tops of the balls. Remove and cool.

ICING: Mix icing sugar with a few drops of vanilla and just enough hot water to give a smooth paste, and stir over simmering water until glossy. Pour the icing over the centre of the cake and decorate, if you wish, with Easter decorations such as chicks or tiny marzipan eggs, tinted with food coloring.

Note: Without the marzipan and special decorations, the mixture for Simnel Cake makes an excellent, well-flavored fruit cake for any time of the year. The egg whites, stiffly beaten and added separately, give it a crusty outside. The top may be iced or decorated with almonds or walnuts, and ½ cup nuts may be added to the mixture. Like all rich fruit cakes, it improves in both flavor and texture with keeping, so long as it is stored in an airtight tin.

Passionfruit, pawpaw and mango whip

A perfect dessert, light-textured and fresh-flavored.

1 large ripe mango, peeled, seeded and chopped or 1 x 425g can mango slices, drained and chopped
1 small ripe pawpaw peeled, seeded and chopped
6 passionfruit
2 tablespoons rum
1 tablespoon lime or lemon juice
2 tablespoons sugar
1 cup cream, whipped

Puree the mango and pawpaw in a food processor or blender, or push through a nylon sieve. Transfer to a bowl and stir in pulp of 3 passionfruit, rum, juice and sugar. Fold in cream.

Cover and chill several hours. Spoon into a serving dish and top with remaining passionfruit pulp. Serve with extra whipped cream and crisp biscuits. Serves 6.

Grilled marinated chicken

This is a specialty of a tiny restaurant Le Languedoc on the island of Nantucket, Massachusetts. It is a simple dish but would make a super Easter luncheon.

6 chicken half-breasts, boned, or 3 halved small chickens
MARINADE
2 tablespoons white wine vinegar
2 tablespoons lemon juice
3 teaspoons ground coriander
3 teaspoons chopped fresh rosemary or 1 teaspoon dried
2 cloves garlic, chopped
½ cup olive oil

Flatten the chicken breasts between 2 sheets of plastic film, or flatten chicken halves and trim off any scraggy skin.

MARINADE: Combine vinegar, lemon juice, coriander, rosemary and garlic in a bowl. Add the olive oil in a stream, whisking constantly until mixture is well combined and thick.

Place the chicken in a large dish and coat with the marinade. Cover and chill for 1½-2 hours. Remove chicken from marinade.

Heat a well-seasoned ridged griddle pan over moderately high heat until it is hot, brush with oil and sear the chicken breasts for 3-4 minutes on each side or until the flesh is springy to the touch. Or arrange the chicken breasts on the rack of a griller tray and grill under a preheated grill about 5 cm from heat for 3 minutes on each side. Transfer the chicken to a heated platter. Serve with baby new potatoes and a green salad. Serves 6.

Caramel oranges

Glamorous enough for a luncheon or dinner party — yet inexpensive.

6-8 large oranges
1 cup sugar
⅔ cup cold water
⅔ cup warm water

Using a swivel-headed vegetable peeler, thinly pare several strips of rind from one orange and cut into shreds. Drop into boiling water for 1 minute, drain and set aside.

Put sugar and cold water into a heavy saucepan and heat, stirring occasionally, until sugar dissolves. Boil without stirring until the syrup begins to color, then drop in the shredded rind and cook for 3-4 minutes to glaze it. Remove rind with a slotted spoon and continue to cook the syrup, rotating the pan frequently so that it will color evenly, until it is a rich caramel brown. Remove pan from heat and, protecting your hand with a cloth, add warm water. Stir to dissolve the caramel, pour into a bowl and leave to cool while preparing oranges.

Peel oranges, removing outside membrane. Cut across into slices, removing any seeds, and re-form the oranges. Place on a serving dish, top with glazed rind and spoon a little caramel over.

Chill oranges and caramel. Pour a little more caramel over each orange as it is served. Serves 6-8.

Chocolate roulade

This is the most sumptuous chocolate dessert I know — rich, dark yet delicate.

5 large eggs, separated
¾ cup castor sugar
185g dark chocolate, broken into pieces
3 tablespoons cold water
Extra 60g grated chocolate
FILLING
1 cup cream, chilled
1 tablespoon icing sugar
1 tablespoon sweet sherry
Dash of vanilla

Grease a baking tray and cover with greased baking paper or aluminium foil.

Beat egg yolks, adding the sugar gradually, until pale and thick.

Place broken chocolate and cold water over gently simmering water to melt. Cool a little, then stir into yolk mixture. Beat egg whites to a firm snow and fold in.

Spread mixture evenly on tray, leaving a 2.5cm margin all round. Bake in a moderate oven 180C (350F) for 10 minutes, then reduce to 150C (300F) and bake 5 minutes longer. Remove from oven and cover with a cloth wrung out in cold water. Cool, then refrigerate 1 hour.

Dust a large sheet of waxed paper with grated chocolate. Remove cloth from roulade and loosen paper or foil from tray. Turn roulade out on to chocolate and carefully peel off backing.

Whip cream with sugar, sherry and vanilla and spread half the cream over the roulade. Roll up from a long

side, using waxed paper to help roll it on to a long board or serving platter. Decorate with remaining cream. Serves 6.

Green cucumber soup

A light refreshing soup, cucumber flavored with dill, this also may be served chilled.

2 large, dark green cucumbers
3 cups chicken stock
30g butter
1½ tablespoons flour
½ cup milk
2 teaspoons chopped fresh dill, or ½ teaspoon dried
Salt and freshly ground white pepper
½ cup cream
Snipped fresh dill or chives to garnish

Using a swivel-bladed potato peeler, peel cucumbers thinly, so that green beneath skin is left on. Halve lengthways, scoop out seeds and cut into pieces. Puree in a food processor or blender until smooth, adding a little stock to help if necessary. Pour into a jug, add remaining stock and set aside.

Above: Grilled Marinated Chicken, boiled new potatoes and green salad, plus pretty Caramel Oranges — an elegant meal.

Melt butter in a large saucepan, stir in flour and cook gently for 1 minute. Remove from heat, cool a little, and stir in milk. Blend until smooth, stir until boiling.

Add cucumber mixture, dill, salt and pepper. Stir in cream. Reheat gently until piping hot. Serve in heated bowls, garnished with dill or chives. Serves 6.

Healthy fare

All over the world, there are people who live longer and happier lives because they have always eaten foods that have contributed to their spectacular state of good health. Specifically, they have eaten wholefoods — unrefined foods to which nothing has been added or taken away. Essentially, wholefoods are used as close as possible to their original state. They contain no artificial colorings, preservatives or additives. Fresh vegetables and fruits are wholefoods. So too are fresh fish, poultry and meats. Dried beans, peas, lentils, rice are interesting wholefoods. These all provide valuable nutrients as well as fibre which is essential for the normal working of our digestive systems.

Peppers stuffed with sprouts and tabouli

4 red or green peppers
2 cups tabouli
1½ cups bean sprouts (mung, alfalfa etc.)
1 small cucumber, peeled, seeded and chopped
1 small carton natural yogurt
2 tablespoons finely chopped fresh mint
Salt and freshly ground pepper
Mint leaves to garnish

Leave peppers whole. Cook in boiling salted water to cover until barely tender, about 6 minutes. Drain, and refresh under cold running water. Cut tops off (stalk ends), remove seeds and ribs, and invert on paper towels to drain. If large, cut in half lengthwise.

Combine tabouli, bean sprouts, cucumber, yogurt and mint. Taste, and season with salt and pepper. Arrange peppers on a serving plate, fill with tabouli mixture, mounding it up, and garnish with fresh mint leaves. Serves 4.

Note: Fresh sprouts are available from vegetable sections of large supermarkets, health food shops and many greengrocers.

Tabouli

This refreshing salad is one of the national dishes of Syria and Lebanon. The burgul gives it a delicious nutty flavor that will appeal to all health food enthusiasts and those who just like good things to eat.

1 cup burgul (cracked wheat)
2 large tomatoes
3 tablespoons finely chopped spring onions or 1 mild spanish onion, chopped
Salt and freshly ground pepper
1-1½ cups finely chopped parsley
½ cup chopped fresh mint
4 tablespoons olive oil
4 tablespoons lemon juice

Soak burgul in cold water for about 1 hour before preparing salad. Drain and squeeze out as much water as possible (place in a Chux cloth or in a sieve and squeeze with hands). Peel and chop tomatoes. Combine tomatoes and spring onions with burgul and season to taste with salt and pepper. Add parsley, mint, oil and lemon juice and mix well. Taste to see if more seasoning is required — the salad should taste lemony. Stand for at least an hour to allow the burgul to absorb the dressing.

Serve in individual bowls with pita bread or fresh cos lettuce leaves for scooping up the salad. Or pile the salad in a pyramid and garnish with halved stoned black olives. A lovely simple first course or as part of a salad meal. Delicious also with thinly-sliced grilled steak in pita bread. Serves 6-8.

Swiss health breakfast

A variation of the original muesli. It is a good idea to store wheatgerm in the freezer, as this is one food that quickly goes rancid. It is easy to take out enough for each day as you need it.

1 tablespoon fresh wheatgerm
1 tablespoon whole oats
5 tablespoons water
1 teaspoon lemon juice
Honey to taste
Cream or milk
1 unpeeled apple
Chopped nuts if desired

Soak the wheatgerm and whole oats in the water overnight in the refrigerator. Next morning add the lemon juice in honey and cream or milk, and mix well. Shred the unpeeled apple into this and serve at once. Scatter a handful of chopped nuts on top if you like — it makes the cereal more nutritious. Serves 1.

There are as many variations of the swiss health breakfast as there are fruits on the market. Fresh grapes, peaches, bananas, or any other favorite fruit can be mashed or shredded into the cereal.

Lentils and rice

In this cheap and nourishing dish, called Mujaddarah, the lentils and rice complement each other in providing protein. In the Middle East, the proportions vary with every family. Olive oil gives a distinctive

Left: Peppers (green or red) Stuffed With Sprouts And Tabouli are attractive and tempting.

flavor to the dish, but a lighter vegetable oil will do.

1 cup brown lentils, well washed and soaked for 1-2 hours
1 onion, finely chopped
7-8 tablespoons oil
Salt and freshly ground black pepper
½ cup long grain rice
2 extra onions, sliced downward into half-moon shapes

Drain lentils, cover with fresh water and boil for 20 to 30 minutes or until tender. Fry chopped onion in 2 to 3 tablespoons of the oil until soft and golden. Add it to the lentils and season with salt and pepper. Mix well and add to the rice together with enough water to make the volume of liquid in the pan about equal to that of the rice.

Season again and simmer gently, covered, for about 20 minutes or until rice is tender; add a little more water during the cooking if needed — it should be just absorbed when the rice is cooked. Fry sliced onions briskly in remaining oil until dark brown, sweet and almost caramelised.

Serve the lentils and rice in a large shallow dish garnished with the fried onion slices. Either hot or cool, it is a delicious light supper dish to have, dressed with yogurt. Serves 4.

Rizogalo

Milk is plentiful in Greece and is often used in this everyday Greek pudding. At one time it was made with ewe's milk but now it is usually cow's. Never serve the pudding hot — room temperature is about right.

5 cups milk
⅔ cup short grain rice
2-3 strips lemon rind
2 teaspoons cornflour
⅔ cup sugar
Ground cinnamon

Put milk, rice and lemon rind into a saucepan. Stir well and cook over gentle heat for about 30 minutes or until rice is soft. Mix cornflour into sugar, distributing it evenly to avoid lumps when cooking, and stir into the rice. Continue cooking gently for a further 20 to 30 minutes until the pudding is like very thick cream. Stir from time to time to prevent sticking.

Cool slightly, discard the lemon rind and spoon the rice into individual shallow glass bowls. Set aside until cooled to room temperature and covered with a skin.

Sprinkle lightly with cinnamon to serve. Serves 6.

Yakni

The most popular Arab way of feeding a large family is a rib-warming stew with one, two or three vegetables in season, very little meat, some dried beans and a dish of rice. Lamb is the usual meat and favorite vegetables and all types of beans, chick peas, lentils and split peas, soaked and boiled, are added for extra nourishment. Cubes of meat can be used instead of the meatballs.

500g assorted vegetables — zucchini, tomatoes, okra, eggplant, green beans, cabbage, etc
1 large onion, chopped
2 tablespoons oil or butter
500g lamb or beef, minced
2-3 tablespoons tomato paste
¼ cup chopped parsley or coriander
½ teaspoon ground allspice, cumin or coriander (optional)
Salt and pepper
2 potatoes, cut into small pieces and sauteed in oil
or 1 cup dried beans, soaked then cooked until tender.

Wash and trim the vegetables and cut into pieces. Peel tomatoes if using, cut off the hard stems of okra, sprinkle eggplant pieces with salt and leave to drain in a colander for 1 hours.

Fry onion in oil or butter until lightly browned. Roll meat into small balls and fry these until they change color. Add vegetables and stir for a minute or so. Cover with water, stir in tomato paste, parsley and spice if used, and season with salt and pepper.

Simmer gently for about 1 hour, until the sauce is rich and reduced; add water if the stew becomes too thick. Near the end of the cooking time, add the potatoes or beans if using.

Your stew will have an aroma reminiscent of millions of kitchens in the Middle East if you include okra or spinach and fry 4 cloves of peeled and crushed garlic and ½ teaspoon ground coriander with the onions for 2 minutes, before putting in meat and vegetables.

Serve as a main course with fluffy rice. Serves 4 to 6.

Oriental vegetables with tofu

Tofu, or fresh bean curd, is available from Asian and health food shops. It is high in protein, low in cholesterol and kilojoules. Covered with water, which should be changed daily, it will keep for two or three days in the refrigerator.

3 cups mixed prepared vegetables — choose from 3 or more of these: green beans, carrots, zucchini, mushrooms, spinach, chinese or ordinary cabbage, snow peas, orinary peas, bean sprouts
1 onion
3 sticks celery
1 green pepper
250g tofu
3 tablespoons peanut oil
2 cloves garlic, sliced
2 teaspoons grated fresh ginger
Soy sauce
2 tablespoons toasted sesame seeds

Trim vegetables and cut the larger ones into bite-size diagonal shapes, squares or slices. Peel the onion and slice downward into wedges, then separate into petal shapes. String celery and slice on the diagonal, remove seeds and ribs from pepper and cut into squares. Dry the tofu on paper towels and cut it into bite-size squares.

Heat the oil gently with the garlic and ginger in a wok or frying pan. When oil is hot add tofu and saute until tofu is browned on both sides. Remove with chopsticks or slotted spoon, discard garlic and ginger and set tofu aside.

Add onion, pepper and celery to the pan and saute on medium heat for 3 minutes. Add each of the longer-cooking vegetables in turn and saute for a few minutes between additions and tossing every minute or so, then add fast-cooking vegetables and toss a minute or two longer. Gently stir in tofu, bean sprouts if using, and heat through.

Season with soy sauce to taste, sprinkle with sesame seeds and serve immediately, with a bowl of steaming white or brown boiled rice if you wish. Serves 4.

Above: Tofu is high in protein, low in cholesterol, and delicious in Oriental Vegetables With Tofu.

Sashimi

A great change is taking place at fish markets throughout Australia. More and more people are lining up to buy very fresh raw tuna and other fish for sashimi — one of the glories of Japanese cuisine. You may also find wasabi — the pungent green horseradish that makes all the difference.

500g raw fresh fish (tuna, snapper, squid, prawns — alone or a mixture)
DIPPING SAUCE
3 tablespoons Japanese soy sauce
2 teaspoons sake or sherry
Pinch sugar
GARNISH
2½ teaspoons wasabi (powdered green horseradish)
2 sticks celery
1 carrot
Daikon (long white oriental radish)
6 green spring onions
2 cups boiled rice (if liked)

Prepare the fish, first remove the skin and any bones. Tuna and other fish may be cut into thin slices or thicker strips. The squid is cleaned, opened out and cut into wide strips, then the flesh is scored diamond fashion, prawns are shelled, deveined and the 2 halves opened like butterfly wings.

Make the sauce by combining ingredients.

PREPARE THE GARNISH: Mix the wasabi with enough water to form a paste — like mustard. Finely chop or shred the celery, carrot, daikon and spring onions, including some of the green tops.

TO SERVE: On four individual plates arrange the fish. Slices are overlapped, strips are formed into a little mound, the prawns are placed decoratively. Or, if using only one fish aim at arranging it attractively on the plate. Garnish each plate with about a teaspoon of the wasabi. Group the vegetables in a decorative mound. Cover each plate with a sheet of plastic and refrigerate for no more than an hour before using.

Pour the dipping sauce into 4 tiny individual bowls and accompany each serving of sashimi with its own sauce. A bowl of rice may be placed on the side. Offer chopsticks or forks. Each guest dips the fish in wasabi or dipping sauce or takes a little rice or vegetables and enjoys eating the fish with his or her own combination.

Kasha

Outside Russia, kasha is the name of a coarse buckwheat meal, but in Russia both buckwheat and other cooked grains are called kasha. Buckwheat kasha has an assertive, almond-like flavor. It can be served with all meat dishes, especially with rich meats like pork, duck or goose.

2 cups buckwheat meal (kasha), or 1 cup buckwheat and 1 cup burgul (cracked wheat)
3 cups stock or water
1 teaspoon salt, if needed
45g butter

If grain is not toasted (brown) already, place it in a dry frying pan and toast over a medium heat, stirring often, until golden brown.

Bring stock or water to the boil in a heavy saucepan, adding salt unless stock is already seasoned. Pour toasted grain in slowly, stirring constantly. Bring to the boil over gentle heat and simmer a few minutes until thick. Stir in butter, cover and cook gently 10 minutes.

Remove lid and fluff up kasha with a fork. Leave uncovered over very low heat for 1 hour, tossing and turning it with a fork every 5 minutes to separate grains. Serves 2, or 8 as an accompaniment.

KASHA WITH MUSHROOMS AND ONIONS: Cook kasha as described in recipe and fold through 90g sliced mushrooms and 1 large chopped onion which have been sauteed in butter.

KASHA WITH PICKLED PORK AND ONIONS: Cook kasha as described in recipe, and fold through 125g diced pickled pork and 1 large chopped onion, which have been sauteed together in a little butter until pork is crisp and brown.

HERBED SESAME KASHA: Cook kasha as described in recipe, and fold through 2 tablespoons each of toasted sesame seeds and chopped fresh herbs.

Poor man's caviar

A great-tasting pate, this is every bit as good as rich man's caviar. Use as a sandwich spread or dip.

2 large eggplant
1 clove garlic, crushed
2 teaspoons lemon juice
2 tablespoons olive oil
Salt and pepper
GARNISH
Chopped parsley
Lemon wedges

Prick the eggplant all over with a fork, cut in half and place cut side down on a greased baking tray. Bake in a preheated moderately hot oven, 190C (375F), for 30 to 40 minutes until softened.

Peel, then blend the eggplant in an electric blender with the garlic and lemon juice, adding the oil a teaspoon at a time. Alternatively, chop the flesh finely and rub through a sieve, then add the garlic, lemon juice and oil in a steady stream, beating until smooth. Season to taste. Chill until required. Pile into a bowl and top with chopped parsley. Serve with lemon wedges and wholemeal toast.

Lentil soup

The lovely lemony flavor of cumin adds interest to this healthy, hearty soup.

3 tablespoons oil
2 onions, chopped
1 carrot, chopped
2 celery sticks, chopped
1 clove garlic, crushed
⅔ cup lentils
1 teaspoon ground cumin
4 cups stock or water
Salt and pepper
3 tomatoes, peeled, seeded and chopped
1 tablespoon chopped parsley to garnish

Heat the oil in a large pan, add the onion, carrot and celery and fry until softened. Add the remaining ingredients (except tomatoes) with salt and pepper to taste. Bring to the boil, cover and simmer for 40 minutes, stirring occasionally. Add tomatoes and cook further 5 minutes. Check the seasoning.

Pour into a warmed tureen and sprinkle with parsley. Serves 6.

Chick pea salad

An unusual Mediterranean-type salad.

1 cup dried chick peas or 2 cups canned
2 small onions (red salad ones, if available)
1 bay leaf
1 clove garlic
1 teaspoon salt
1 orange and 1 grapefruit, cut into segments
2 stalks celery, sliced
½ green or red pepper, sliced
1 tablespoon chopped mint

Soak chick peas in water overnight. Next day, drain. Place in a saucepan, cover with water, add 1 small onion halved, bay leaf, garlic and salt. If using canned chick peas, drain and wash.

Bring to the boil. Skim off any scum that rises to the surface. Simmer for 1-1½ hours or until tender. Drain and leave to cool.

Prepare orange and grapefruit segments (see method). Cut remaining onion into rings. Mix orange and grapefruit segments, celery, sliced pepper and onion rings and mint. Toss with Vinaigrette Dressing (1 tablespoon vinegar, 3 tablespoons oil, pinch mustard, salt and pepper beaten together until slightly thickened). Serves 4.

TO SECTION CITRUS FRUIT: Hold the fruit over a bowl to catch all the juice, and use a sharp, serrated knife to remove all the rind and white pith. Pare it around and around like an apple, so the cells are exposed. Loosen the sections by cutting down along the membrane. Lift out the segments in one piece and remove any seeds. Squeeze the core with remaining membrane over the segments. This juice may be added to the dressing.

Hopping John

This traditional dish of black-eyed peas and rice from America's Deep South shows the early settlers knew a thing or two about healthy eating. The combination adds up to good nutrition, the texture is delicious and only a small amount of pork is required for excellent flavor. Serve hopping john with a fresh green vegetable for a complete main course — or add a slice of pan-browned ham for those who feel hard-done-by without meat.

1 cup black-eyed peas
1 smoked pork hock or 1 small piece pickled pork, or 1 ham bone
1 large onion, chopped
1 cup raw long grain rice
Salt and freshly ground pepper

Soak peas overnight in cold water or cover with boiling water and soak for 4 hours.

Drain peas, rinse in cold water and place in a large saucepan with the pork, onion and enough water to measure twice the depth of the peas. Simmer covered for 1 hour or until peas are tender. Remove pork with slotted spoon, discard any bone and gristle and chop meat into small pieces. Drain peas in a sieve placed over a bowl and add enough water, if necessary, to measure 2 cups liquid. Return chopped meat, peas and liquid to the saucepan, bring to a boil and add the rice. Simmer covered until the rice is tender and the liquid is absorbed. Stir in salt and pepper to taste and spoon into a heated serving bowl. Serves 6.

April

Great cakes

At weddings, birthdays, christenings, bon voyage parties and even the simplest of get-togethers, a cake is often the centre of interest, and this interest happily extends to the cook. Everyone wants to know who made the cake. Thirty years of fan mail proves to me that most cooks want to be able to make a perfect cake. It's not all that difficult — just follow the instructions carefully. Here are some favorite recipes.

Basic butter cake

This basic butter cake keeps fresh for about 4-5 days because of the eggs and butter. Try a few simple variations or even increase the quantity and bake it in a fancy ring tin.

125g butter
¾ cup castor sugar
1 teaspoon vanilla
2 eggs
2 cups self-raising flour
Pinch salt
½ cup milk

Grease two 20cm sandwich tins or one 20cm deep round or square cake tin, and line bases with greased greaseproof or baking paper. Set oven temperature at moderate 180C (350F).

Using an electric mixer, cream butter and sugar with vanilla until mixture is white, light and fluffy. Add eggs one at a time, beating well after each.

Sift flour and salt together and fold into creamed mixture alternately with milk, beginning and ending with flour. Do this by hand (beating at this stage will cause tunnels through the cake). When mixture is smooth, pour into prepared tins.

Lightly smooth top and bake in moderate oven 25-30 minutes for sandwich tins, 45-50 minutes for deep tin. Cake is done when a fine skewer inserted in the centre comes out clean. Cool in tins for 5 minutes then turn out and cool on wire racks. Fill and ice as liked.

FOR A LARGER CAKE: For two 23cm sandwich layers or one deep cake made in a plain tin or a fancy ring (ours was made in a springform tin with ring insert).

Follow recipe for Basic Butter Cake or one of the variations given below, but use 185g butter, 1¼ cups castor sugar, 1½ teaspoons vanilla, 3 eggs, 3 cups self-raising flour, large pinch of salt and ¾ cup milk.

VARIATIONS

Lemon Cake: Add the grated rind of 1 lemon and 2 teaspoons lemon juice but omit vanilla.

Sultana Cake: Add ⅔-1 cup sultanas and 1 teaspoon mixed spice.

Seed Cake: Add 1 tablespoon caraway seeds to mixture and sprinkle 1 teaspoon of seeds on top before baking.

Spice Cake: Sift 1 teaspoon mixed spice with flour and salt. Add 125g chopped dates or chopped walnuts to mixture.

Hazelnut cake

A luscious continental cake, flavored with hazelnuts, this is topped with apricot glaze and filled and decorated with chocolate butter cream — perfect for a very special coffee party or to serve as a dessert.

½ cup castor sugar
5 large eggs
1 slightly heaped cup ground hazelnuts
2 tablespoons melted butter
1 tablespoon honey
½ cup plain flour
Chocolate butter cream
½ cup apricot jam
Toasted hazelnuts

Set oven temperature to moderate 180C (350F). Line the base of a 20cm spring form tin with greaseproof paper. Butter the tin and paper and sprinkle with a teaspoonful of the castor sugar. Separate eggs, beat yolks with sugar until thick and pale. Stir in ground hazelnuts, melted

Right: Great tastes — Basic Butter Cake and Hazelnut Cake.

butter and honey, sift flour over and mix well.

Beat egg whites until they hold soft peaks and fold into the egg yolk mixture. Turn into the preparèd tin and bake in moderate oven for 35-40 minutes or until a fine skewer inserted in the centre comes out clean.

Remove sides of tin, lift cake on to a rack and cool, then split into two and fill with about half the chocolate butter cream.

Heat apricot jam with 2 tablespoons of water in a small saucepan, stirring until dissolved. Rub the mixture through a wire sieve then return it to the saucepan and boil gently until the glaze is clear and drops heavily from the spoon. Pour on to the top of the cake and spread to the edges.

Allow to cool and set. Fill remaining butter cream into bag fitted with a star tube, pipe rosettes round the cake and top each with a whole toasted hazelnut (prepared by baking in a slow oven until skins are brittle, then rubbing skins off in a cloth).

CHOCOLATE BUTTER CREAM: Cream 2 egg yolks with ¼ cup castor sugar until pale. Dissolve ¼ cup additional castor sugar in ½ cup milk, bring it to the boil and stir into the yolks. Return this mixture to the saucepan and stir on very low heat until it thickens and coats the back of the spoon. Cool completely, then cream 250g butter until soft and beat butter and 125g chocolate gradually into the custard.

Austrian coffee cake

185g butter
¾ cup castor sugar
3 eggs, slightly beaten
1½ cups self-raising flour
Pinch salt
1-2 tablespoons milk
COFFEE SYRUP
1 cup strong black coffee
⅓ cup sugar
½ cup water
2 tablespoons rum

Grease a 5-cup ovenproof mould or ring tin (we used a savarin mould). Sprinkle with fine breadcrumbs. Set oven temperature at moderate 180C (350F).

Beat butter until soft, add sugar, a little at a time, and continue beating until light and fluffy. Gradually add eggs, beating thoroughly after each addition. Fold in sifted flour and salt alternately with enough milk to make a dripping consistency.

Spoon into prepared mould and bake in a moderate oven for 40-45 minutes or until skewer inserted in the centre comes out clean. Leave to cool in mould for a few minutes then turn out on to wire rack. When cold replace cake in mould. Slowly pour coffee syrup over cake. Refrigerate until ready to serve. Turn out on to plate and, if liked, coat with whipped cream and toasted flaked almonds. Or serve with a bowl of whipped cream and strawberries. Serves 8-10.

COFFEE SYRUP: Put coffee into a jug. Heat sugar and water in a saucepan until sugar dissolves then boil for 2 minutes. Add to coffee and allow to cool. Stir in rum.

Caramel nut cake

1¾ cups flour
Pinch salt
1¾ teaspoons baking powder
1 cup firmly packed brown sugar
125g butter, softened or soft margarine
2 eggs
½ cup milk
1 teaspoon vanilla
¾ cup chopped walnuts or pecans
Sifted icing sugar

Sift flour, salt, baking powder and sugar into a bowl. Add butter, eggs, milk and vanilla and beat vigorously until well blended. Fold in nuts. Spoon into a greased and bottom-lined 23 x 33cm cake tin. Bake cake in a preheated moderate oven 180C (350F) for 30-35 minutes or until a skewer inserted in the centre comes out clean. Cool on a wire rack, then dust with icing sugar. Cut into squares to serve.

Sour cream chocolate cake

This is a truly superb cake, which I like to serve as a dessert with whipped cream, or in thin slices with afternoon coffee.

TO COAT TIN
15g butter
4 tablespoons flaked almonds
CAKE
1 cup boiling water
125g dark chocolate, chopped
1 teaspoon bicarbonate of soda
250g butter
1½ cups castor sugar
3 eggs, separated
1 teaspoon vanilla essence
2½ cups flour
Pinch of salt
1 teaspoon baking powder
⅔ cup light sour cream

Generously butter a 12-cup bundt tin or two 20cm fluted ring tins. Sprinkle with flaked almonds, pressing them well into the butter to coat the bottom and sides of the tin.

Put the boiling water, chocolate and bicarbonate of soda in a bowl and stir until smooth. Cream the butter and sugar until light and add the egg yolks one at a time, beating after each addition. Stir in the vanilla, then add the chocolate mixture a little at a time. Sift the flour, salt and baking

Far left: Austrian Coffee Cake, with cream or strawberries. Left: Use ripe fruit in Banana Cake.

powder and fold in alternately with the sour cream, mixing lightly until just combined. Beat the egg whites until stiff and fold into the creamed mixture with a large metal spoon.

Turn gently into the prepared tin and bake in a preheated moderate oven 180C (350F) for 1 to 1¼ hours for the large cake or 45 minutes for the small cakes, or until cooked when tested with a skewer. Leave in the tin for a minute, then turn out and cool on a wire rack.

Note: A bundt tin is used to give a pretty shape to continental cakes. It is a deep tin with fluted sides and a hole in the middle and should be available at kitchen shops and department stores.

Banana cake

Whenever I have very ripe bananas on hand I use them up by making this lovely banana cake.

2 teaspoons lemon juice plus enough milk to make ⅔ cup
2⅓ cups self-raising flour
1⅔ cups sugar
1 teaspoon bicarbonate of soda
1 teaspoon salt
185g butter, softened
⅔ cup mashed, very ripe bananas (about 2 large bananas)
2 eggs
⅔ cup chopped walnuts
Whipped cream

Set oven temperature to moderate 180C (350F). Grease two 23cm sandwich tins.

Leave the lemon juice and milk for 5 minutes until the milk thickens a little. Sift flour into a large bowl and add sugar, soda and salt. Add softened butter, mashed bananas and milk. Mix well by hand with a wooden spoon, or with an electric mixer at low speed. Add eggs and beat 2 minutes longer. Stir in walnuts.

Pour mixture into sandwich tins and bake in moderate oven for about 35 minutes or until cooked when tested with a skewer. Cool for 5 minutes in the tins, then turn out.

When layers are cool, sandwich with whipped cream. Chill until ready to serve.

Swedish thousand-leaves torte

The French make a version of this cake using jam in place of the apple sauce and call it Millefeuilles — a thousand leaves. It's easy to make with ready-made pastry.

1 x 375g packet ready-to-roll puff pastry
2 cups sweetened apple pulp
1½ cups cream, whipped
Glace cherries (optional)

Cut pastry into 4 portions and roll each portion out thinly on waxed paper. Cut into 20cm rounds. (If using ready-rolled pastry, simply cut out the rounds on the dividing paper from the packet.) Prick pastry all over with a fork.

Brush 2 baking trays with iced water and place pastry rounds (still on paper) on them. Place all trimmings on the trays as well. Bake in a very hot oven 230C (450F) for 6-8 minutes until pastry is delicately browned. Leave on paper until cold.

Place one round on a serving plate, spread with apple, then with cream, and continue building the pastry rounds and filling like a layer cake. Using a palette knife or spatula, spread cream around sides of cake. Crush the pastry trimmings and press gently on to the sides of the cake.

Decorate top of cake with cream and glace cherries if liked.

Citrus halvah cake

This is a deliciously fresh-tasting dessert cake.

185g butter
¾ cup castor sugar
Grated rind and juice of 1 orange and 1 lemon
3 eggs, beaten
1½ cups semolina
1¼ cups ground almonds
3 teaspoons baking power
SYRUP
¾ cup castor sugar
5 tablespoons water
2 tablespoons lemon juice
½ tablespoon ground cinnamon
2 tablespoons chopped candied peel
3 tablespoons orange juice
TO DECORATE
½ cup cream, whipped
¼ cup flaked almonds, toasted

Cream the butter and sugar together with the grated citrus rind until pale and fluffy. Beat in the citrus juice and eggs a little at a time, then continue to beat, fold in the semolina, ground almonds and baking powder.

Turn into a greased and floured 23cm ring tin. Bake in a preheated very hot oven 220C (425F) for 10 minutes, lower the heat to 180C (350F), and bake for a further 30 minutes.

Meanwhile, prepare the syrup. Place the sugar, water, lemon juice, cinnamon and peel in a pan and bring to the boil, stirring. Simmer until slightly thickened, then add the orange juice.

Turn the cake on to a serving plate straight from the oven. Pour the syrup over the hot cake slowly until it is all absorbed. Leave to cool.

To serve, fill the centre of the ring with the whipped cream and sprinkle the almonds on the cake. Serves 10.

Lindy's famous cheesecake

Lindy's restaurant in New York was a famous actors' haunt. People went there to see and be seen — and to eat the smooth, rich cheesecake. This is my version, the ingredients scaled down to family size.

CRUST
250g plain sweet biscuits
1 tablespoon sugar
½ teaspoon mixed spice
90g melted butter
FILLING
750g neufchatel or philadelphia cream cheese
½ cup sugar
1 teaspoon vanilla essence
¼ teaspoon salt
Grated rind 1 lemon
1 tablespoon lemon juice
4 eggs, separated
1 cup cream
2 tablespoons plain flour, sifted
TOPPING
1 cup cream, whipped
Freshly grated nutmeg

Grease a 23cm spring form tin and set oven temperature at 170C (325F).

Crush biscuits into fine crumbs, and blend with remaining crust ingredients. Press over bottom and sides of tin and chill while preparing filling.

FILLING: Have cream cheese at room temperature. Beat until soft, then add sugar, vanilla, salt, lemon rind and juice and beat until creamy. Beat in egg yolks one at a time, then beat in cream. Lightly stir in sifted flour, and finally fold in stiffly beaten egg whites.

Pour into prepared crust and bake in preheated slow oven for 1 hour 10 minutes. Turn off heat and leave cake in oven until cold. Chill until ready to serve, spoon whipped cream on top and sprinkle with nutmeg. Serves 10-12.

VARIATION: Instead of nutmeg, the cake may be decorated with strawberries, passionfruit, grated chocolate etc.

Honey spice sponge roll

Honey not only gives this sponge roll a very special flavor but it has remarkable keeping qualities. Store in a tin, but leave lid slightly ajar.

3 eggs
½ cup castor sugar
½ cup arrowroot
1 tablespoon plain flour
½ teaspoon ground cinnamon
1 teaspoon mixed spice
1 teaspoon cream of tartar
½ teaspoon bicarbonate of soda
1 tablespoon honey (at room temperature)
HONEY CREAM FILLING
90g butter
2 tablespoons honey
1 tablespoon water

Line a 30 x 25cm swiss roll tin with greased greaseproof or baking paper.

Set oven temperature at moderately hot 190C (375F).

Beat eggs until thick and gradually add sugar. Continue beating until mixture is thick and will hold its shape, about 10 minutes. Sift arrowroot, flour, cinnamon, mixed spice, cream of tartar and soda together three times. Lightly fold into egg mixture and add honey, mixing gently until evenly distributed.

Turn into prepared tin and gently shake to spread mixture evenly. Bake in preheated hot oven 190C (375F) for 15-20 minutes. Turn out on to a tea towel which has been lightly dusted with castor sugar and quickly peel off paper and trim edges. Roll up immediately in tea towel, starting with narrower side. Allow to cool and then unroll, fill with Honey Cream Filling and roll again. (If serving as dessert, roll cake beginning with wider side, and cut into diagonal slices.)

HONEY CREAM FILLING: Beat butter until light and add honey a tablespoon at a time, then add water. Continue beating until mixture is smooth and creamy.

Croquembouche

A traditional celebration cake of France, this is popular for weddings, special birthdays or even Christmas.

40-50 small profiteroles (see Choux Pastry)
2-2½ cups Creme Patissiere
1 cup castor sugar

Choose a serving platter the size you want your croquembouche base to be. Fill profiteroles with Creme Patissiere. Place sugar in a small, heavy saucepan and cook slowly, tilting frequently from side to side so that sugar heats evenly, until it melts and caramelises to a rich brown. Dip saucepan in cold water to stop further cooking.

Lifting profiteroles with two fine skewers, dip tops in the toffee and arrange in a ring, touching each other, on the plate. Dip more profiteroles and arrange in a slightly smaller ring on top, holding each profiterole steady until toffee sets to secure it in place. Continue, using 1-2 fewer profiteroles for each layer, to make a tall cone shape ending in one profiterole on top. Gently reheat toffee if it becomes too thick.

Put croquembouche in a cool, dry place until required (in humid weather, use a fan to keep toffee from getting sticky). Reserve remaining toffee.

Just before serving, decorate with spun sugar. Heat remaining toffee, dip in the backs of two metal spoons, touch together then pull apart to pull a long fine thread of toffee. Repeat until you have a bunch of threads then break off and drop over the croquembouche. Spun sugar cannot be made far ahead of time as it becomes damp and collapses.

Choux pastry

Use for profiteroles. Baked choux pastries can be stored in an airtight container for one to two weeks or in the freezer for one to two months. Crisp for a few minutes in a moderate oven if necessary.

1 cup plain flour
1 cup water
125g butter cut into pieces
½ teaspoon salt
1 teaspoon sugar (for sweet puffs)
4 eggs
1 egg beaten with pinch of salt for glazing

Sift flour on to a piece of greaseproof paper. Put water, butter, salt and sugar, if using, into a medium-size saucepan. Bring slowly to the boil (butter must be melted before water boils).

Immediately remove from heat, tip in flour all at once and stir vigorously. Return to heat and continue stirring until mixture forms a mass, leaves sides of saucepan and begins to film the bottom — this will take only a short time. Remove from heat and cool a little. Mix the 4 eggs together and beat into dough, a little at a time, until dough is as shiny as satin and holds its shape on a spoon. You may not need to add all the egg.

Take spoonfuls of the pastry and push off in mounds on to a greased baking tray. Alternatively, fill into a piping bag fitted with a 1cm plain tube and pipe pastry into small, high mounds. Pastry will swell to about twice its size when baked, so allow for this.

Brush pastries with egg glaze and bake in a very hot 220C (425F) oven for 10 minutes; reduce heat to moderate 180C (350F) and bake 15-25 minutes more (depending on size) until pastries are golden-brown, firm to touch, and feel very light in the hand.

Make a slit or hole in the side of each puff and return to turned-off oven with the door slightly ajar for 20 minutes. This ensures that they are thoroughly dried out — the secret of puffs that will hold their shape without collapsing.

Cool on a rack. Fill by piping filling through holes in sides, or by carefully cutting off tops with a serrated knife, spooning in filling and replacing lids. This quantity of pastry makes about 20 x 5cm puffs, 12 x 8-10cm puffs or one 23-25cm ring.

Creme patissiere

This rich pastry cream is used to fill fine pastries and cakes. Unlike whipped cream, it will not turn pastries soggy if they are filled ahead of time.

1½ cups milk
1 vanilla bean or 1 teaspoon vanilla essence
½ cup sugar
¼ cup plain flour
2 eggs
2 egg yolks

Bring milk to the boil with vanilla bean, if using, and set aside. Mix sugar and flour together, add eggs and egg yolks and beat until thick and pale. Remove vanilla bean from milk or add vanilla essence, if using, and gradually pour milk into egg mixture, stirring constantly until well blended. Return to the saucepan and cook over gentle heat, stirring, just until boiling point. Remove from heat and continue stirring for a few minutes to release steam. Turn into a bowl to cool and chill, covered with plastic film laid directly on the surface of the cream, until needed. Makes about 2 cups.

Sacher torte

This is Vienna's most famous cake, elegantly simple but really luscious. It has become fashionable to serve whipped cream with sacher torte. This is not traditional, but it is really delicious.

200g dark cooking chocolate
125g unsalted butter
1 teaspoon vanilla
8 egg yolks
10 egg whites
Pinch salt
¾ cup castor sugar
1 cup plain flour
¾ cup apricot jam
GLAZE
100g dark cooking chocolate
1 cup cream
250g sugar
1 teaspoon golden syrup
1 egg white
1 teaspoon vanilla

Preheat oven to moderate 180C (350F). Grease and line two 23cm sandwich tins with circles of greased greaseproof or baking paper.

Above: Smooth and rich, Lindy's Famous Cheesecake is a speciality of a popular old New York restaurant.

Place chocolate and butter in a bowl and stand over hot water until melted, stirring occasionally with a wooden spoon. Add vanilla, cool slightly and beat in the egg yolks one at a time.

Beat egg whites slowly with a pinch of salt until frothy.

Increase speed and beat until soft peaks form, then add the sugar, 1 tablespoon at a time; continue beating until thick and glossy.

Stir 3 tablespoons of this meringue into the chocolate mixture — this makes it easy to combine the chocolate mixture and the meringue.

Sift the flour over the chocolate mixture. Using a metal spoon or rubber spatula with an over and under cutting motion, fold together the remaining meringue, chocolate mixture and flour. Do not over mix.

Pour the mixture into the prepared tins and bake in a preheated moderate oven 180C (350F) for 20-30 minutes or until a fine skewer comes out clean when inserted in the centre of cakes.

Remove tins from oven and stand on wire racks for 20 minutes; run a knife around cakes, turn out. When completely cold, store in sealed tins for 24 hours.

Sieve jam into a small saucepan, add 1 tablespoon of hot water and heat slightly. Join cakes with ⅓ of the jam and brush top and sides with the rest of it.

Stand cake on rack over a baking tray and, holding the saucepan over the cake, pour the glaze over. When icing stops dripping and starts to set, move to a serving dish. Refrigerate until the glaze has hardened.

Sacher torte can be stored in the fridge for several days.

GLAZE: In a small heavy saucepan combine chocolate, cream, sugar and golden syrup. Heat gently until sugar dissolves, stirring with a wooden spoon, then boil without stirring for 5 minutes.

In a small bowl, lightly beat egg white, then pour in the hot chocolate mixture, beating constantly. Pour back into saucepan. Cook, stirring, over a gentle heat for 3 minutes. Stir in vanilla. Allow to stand for only a minute before pouring over cake.

• *For more delicious cake recipes, see index.*

Chinese favorites

Eating with chopsticks is the best way to enjoy Chinese food, as it allows just the right amount of sauce on each morsel of food. Once adept, you will want to extend your skills by cooking Chinese food with chopsticks. Gold, silver, ivory, wood and plastics are available, but plain bamboo chopsticks are cheapest and perhaps best. Bamboo and wooden chopsticks are used in the kitchen as they can withstand high temperatures and do not alter the taste of the food. Chinese cooks never use anything except chopsticks. They are used as beaters, cooking forks, mixing spoons and draining spoons. Hold 3 or 4 chopsticks, separating each between the fingers and practise beating an egg or mixing seasonings. Invest a few dollars in a bundle of bamboo chopsticks and a wok, and start on these simple recipes. Don't be discouraged by an early clumsiness, as with any manual skill it takes practice! It is great fun and amazingly simple — once you get the hang of it.

Stir-frying

There is a sequence to using a wok and stir-frying. This is the general system:

- All meat and vegetables should be on hand before stir-frying begins. Meat and vegetables should be thinly sliced, diced or cubed, the seasonings measured and in small bowls. Check your ingredient list thoroughly before you start.
- Heat wok over high heat until it is hot enough for a drop of water to sizzle. When the water evaporates add a tablespoon or two of oil, peanut or vegetable oil but not olive. Spread the oil over the pan by tilting or rotating the pan itself. Heat the oil until it is bubbling and easy flowing, but not quite smoking.
- The first seasonings like garlic, ginger and green shallots are sometimes added and stirred until they become lightly browned and the oil aromatic. Remove if recipe advises. With strong heat, add the meat, small batches at a time, and toss and flip it vigorously to assure even cooking and prevent burning. At this point add no other liquid, if the meat is raw the liquid will toughen it. However if the pan becomes too dry drizzle a little oil around rim of pan; as it runs down it will get hot. The hot oil seals the flavor and serves to partially cook the meat.
- Add liquid seasonings such as soy sauce and sherry. These are never poured directly on the food, since they might be absorbed in concentration in one part of the food, they are added like the oil around the rim.
- Transfer the partially-cooked meat to a dish and reserve it. Rinse out the pan, add more oil and heat it, add the vegetables a handful a a time (this keeps the temperature of the oil from dropping too quickly). The stock is added in the same manner as the oil, around the rim.
- When the vegetables are almost cooked, return the meat and quickly stir-fry. Sometimes liquid seasonings are added at this point.
- The sauce or pan liquids are sometimes thickened with cornflour if desired. The ingredients are pushed aside, the cornflour blended with a little stock or water is stirred in to thicken the liquids. The ingredients are then tossed briefly and the dish is finished. This whole process should take only from one to three minutes.
- Transfer the food to a heated platter and serve at once.

To cook Chinese noodles

Allow 1 bundle Chinese egg noodles for each person or approximately 60g. Soak noodles in hot water for about 10 minutes. The strands will separate and enable the noodles to cook evenly. Bring a large saucepan of water to the boil and add a spoonful of peanut oil. Drain the soaked noodles and drop them into the boiling water.

When water returns to the boil, cook fine noodles for 2-3 minutes, wide noodles for 3-4 minutes. Do not over-cook. Like properly-cooked pasta, noodles should be tender but still firm to the bite.

Right: Chinese food to delight the taste buds — Fried Rice, Sweet And Sour Pork and Ginger Chicken.

At end of cooking time, drain noodles in a large colander, then run cold water through the noodles to rinse off excess starch and to cool them so they don't continue to cook in their own heat. Drain thoroughly. Use in soups, or braised noodle dishes — spread noodles out on a damp (not wet) towel, to dry out a little before using as directed in recipe.

SOFT FRIED CHINESE NOODLES: Cook noodles as described above and spread out to dry. A little peanut oil may be sprinkled over them to prevent them from sticking.

Heat 2 tablespoons each of peanut oil and sesame oil in a wok or frying pan, and when very hot add a handful of noodles. When golden on one side, turn and fry other side. Repeat with remaining noodles, draining on paper towels before serving at once. It may be necessary to add more oil to the pan if a large quantity of noodles is being fried, but make sure the fresh oil is very hot before adding noodles.

Serve them with beef, pork, poultry or vegetable dishes, or combine with stir-fried ingredients.

CRISP FRIED CHINESE NOODLES: These crisp noodles are used mainly as a garnish. Rice vermicelli and cellophane noodles may be fried in deep hot oil straight from the packet. Egg noodles need to be cooked first as for soft-fried noodles. Use a larger amount of peanut oil and deep-fry in handfuls until crisp and golden-brown. Drain on paper towels before serving.

Fried rice

You can vary the additions to the basic fried rice mixture, substituting prawns or cold roast pork for the chicken or ham. Serve as a light, nourishing main course or with other Chinese dishes.

6-8 dried Chinese mushrooms
½ teaspoon sugar
1 teaspoon soy sauce
Few drops Oriental sesame oil
1 chicken fillet, diced
1 egg white, lightly beaten
2 teaspoons cornflour
4-6 tablespoons peanut or vegetable oil
2 large eggs, beaten
½ cup diced ham or bacon or barbecued pork
Salt
3 cups cold, cooked rice
½ cup cooked peas
Pinch pepper
1-2 tablespoons rice wine or dry sherry

Soak the mushrooms in warm water to cover for 20 minutes then drain, rinse and remove stalks. Sprinkle with sugar, soy sauce and sesame oil mixed together then cut into dice or strips.

Mix chicken with egg white then cornflour. Stir fry in a little oil (see Stir-Frying), taking care that pieces do not stick to each other. Remove chicken, drain wok and wipe out quickly with paper towels.

Heat wok, add 1-2 tablespoons oil and heat. Pour in beaten eggs, stir and, when cooked, remove and cut into pieces about 2.5cm square.

Wipe out wok again and heat remaining oil. Add mushrooms, ham, bacon or pork and chicken, Stir-fry over moderate heat and season lightly with salt. When oil and salt are absorbed, add rice, mixing and turning thoroughly to prevent ingredients sticking together. Add peas and cooked eggs, season with salt and pepper, sprinkle with rice wine or sherry and stir-fry over high heat until heated through, taking care that rice does not scorch and that grains remain separate. Serve immediately. Serves 4-6.

TO COOK RICE: Place 1½ cups well-rinsed medium grain rice in a heavy saucepan with ½ teaspoon salt and cold water to come 2cm above level of rice. Bring to the boil then lower heat to medium and continue cooking until steam holes appear in rice. Reduce heat to very low, cover tightly and cook 12-15 minutes or until rice is tender. Set aside, covered, 5 minutes then turn on to a large, shallow dish. Spread out and cool, then chill, covered, overnight.

Ginger chicken

3 chicken fillets
Salt
2 tablespoons rice wine or dry sherry
125g snow peas
1 egg white
1 tablespoon cornflour
Peanut or vegetable oil
1 teaspoon finely chopped garlic
2 thumb-size pieces fresh ginger, peeled and cut into thin shreds
SAUCE
½ teaspoon salt
1 tablespoon vinegar
2 tablespoons chicken stock
1 tablespoon sugar
1 tablespoon tomato sauce
1 teaspoon cornflour
2 teaspoons water

Hold each chicken fillet firmly and, with the knife at a 45-degree angle to the surface, cut into slices across the grain of the meat. Place meat in a bowl and mix with ½ teaspoon salt and 1 tablespoon rice wine or sherry. Set aside.

Remove strings and stems from snow peas.

Place all sauce ingredients except cornflour and water in a small saucepan and heat, stirring. As soon as it boils, remove from heat and set aside. Mix cornflour and water for sauce in a small bowl and set aside.

Mix chicken with egg white, then with the 1 tablespoon cornflour. Stir-fry in batches in a little fairly hot oil, just until chicken changes color, being sure to keep the pieces moving to prevent crisping and browning. Set chicken aside, drain wok and wipe out quickly with paper towels.

Heat 2 tablespoons oil in the wok, stir-fry garlic until it releases its aroma, then add snow peas and ginger. Stir-fry for 30 seconds, add chicken, sprinkle with remaining rice wine or sherry and continue to stir-fry 2 minutes longer. If the sauce is too thin, thicken with prepared cornflour and water mixture. Serve immediately with boiled rice. Serves 4.

GINGER CHICKEN WITH BROCCOLI OR GREEN PEPPER: Substitute 1½ cups broccoli florets or 1 large green pepper, seeded and cut into triangular pieces, for the snow peas. Stir-fry 2-3 minutes with garlic and ginger before adding chicken, then 2-3 minutes with chicken.

Sweet and sour pork

This is one of the best-loved Chinese-style dishes around the world.

500g pork fillet
1 red chili
2 peppers
1 x 225g can pineapple rings, drained
1 leek
Cornflour
1 tablespoon water
1 egg, beaten
Peanut or vegetable oil
1 teaspoon chopped garlic
1 tablespoon rice wine or dry sherry
SAUCE
⅓ cup vinegar
1 teaspoon soy sauce
3 tablespoons sugar
1 tablespoon tomato sauce
1 tablespoon worcestershire sauce
½ teaspoon salt

Slice pork thinly on the diagonal and beat each slice lightly with the back of the knife to tenderise the meat. Cut chili into thin rings, discarding seeds. Remove seeds and ribs from peppers and cut into squares. Cut pineapple into pieces about same size as peppers. Quarter leek lengthwise, wash well and cut into 4cm lengths. Mix sauce ingredients together. Mix 2 teaspoons cornflour in water in a small bowl.

Dip pork pieces into beaten egg, then coat with cornflour. Stir-fry in batches in a little oil over medium heat. Set pork aside, drain wok and wipe out quickly with paper towels.

Heat 2 tablespoons oil in the wok and stir-fry the chopped garlic; as soon as it releases its aroma, add leek then peppers. Stir-fry until vegetables are slightly softened, then add chili, pineapple and pork and continue to stir-fry, mixing and turning ingredients briskly, for 2-3 minutes. Moisten with rice wine or sherry, then add sauce. Thicken sauce with prepared cornflour mixture, toss briefly. Serve immediately with boiled rice. Serves 4-6.

Stir-fried squid with crab

Squid has an interesting, chewy texture and needs only a very short cooking time — overcook it, and it toughens.

375g squid
½ teaspoon salt
3 teaspoons oil
2 slices fresh ginger, finely chopped
6 shallots, cut into short lengths (include some green tops)
4 tablespoons crabmeat, flaked (fresh or canned)

SEASONINGS
2 teaspoons tomato paste
2 teaspoons sugar
1 tablespoon light soy sauce
4 tablespoons chicken stock
1 tablespoon rice wine or dry sherry
2 teaspoons cornflour blended with 2 tablespoons water

Clean squid thoroughly and rub in the salt. Cut into strips 5 x 2cm and make criss-cross cuts over the fleshy side of all the strips.

Heat the oil in a wok or frypan over moderate heat. Stir-fry the ginger and shallots for 30 seconds. Add the squid and stir-fry for 1 minute, then add crab and fry 30 seconds longer. Combine seasoning ingredients, stir into mixture, and cook over moderate heat for 1 minute, or until sauce is clear and thickened. Serves 4-6.

Above: Stir-fried Squid With Crab is a dish that is as good as it looks. Serve it with boiled rice.

Honey prawns

Use the wok first as a frypan then as a saucepan to produce this dish.

750g green king prawns, shelled and deveined
¼ cup cornflour
1 cup self-raising flour
½ teaspoon salt
¼ teaspoon white pepper
1¼ cups water
1 egg, beaten
Oil for frying
2 tablespoons honey
2 tablespoons sesame seeds

Dust prawns lightly with cornflour. Sift flour, salt and pepper into a bowl, make a well in centre and gradually add water and egg, mixing to a smooth batter free of lumps. Put 3 or 4 prawns in a bowl, pour over a small amount of batter to coat and remove. Repeat with remaining prawns.

Heat a wok then add the oil and heat until haze rises. Add prawns a few at a time and fry for 3 minutes or until prawns are golden and cooked through. Drain and keep warm. Remove oil from pan and wipe clean. Heat 1 tablespoon fresh oil in pan, add honey and stir over gentle heat until warm. Add prawns, toss quickly, remove and sprinkle with sesame seeds. Serve immediately. Serves 4-6.

Fragrant noodles

This is a dish you find Orientals eating in Chinese restaurants.

20 dried shrimp (from Chinese groceries)
8 dried Chinese mushrooms
½ cup peanut oil
3 medium onions, diced
1 tablespoon light soy sauce
2 teaspoons Chinese wine or dry sherry
2 cups water
500g Chinese egg noodles

Soak dried shrimp and mushrooms separately in cold water for 10 minutes, then drain and clean. Remove stems and halve or slice mushrooms. Heat half of the oil in a frying pan or wok, add onions and stir-fry 2-3 minutes. Lower heat slightly, add shrimp and mushrooms and cook, stirring, until only residual moisture is left and oil spatters when in contact with moisture.

Remove from heat. Heat rest of oil in a small saucepan, add shrimp mixture, soy sauce and wine or sherry and stir-fry 1-2 minutes. Add water and simmer 20 minutes or until water has nearly evaporated. Meanwhile, cook noodles according to packet directions or instructions on these pages. Drain, rinse quickly under cold running water and drain again. Reheat all ingredients together and serve. Serves 4.

Crispy noodles with chicken

250g Chinese egg noodles boiled in water until tender, drain (see instructions on page 58).
2 boneless, skinless Chicken breasts (4 fillets)
1 tablespoon shredded green ginger
1 tablespoon Chinese rice wine or sherry
1 teaspoon cornflour
3 slices cooked ham
90g canned bamboo shoots
6 dried Chinese mushrooms
1 small bunch green shallots
7 tablespoons peanut oil
Extra 1½ teaspoons cornflour
SAUCE
1 cup chicken stock
1 teaspoon sugar
2 tablespoons rice wine or sherry

First prepare noodles, set aside to dry on paper towels. Shred the chicken into long thin strips, mix with ginger, wine and cornflour. Cut the ham and drained bamboo shoots into long strips. Soak the mushrooms in hot water, when soft cut into strips. Cut shallots into short finger lengths. Heat 3 tablespoons oil in another wok. Add cooked, drained noodles, stir-fry over high heat, turning and stirring noodles then shaping into a 'cake'. Lower heat and cook until crisp and golden then turn to brown the other side. This takes about 6-8 minutes. Meanwhile prepare chicken.

Heat 2 tablespoons oil in the wok and stir-fry the chicken 2-3 minutes, drain and set aside, discard oil.

Pour 2 tablespoons oil into wok and stir-fry mushrooms, bamboo shoots and shallots for 1 minute, add the ham and chicken and stir-fry over high heat. Mix the sauce ingredients and pour into the wok, cook for 2 minutes. Mix the extra cornflour with a little water and add to wok, stirring to thicken mixture.

Place crispy noodles on a serving platter and top with chicken mixture. Serves 4.

Five-spice duck

Devotees of Chinese food enjoy crispy-fried chicken and duck and the five-spice powder that often flavors these dishes. This recipe is for braised duck. The five-spice powder is available from Oriental food shops. It is a mixture of ground star anise, anise pepper, fennel, cloves and cinnamon.

1 duck
3 leeks
¼ cup sherry or Chinese Shaoshing cooking wine
¼ cup soy sauce
1 tablespoon honey
2 cups water sauce
1 teaspoon five-spice powder

Prick the skin of the duck. Roast the duck in a moderately hot oven 190C (375F) for 1 hour. Halve the leeks lengthwise. Wash sandy grit from between layers of leeks, cut into 5cm lengths. In a flameproof casserole place half the leeks, top with roasted duck. Pour the sherry or wine, soy sauce and honey over the duck, add the water and bring quickly to the boil. Cover and cook over a medium heat for 30 minutes, basting several times. Place remaining leeks over the duck, cover and cook for another 15 minutes. Sprinkle the five-spice over the duck and cook for another 15 minutes.

Remove duck, split in two, then remove wings and legs and cut each half into sections. Spoon leeks on to serving dish, top with duck. Serve with boiled rice or as part of a Chinese meal. Serves 4-6.

Beef and peppers in black bean sauce

500g lean fillet or rump steak
1 tablespoon soy sauce
1 tablespoon hoisin sauce (optional)
1 tablespoon tomato paste
1½ tablespoons cornflour
5 tablespoons vegetable oil
1¼ teaspoons sugar
2 tablespoons Chinese salted black beans
2 medium red or green peppers, scored and seeded
1 teaspoon grated fresh ginger
3 tablespoons Chinese wine or dry sherry

Slice beef thinly across the grain and cut into finger-length strips. Mix soy sauce, hoisin sauce, tomato paste, cornflour, 1 tablespoon oil and sugar. Add beef, turn to coat the strips all over, and leave 15 minutes. Meantime, soak beans in cold water for 15 minutes. Cut peppers into 4cm squares. Heat wok then add remaining oil over high heat. When it begins to give off a haze, add ginger and drained black beans and stir-fry 30 seconds. Add beef and stir-fry 2 minutes. Add peppers, sprinkle with wine or sherry and stir-fry 1 minute more. Serve at once. Serves 4-6.

Far left: Crispy Noodles With Chicken. Left: Chinese Smoked Meatballs — for the adventurous.

Sesame chicken with rice noodles

This soup/stew from China's Fukien province is said to rejuvenate the body. The pungent, nutty sesame oil beautifully offsets the chicken and delicate rice noodles.

750g chicken joints (thighs, breasts)
250g Chinese rice noodles
1 tablespoon Oriental sesame oil
2 tablespoons vegetable oil
1 tablespoon shredded fresh ginger
½ cup Chinese rice wine or dry sherry
3 cups chicken stock
1 teaspoon sugar
1 teaspoon salt
6 leaves spinach or silverbeet, chopped

With a cleaver or heavy knife chop chicken into bite-sized pieces. Soak noodles in warm water to cover for 5 minutes, then drain in a colander. Heat sesame oil with vegetable oil in a wok until it forms a haze. Add ginger and stir-fry for 30 seconds then add chicken and stir-fry until pieces are golden, about 3 minutes. Add wine, bring to the boil and add stock, sugar and salt. Simmer for 15 minutes or until chicken is tender. Stir in noodles and cook further 5 minutes; add spinach for the last minute. Ladle into 4 heated bowls. Serves 4.

Chicken noodle and corn soup

A thick Oriental soup that is almost a meal in itself.

1 chicken or 6 chicken joints, thighs, breasts, legs etc.
8 cups water
½ teaspoon salt
125g Chinese egg noodles
2 cups fresh corn kernels, cut from cob or 1 x 440g can creamed style sweet corn
Freshly ground black pepper
½ cup snipped coriander leaves or chopped parsley

Remove fat and trim off fatty skin from chicken, cut into joints. Cover chicken with water in a saucepan, add salt and bring to the boil. Lower heat, cover and simmer until tender, about 30 minutes. Remove chicken from stock and take meat from skin and bones. Shred the meat and return to stock. Bring back to the boil. Add noodles and corn and cook until noodles are tender. Season with salt and pepper, and stir in coriander leaves. Serves 6.

Chinese smoked meatballs

Here is a recipe for the adventurous. The humble meatball is transformed with Chinese flavorings and then smoked over black tea and fennel seeds. Meatball one-upmanship, indeed!

4 dried Chinese mushrooms
1 small can water chestnuts
500g lean minced beef
2 tablespoons soy sauce
2 tablespoons cornflour
1 tablespoons finely chopped spring onions
1 tablespoon finely chopped fresh ginger
1 medium carrot, grated
1 tablespoon rice wine or dry sherry
1 teaspoon Chinese sesame oil
FOR SMOKING
2 tablespoons each brown sugar, black tea and fennel seeds
TO SERVE
2 teaspoons sesame oil mixed with 2 tablespoons soy sauce
2 spring onions, finely chopped or shredded

Soak the mushrooms in hot water to cover for 15 minutes or until soft. Drain, remove stems and chop caps finely. Drain chestnuts, rinse under cold running water and chop finely. Place mushrooms and chestnuts in a large bowl with remaining ingredients and mix very well by hand until mixture is firm and compact. Shape into walnut-sized balls and arrange in one layer on a greased cake rack or Chinese bamboo steamer. Cover, and steam over boiling water in a wok or deep frying pan for 15 minutes.

To smoke the meatballs, you need an old frying pan, wok or other metal container. Combine brown sugar, tea leaves and fennel seeds and place in the bottom. Set over high heat and, when the mixture starts to smoke, put the rack containing the meatballs over the smoke. Cover tightly with a lid or foil and leave for 5 minutes over high heat. Reduce heat to moderate and smoke for another 5 minutes, then turn heat off and leave meatballs for a further 10 minutes, still covered.

To serve, brush the meatballs with a little of the sesame-soy mixture and sprinkle with spring onions. Serve remaining sesame-soy separately, for dipping. Serves 6-8 as a first course or 4 as a main course with rice.

Note: The burnt-sugar mixture used for smoking will lift off the wok if you soak for several hours in hot water and scrub with a stiff brush.

A wedding at home

A wedding at home is one of the happiest of occasions. I was reminded of this when a friend of my daughter elected for a garden wedding in her lovely family country home with its spacious gardens and wide verandas where grandparents, aunts, cousins as well as family and friends had so many happy memories. It took planning. Lists were made, supplies checked. Platters were borrowed, knives sharpened, paper napkins bought. China, glasses and cutlery were hired from the local RSL club, along with additional tables and seating. On the day before the wedding friends arrived to do the flowers. Others whose skills were better employed in the kitchen were washing potatoes, crisping the greens, making salad dressing and so forth. It was a hive of activity. The bride's mother had pretty floral tablecloths made for the tables, a lovely touch and as there are six children in the family, those cloths will surely get plenty of use and become family treasures! As far as help on the day they took advantage of the fact that there are nearly always local people who can be enlisted, who have had experience at serving food. Advise them of the arrangements well in advance so there is no need even for last-minute instructions. There is enough excitement without that! Informality was the keynote, food arranged on a buffet table, then tables and chairs for guests to seat themselves with friends. Pretty floral arrangements, the wedding cake, tempting food and some light music all contributed to the special atmosphere.

Wedding menu for 50 guests

Champagne Punch (alcoholic)
Fruit Tea Punch (non-alcoholic)
Sandwiches
Golden Fruit Cocktail (optional)
Wedding Chicken
Persian Rice Salad
or
Rice Salad
Greens And Avocado Salad
Baby New Potatoes
Glazed Ham (see index)
or
Roast Fillet Of Beef
or
Smoked Turkey Buffe
Golden Rum Cream Trifle
or
Babas au Rhum
Coffee
Lovers Knots
Wedding Cake

Buy the smoked turkey buffe ready to serve.

For additional guests another ham, turkey or fillet of beef may be added. Golden fruit cocktail makes a refreshing first course but is not essential. Dainty sandwiches are a welcome addition as guests usually appreciate a nibble during the wait between the service and the reception.

Most people find it easier to order a wedding cake well in advance of the big day. However, if you want to make and decorate your own, use the recipe for Christmas Cake (see index) or your special favorite cake.

A guide for beverages

COFFEE: 250g finely ground coffee makes 5 litres or 20 metric cups, giving 20-25 large cups of coffee or 40 demitasse; 60g instant coffee makes 5 litres. Allow 1 carton (300ml) cream, 2 cups milk and 500 to 750g coffee sugar for this quantity.
SOFT DRINKS: 2 litres serves 10 drinks.
BEER: 4 drinks to 1 bottle (kegs might be simpler to handle and keep colder if a barman is available to handle the equipment).
WINE: 1 bottle serves 6 drinks.
SHERRY OR PORT: 1 bottle gives 20 to 24 drinks.
CHAMPAGNE: 1 bottle champagne pours 6 to 8 glasses; on this basis 9 to 15 bottles champagne will provide drinks throughout the meal for 30 guests. Nine bottles will pour about 68 glasses, giving 2 glasses per person with a little extra. Fifteen bottles will pour about 3½ glasses per guest. Make your own calculations on how much you would like to serve.

Right: Clockwise from upper left corner Babas Au Rhum, Smoked Turkey Buffe, Golden Fruit Cocktail, Wedding Chicken, Rice Salad, Greens And Avocado Salad.

Store food with care

One of the dangers of home catering is a lack of awareness of handling bulk foods. Please read and treat this matter with the seriousness it deserves. Spoilage is an ever-present danger and is not always detectable by appearance, taste or smell.

● It is not advisable to multiply quantities; it is better to make up the recipe several times, cooling and storing each batch correctly as it is done. Leave meat and other perishables in the refrigerator until you are ready to use.

● Food that is to be held must be covered, cooled quickly and kept cool until it is time to serve or reheat it. If it contains meat, eggs, fish, cooked vegetables, milk or cream it must be refrigerated for the holding time.

Note that these precautions apply to cold foods, including sandwiches, as well as hot ones. Once food is reheated, don't hold it for long below 100C (212F) or boiling point. Reheating should be done as close to serving time as possible.

● Be certain that working surfaces, hands and anything with which the food comes in contact are perfectly clean.

● Have ready a good supply of very sharp knives. Don't slice raw meat then cooked meat with the same knife unless it is well washed and cleaned before re-using.

Wedding chicken

The chicken and sauce are cooked ahead (2 or 3 days, if necessary) and assembled on the wedding day. This is a variation of the dish I served at my daughter's wedding.

1 onion, halved
6 cloves
8 peppercorns
4 sticks celery
2 carrots
1 teaspoon salt
1 cup white wine
20 large half breasts of chicken
SAUCE
1 onion, finely chopped
1 tablespoon oil
1 tablespoon ground cumin
1 tablespoon curry powder
1 tablespoon tomato paste
¾ cup white wine
¾ cup stock
2 bay leaves
12 dried apricots
Salt
Freshly ground pepper
2 cups mayonnaise
1 cup chopped walnuts or pecans

TO GARNISH
Lettuce, watercress or parsley
Tomato slices

Cooking this large quantity of chicken is easier if done in several batches. Place all the ingredients, except the chicken, in a large wide saucepan baking dish and add one layer of chicken breasts. Pour in enough water to cover the chicken (return remaining breasts to refrigerator). Cover the dish with a lid or foil, and simmer gently for 20 minutes.

Lift the chicken from the liquid as soon as it is cool enough to handle. Remove the bones and skin, Place them in a clean saucepan an set aside. Cut each chicken breast diagonally into 2 neat pieces. As soon as they are cool, store in the refrigerator in a covered container. Repeat the process with the remaining chicken, adding water as required.

To prepare the stock for the sauce, add the poaching liquid and 4 cups of water to the skin and bones saved from the chicken. Bring slowly to the boil, reduce the heat, and simmer for 1 hour. Strain, cool and refrigerate.
IMPORTANT: Take great care when cooking in bulk. Food should be cooled quickly to prevent bacteria multiplying, and stored at once in the refrigerator.
SAUCE: Cook the onion gently in hot oil until soft but not brown, about 4 minutes. Add the cumin and curry powder and cook for 3 minutes longer, stirring. Add the tomato paste, wine, stock, bay leaves and apricots. Bring to the boil, and add salt and pepper to taste. Simmer uncovered, for 10 minutes. Strain, pushing solids through the sieve, and cool.

Gradually add the cooled sauce to the mayonnaise. Taste, and adjust the seasoning, fold in the chopped nuts. Take the poached chicken pieces from the refrigerator and gently spoon over enough sauce to moisten them lightly; you will need about one-third. Cover, and replace in the refrigerator. Also cover and chill the remaining sauce.
TO SERVE: Arrange the chicken pieces carefully on platters. Spoon a little sauce over each. Serve with rice salad. Serves 25.

Golden fruit cocktail

3 x 425g cans grapefruit segments
3 x 283g cans mandarin segments
2 x 227g cans maraschino cherries in syrup
2 x 425g cans pineapple pieces
2 teaspoons Angostura bitters
3 cups shredded coconut
25 mint sprigs

Drain the fruits, reserving the liquid from the grapefruit and cherries. Gently mix the fruits together with the grapefruit and cherry syrups and bitters. Cover and chill. Wash the mint and store it, covered, in the refrigerator. At serving time, spoon the cocktail into small glass coupes (strewing some of the coconut through) and top with a sprig of mint. Serves 25.

Greens and avocado salad

When making green salad for a large party, prepare and dry lettuce, store in plastic bags in refrigerator.

2 iceberg or cos lettuce
3 mignonette lettuce
3 avocados, peeled, stoned and sliced
1 cup pecans
1 cup sliced green shallots
DRESSING
6 tablespoons white wine vinegar
Salt and freshly ground black pepper
¾ olive oil

Wash and dry lettuce — a whirling salad basket is ideal for this. Store in plastic bags in refrigerator until required. Prepare avocados at the last minute.

Whisk vinegar, salt, pepper and oil together until well blended. Arrange lettuce in large bowl, pour dressing over and toss well. Add avocado, nuts and shallots and toss again gently, but avoid breaking avocado.
Serves 25.

Babas au rhum

4 cups flour
½ teaspoon salt
30g compressed yeast
1½ tablespoons sugar
1 cup warm milk
4 x 60g eggs
250g butter, softened
4 tablespoons currants
SYRUP
2 cups water
2 cups sugar
2.5cm piece vanilla bean
6 tablespoons rum

Sift flour and salt into a large warmed bowl. Cream yeast and sugar in a small bowl, then add warm milk. Make a well in centre of flour and add yeast mixture. Sprinkle a little flour from sides over top, cover with a cloth and leave in a warm place for 15 minutes for yeast to sponge.

Beat eggs into butter and add to yeast mixture. Beat vigorously with your hand until all flour is incorporated and dough is smooth and elastic, add currants and give another few beats. Cover bowl with greased plastic film and a cloth and leave to rise in a warm place until dough is doubled in bulk, 30-40 minutes. Spoon dough into two well-greased 23cm savarin moulds or deep ring tins. Allow to rise in a warm place until dough reaches top of tin. Bake in a hot oven 200C (400F) for about 20 minutes or until babas are golden-brown and beginning to shrink a little from sides of mould.

To make syrup, boil water, sugar and vanilla bean for 10 minutes, then remove from heat, discard vanilla and stir in rum.

Cool babas in tins for five minutes, then pierce all over with a fine skewer. Place tin on a plate and drizzle syrup over a little at a time. Turn out of tin, allow to cool. Serve with creme chantilly (whipped cream). Each baba serves 8-10.
Note: Babas may be cooked several weeks before the wedding and frozen. Do not pour syrup over before freezing. Wrap the cooled babas in foil then freeze. To thaw, remove from freezer 12 hours before required. At serving time heat in moderate oven 180C (350F). Pour hot syrup over and allow to cool. Good kitchen shops are now selling proper savarin tins for the cake; buy two.
CREME CHANTILLY: Allow 1 x 300ml carton cream, whipped with a little sugar and vanilla, for each baba.

Rice salad

4 cups raw basmati or long grain rice
1 cup vinaigrette
500g frozen peas
1 green pepper, seeded and finely chopped
4 tender sticks celery, sliced

Cook the rice 2 cups at a time, in plenty of boiling salted water. Drain, rinse with hot water to remove any trace of starch and drain again. When all the rice is cooked, moisten with ½ cup of the dressing and store, covered, in the refrigerator. The night before the wedding, cook the peas in boiling salted water until just tender. When cool, add to the rice with the peppers and celery and remaining vinaigrette. Keep refrigerated until ready to serve.
Serves 25.

Sandwiches

Small, perfect sandwiches can't be beaten as an hors d'oeuvre to serve to wedding guests when they arrive from the church, or for any time when you want something simple and delicate. Remember that 'perfect' is the key word, meaning that the sandwiches must be prepared and stored with great care to be temptingly fresh and dainty. Buy the bread unsliced and ask your grocer or delicatessen dealer to slice it thin on the machine, or firm the loaf in the freezer for 1 hour before slicing it yourself. I like to wrap 6 rounds of bread, 3 sandwiches with crusts still on, in the outside lettuce leaves normally discarded, then in plastic film wrap, label them, then pack them in a flat container so they keep a good shape. Store in refrigerator overnight. When required, unwrap and trim and cut with a good, sharp knife — preferably a serrated bread knife.

Persian rice salad

4 cups long grain rice
2 slices fresh ginger, finely chopped
2 teaspoons ground coriander
2 teaspoons ground cumin
½ teaspoon nutmeg
6 green shallots, finely chopped (including some of green tops)
½ cup each raisins, sultanas and dried apricots
1 tablespoon grated orange rind
½ cup toasted pine nuts
About ¾ cup olive oil
Salt and freshly ground black pepper
GARNISH
12 dried apricots, poached in water for 3-4 minutes
Toasted pine nuts

Cook rice, 2 cups at a time, in plenty of boiling salted water for 15 minutes. Drain well. Cut apricots in thin slices.

Place warm rice in a large bowl and add remaining ingredients, seasoning with salt and pepper. You need just enough oil to moisten rice without making it mushy, so add it gradually. Serve salad warm or at room temperature, garnished with apricots and nuts. Serves 25.

Golden rum cream trifle

A rich yet fresh-tasting dessert for a wedding. This can be made a day ahead.

40 coconut macaroons, approx.
½ cup sherry
3 x 425g cans apricot halves
3 x 425g cans pineapple pieces
10 passionfruit, pulped
1 tablespoon grated lemon rind
2 tablespoons gelatine
½ cup water
10 eggs, separated
1¼ cups sifted icing sugar
1 cup rum
4 x 300ml cartons cream
Extra whipped cream and passionfruit to decorate

Crush the macaroons and put them in a layer in the bottom of two large or 4 small glass serving bowls. Sprinkle with sherry. Cover with the apricots, pineapple and the passionfruit pulp and ½ cup juice, reserving a few apricots for decoration. Sprinkle with lemon rind. Soften gelatine in water and stand the container in hot water until gelatine is dissolved. Beat egg yolks with sifted icing sugar until pale and thick; stir in rum and dissolved gelatine.

Whip cream and fold in, beat egg whites until they hold soft peaks and fold in. Pour over fruit and chill overnight covered with plastic wrap. Decorate with whipped cream rosettes and reserved apricots and drizzle over additional passionfruit pulp. Serves 25.

Champagne punch

This lovely punch is perfect for a wedding and is not too expensive when locally made champagne is available at reasonable prices

2 large ripe pineapples
3 cups castor sugar
½ cup fresh lemon juice
1½ cups fresh orange juice
2 cups brandy
2 cups light rum
2 punnets strawberries, sliced
6 bottles chilled champagne

Peel, core and slice the pineapples and whirl the fruit in an electric blender until crushed, or process in a food processor fitted with the steel blade. (Failing this, chop very finely by hand.) Place in a bowl, sprinkle with sugar and allow to stand for 1 hour or more. Stir in the remaining ingredients, except the strawberries and champagne, then cover and chill for 4 hours.

Pour over a block of ice in a punch bowl and just before serving add the strawberries and chilled champagne. Serves 35.

Fruit tea punch

A large bowl of sparkling non-alcoholic punch is a must at any wedding.

1¼ cups sugar
1¼ cups water
4 cups strong tea
1 x 440g can crushed pineapple
1 x 425 ml can apricot nectar
6 oranges
6 lemons
1 punnet strawberries, hulled and sliced
4 large bottles soda water
Ice, to serve.

Boil the sugar and water for 10 minutes, add the tea and allow to cool. Stir in the crushed pineapple with juice, the apricot nectar, and the juice from the oranges and lemons. Chill until serving time. Add the sliced strawberries and soda water. Pour over large pieces of ice in a punch bowl to serve. Serves 20 to 30.

Roast beef

1 scotch fillet or true fillet in the piece weighing about 1.5kg
Freshly ground pepper
3 tablespoons oil
Salt

Preheat the oven to hot 200C (400C). Season the meat with plenty of freshly ground pepper. Heat the oil in a flameproof baking dish and brown the meat well until crusty on one side, then turn and brown the other side.

Place in the oven and roast for 45 minutes for medium-rare meat. Place the cooked meat on a sheet of foil, spoon the pan juice over, wrap tightly and leave at room temperature. The juices will set in the meat and make it easier to carve. Serve the meat at room temperature, cut in thin slices and season with salt and a little extra pepper. Serves 10.

Lovers knots

250g butter
4 tablespoons castor sugar
2 teaspoons vanilla essence
3 eggs
3 cups flour
¼ teaspoon salt
6 tablespoons ground almonds
Icing sugar for dredging

Soften the butter and cream with the sugar. Add the vanilla essence, then beat in the eggs, one at a time, beating well between each addition. Sift the flour and salt together and fold in the ground almonds. Work into the creamed mixture to form a dough, then knead lightly, and wrap in plastic wrap. Chill for 1 hour.

Divide the dough into pieces about the size of a walnut. Lightly flour a board and roll out each little piece of dough into a sausage shape. It should be about 20cm long and the thickness of your little finger in the middle, but thinner at each end. Twist each piece into a pretzel shape, like a loose knot, and press the ends firmly together to make a double ring.

Arrange the biscuits on greased baking sheets and bake in a hot oven 200C (400F) for 10 to 12 minutes, or until pale golden. Place on wire racks and dredge thickly with icing sugar while still hot. Cool, and store in an airtight tin. Just before serving, sift more icing sugar over the biscuits. Makes about 50.

• *For additional recipes, see listings under 'Crowds' in index.*

May

Quick quickbreads

There has been a great interest in homemade bread with today's home cooks and with good reason. Breads — fruity, nutty, savory, plain or fancy — all are delicious. Some are so quick and easy they can be made for tea on the spur of the moment. Others take more time, but are well worth the effort. Enjoy these fruity, nutty breads spread lavishly with soft creamy butter and serve with a selection of colorful jams and jellies.

Olive damper

A variation on the traditional Australian bush bread and a lovely treat suitable for picnics or a barbecue.

4 cups self-raising flour
1 teaspoon salt
30g butter or dripping
½ cup stoned halved black olives or sliced stuffed olives
1 cup milk
½ cup water

Sift flour and salt into a large mixing bowl. Rub in fat, and toss in the olives with a fork. Make a well in flour and pour in milk and water. Mix with a knife until dough leaves sides of bowl; you may need a little more flour if dough is too slack. Place on a greased and well-floured baking tray and pat out to a round about 20cm across. Cut a cross in the top. Bake in a preheated hot oven 200C (400F) for 25 minutes, then reduce oven heat to moderate 180C (350F) and bake a further 15-20 minutes or until damper sounds hollow when tapped. Serve sliced with butter. Makes 1 x 20cm loaf.

Peanut butter quickbread

Cut in slices and spread with cream cheese. This quickbread can be buttered and made into sandwiches with tomato and lettuce, and is good for the lunch-box. It's best eaten the day after it is made. Buy very fresh peanuts, plain toasted for this bread.

2 cups flour
3 teaspoons baking powder
⅓ cup peanut butter
½ cup rough chopped peanuts
½ cup brown sugar
1¼ cups milk

Grease a 23 x 13cm loaf tin, line with a strip of greaseproof paper. Set oven temperature at moderate 180C (350F).

Sift flour and baking powder together into a bowl. Mix in peanut butter with a fork (or rub in with fingertips) until mixture is crumbly and well blended. Stir in the chopped peanuts and sugar, add milk and beat thoroughly. Turn mixture into prepared loaf tin and bake for about 1 hour.

Mincemeat tea loaf

2 cups flour
½ teaspoon salt
½ teaspoon bicarbonate of soda
1 teaspoon baking powder
125g butter
⅔ cup firmly packed brown sugar
2 eggs
3 tablespoons sour light cream
1 cup mincemeat
½ cup coarsely chopped walnuts or pecans

Sift flour, salt, bicarbonate of soda and baking powder. Cream butter with sugar until light and fluffy. Add eggs one at a time, beating well. Mix in sour cream. Gently fold in dry ingredients; do not overmix. The batter should be stiff. Stir in mincemeat and nuts. Spoon into a greased 21 x 15cm loaf tin, pressing with the back of a spoon to pack mixture solidly in tin. Bake in a preheated moderate oven 180C (350F) for 50-60 minutes or until a skewer inserted in centre comes out clean. Cool on a wire rack before slicing.

Right: Nutty Cheese Bread, Peanut Butter Quickbread and Olive Damper are surprisingly easy — and quick — to make.

Nutty cheese bread

This savory loaf — with its nutty crunch and excellent flavor — is good sliced and made into cheese and celery or fresh tomato sandwiches; if you like radishes, try radish and gruyere sandwiches. It is also nice toasted.

30g yeast
2 cups lukewarm water
6 teaspoons sugar
1 teaspoon salt
½ teaspoon freshly ground black pepper
½ cup non-fat dry milk
Approximately 6½ cups sifted plain flour
45g butter, softened
1 large egg, lightly beaten
1 cup grated sharp cheese
½ cup chopped walnuts or pecans

Dissolve the yeast in ¼ cup of the water with one teaspoon of the sugar. Mix the remaining sugar, salt, pepper, dry milk and 1½ cups of flour. Add the remaining 1¾ cups of water, the butter and egg. Add the dissolved yeast and mix until smooth. Add enough of the remaining flour to make a moderately stiff dough. Turn out on to a floured board and knead until smooth and elastic. Place in a greased bowl and grease the top surface of the dough. Cover with a towel and let rise in a warm place until double in bulk, about one hour. Turn out on to a lightly floured surface, press to flatten and cover with half the cheese and nuts. Knead in the cheese and nuts, repeat with remaining cheese and nuts.

Shape into two loaves and place in two greased loaf pans. Grease the top surface of the loaves, cover and let rise until double in size, about 1½ hours.

Bake the loaves in a preheated 200C (400F) oven 15 minutes. Lower the oven temperature to 180C (350F) and bake 35 minutes longer, or until the bread shrinks from the sides of the pan and is well browned.

Currant cider muffins

The spiced little hot cakes are lovely for dessert with fruit and whipped cream or with coffee. They even freeze well, so can be heated up as needed — a good use for your microwave!

2 cups flour
1 tablespoon baking powder
½ teaspoon salt
½ cup currants
1 cup apple cider
185g butter, melted
1 egg, lightly beaten

TOPPING
¼ cup sugar
1½ teaspoons ground cinnamon

Sift flour, baking powder and salt in a bowl. Add currants and toss to coat evenly with flour.

Combine cider, butter and egg then pour over flour, stirring until just blended. The batter will be lumpy.

Spoon into 12 buttered ⅓-cup muffin pans, filling two-thirds full.

Combine sugar and cinnamon and sprinkle each muffin with a teaspoon of spiced sugar. Bake in a preheated hot oven 200C (400F) for 20-25 minutes or until browned and risen. Makes 12 muffins.

Jasmine tea and walnut bread

You'll find jasmine tea at Chinese groceries and health food shops. Use 3 teaspoons to 1 cup boiling water.

60g butter
¾ cup sugar
1 egg, beaten
1 tablespoon grated orange rind
2 teaspoons grated lemon rind
3 cups flour
1 teaspoon baking powder
1 teaspoon bicarbonate of soda
Pinch of salt
½ teaspoon cinnamon
¼ cup orange juice
1 cup cooled jasmine tea, strained
¾ cup chopped walnuts

Grease a 25 x 10cm loaf pan and line with greased paper.

Cream the butter and sugar until light and fluffy, then stir in the egg and grated rinds. Sift together the flour, baking powder, bicarbonate, salt and cinnamon. Add to the butter mixture with the juice and tea, stirring until combined, then fold in the chopped nuts. Spoon into the prepared tin and bake in a preheated moderate oven 180C (350F) for 45 minutes, or until a skewer comes out clean. Cool in the tin for a minute, then turn on to a wire rack. Serve cold, sliced and buttered.

Apricot nut bread

There's a combination of apricot and walnut flavors in this tea bread which is made with melted butter. Good for school lunches as well as weekend snacks.

3 cups self-raising flour
½ teaspoon salt
½ cup castor sugar
1 cup dried apricots cut into thin strips
½ cup chopped walnuts
Grated rind of ½ lemon
2 eggs
¾ cup of milk
60g (2 tablespoons) butter or margarine, melted.

GLAZE
2 tablespoons sugar
Juice of ½ lemon

Line a 20 x 10 x 6cm loaf tin with greased greaseproof paper.

Sift flour with salt into a large bowl. Stir in sugar, apricots, walnuts and lemon rind. Beat eggs with milk and mix lightly into dry ingredients. Gently stir in the melted butter.

Turn into the prepared loaf tin and bake in a moderate oven 180C (350F) for 1¼ hours. Turn out on a wire rack and brush with glaze while still warm. Serve warm or cold with butter.

GLAZE: Put sugar and lemon juice into a saucepan and heat gently until sugar has dissolved.

Black olive bread

Serve with a salad or wedge of tasty cheese and chilled butter, may also be used to make dainty sandwiches with a slice of cheese in between.

2 x 60g eggs
½ cup black olives, stoned and coarsely chopped
2 tablespoons olive oil
½ cup milk
2 cups flour
1 tablespoon sugar
2 teaspons baking powder
¼ teaspoon salt

Brush a 20 x 10cm or 19 x 9cm loaf pan with olive oil and line with greased greaseproof paper.

Beat the eggs until frothy and stir in the chopped olives, oil and milk. Sift the flour, sugar, baking powder and salt together and add the egg mixture, stirring lightly just until the flour is moistened — be careful not to over mix. Spoon into the prepared tin and bake in a preheated moderate oven 180C (350F) for 1 hour, or until it sounds hollow when tapped. Leave in the tin for a minute, then turn on to a wire rack to cool.

Savory bacon muffins

Hot breads are delicious with a light weekend lunch. Serve them still warm with butter. Good with soups or salads.

6 bacon rashers
1 cup milk
60g butter, melted
1 large egg, beaten lightly
2 tablespoons castor sugar
2 cups plain flour
1 tablespoon baking powder
1 teaspoon salt

Remove rind from bacon, place bacon in a large frypan and cook over moderately high heat until crisp.

Transfer to paper towels to drain, then crumble the rashers.

In a large bowl combine milk, melted butter, beaten egg and sugar. Sift flour, baking powder and salt into egg mixture and stir the batter until it is just combined (the batter should be lumpy).

Fold the bacon into the batter and spoon into 12 buttered ⅓-cup muffin tins, filling them two-thirds full. Bake in a preheated hot oven 200C (400F) for 20-25 minutes or until they are golden.

Nutty gingerbread

2½ cups flour
¾ teaspoon bicarbonate of soda
½ teaspoon salt
1½ teaspoons cinnamon
1½ teaspoons ground ginger
½ cup chopped preserved ginger
⅓ cup chopped walnuts or pecans
⅔ cup firmly-packed brown sugar
½ cup treacle
¼ cup golden syrup
185g butter
¼ cup milk
2 large eggs, beaten
TO FINISH
Lemon or orange icing
Glace ginger

Sift flour, bicarbonate of soda, salt, cinnamon and ginger. Stir in preserved ginger, walnuts or pecans. Put sugar, treacle, golden syrup and butter in a saucepan and heat gently until butter melts, add the milk. Add to flour mixture. Mix in eggs and beat well. Pour into a greased 28 x 19cm lamington tin that has been bottom-lined with greased greaseproof paper. Bake in a preheated moderate oven 180C (350F) for 45-50 minutes or until a skewer inserted in centre comes out clean. Allow to cool, then ice with lemon or orange icing and decorate with slices of glace ginger, if using.

LEMON OR ORANGE ICING: Cream 60g butter until light and fluffy. Sift 1 cup icing sugar into a bowl, add 2 teaspoons lemon or orange juice and the creamed butter and beat well. Spread over gingerbread.

Flyaway lemon muffins

The special lightness of these muffins comes from using mineral or soda water.

2 cups plain flour
1 tablespoon baking powder
½ teaspoon salt
½ cup walnut pieces
1 teaspoon grated lemon rind
1 cup mineral water or soda water
185g butter, melted
1 egg, lightly beaten
TOPPING
¼ cup sugar
1 teaspoon grated lemon rind

Sift flour, baking powder and salt together into a bowl. Add walnuts and lemon rind and toss to coat walnuts with flour. Mix together the mineral or soda water, butter and egg and pour over flour mixture, stirring with just a few strokes until moistened. The batter will be lumpy. Spoon into well-greased muffin tins, filling to two-thirds full. Use a large spoon and try to fill each tin with one spoonful. Mix sugar and rind for topping and sprinkle over. Bake in hot oven 200C (400F) for 20-25 minutes or until browned and well risen. Serve hot with butter.
Makes 12.

Apple pecan bread

Use a large granny smith apple for this delicious, moist bread. Lovely for picnics, morning tea or the school lunch box. Serve as little sandwiches with a light luncheon salad.

125g butter, softened
¾ cup castor sugar
2 large eggs
1 large apple, peeled, cored and grated
½ cup toasted chopped pecans
1 teaspoon vanilla
1¾ cups plain flour
1 teaspoon baking powder
½ teaspoon bicarbonate of soda
½ teaspoon salt

Butter a 20 x 10 x 8cm loaf tin and line base and long sides with paper in a large bowl. Cream butter and sugar until light and fluffy. Add eggs one at a time, beating well after each addition. Stir in grated apple, toasted pecans and vanilla. Beat lightly until combined well. Sift in the flour, baking powder, soda and salt and stir the batter until just combined.

Turn the batter into prepared loaf pan and bake in the middle of a preheated oven 180C (350F) for 1 hour, or until a cake tester inserted in the centre comes out clean. Let the bread cool in the pan on a rack for 10 minutes. Turn it out on to the rack and let it cool completely. Serve sliced with butter.

Banana nut bread

This lovely banana bread comes from the Hotel Hana-Maui in Hawaii. Serve it sliced and buttered with a fresh green salad for lunch or enjoy it with morning coffee or a cool, refreshing pineapple juice.

125g unsalted butter
1 cup castor sugar
2 large eggs
3 very ripe bananas
2 cups plain flour
1 teaspoon bicarbonate of soda
¼ cup chopped macadamia nuts or walnuts

Grease and line bottom and long sides of a 20 x 10 x 8cm loaf pan. In a large bowl cream butter and sugar until mixture is light and fluffy. Add eggs one at a time, beating well after each addition, then add the bananas one at a time.

Sift together plain flour and bicarbonate of soda and fold into the banana mixture.

Stir in the nuts and pour the batter into the prepared loaf pan.

Bake in a preheated moderate oven 180C (350F) for 1 hour, or until cake tester comes out clean.

Let the bread cool on a cake rack for 20 minutes, turn it out of the pan on to the rack and let it cool completely before slicing it. Serve plain or spread with butter.

Pepperoni bread

During a holiday in Venice, Italy, I enjoyed a lovely cheese bread flavored with chopped peppers. Serve with a salad or grilled meat or chicken or make into sandwiches with slices of cheese in between, if liked.

2 x 60g eggs
1 large red and green pepper
½ cup grated tasty cheddar cheese
2 tablespoons olive oil
½ cup milk
2½ cups flour
2½ teaspoons baking powder
½ teaspoon salt

Brush a 20 x 10cm loaf pan with olive oil and line with greaseproof paper.

Beat the eggs well. Halve, seed and chop the pepper and add to eggs with cheese, olive oil and milk. Sift flour, baking powder and salt into large bowl.

Make a well in the centre and add the egg mixture, stirring lightly just until the flour is moistened — do not over mix. Spoon into the prepared tin and bake in a preheated moderate oven 180C (350F) for 50-60 minutes. Leave in tin for 1 minute, turn on to wire rack. Serve cold, sliced and buttered.

Note: If only green peppers are available use ½ green pepper and 1 drained, canned red pepper (pimiento).

Budget dinners

It is surprising how well you can eat, even on a budget, when you use a little care and imagination. Even more surprising, you will find it fun to investigate new ideas with the food you buy, eat and cook, the special bonus being the reaction of all the family. Learn to be a good cook and live like a millionaire.

Helpful hints

- Successful budgeters know that before eating well comes shopping well. They plan a few days' meals at a time, make a list of what they'll need and shop from it. Sounds obvious, but for every organised shopper there are dozens of impulse buyers.
- Good budgeters use all the food they buy because they use it promptly. Storing food too long so that it's eventually thrown out wrecks a budget.
- The meals a good manager provides often seem surprisingly lavish, with soup or another first course and a substantial dessert. There's good sense behind this — it means the main course can be a moderate one and it makes the family feel that they're eating well, too.
- For the most part, providing well on a budget means that time has to replace money. Convenience foods and take-aways cost much more than the food you prepare yourself — and, when you consider some of the easy and delicious dishes suggested here, expensive 'convenience' seems unnecessary.
- Don't be rigid in your approach to food. International dishes using grain products, dried peas and beans and vegetables in new and interesting ways are not only economical and healthy but may have your family feeling that they're eating better than ever!

Knackwurst with sauerkraut

If your family likes a smoked continental sausage or good Vienna frankfurters, serve them this way for a casual meal. Crusty bread is a good accompaniment.

2 onions, sliced
30g butter
1 tablespoon oil
1kg sauerkraut, rinsed in cold water
2 cooking apples, peeled, cored and sliced
1 tablespoon brown sugar
1 teaspoon dry mustard
½ cup dry white wine
Salt and freshly ground black pepper
1 tablespoon caraway seeds, optional
750g knackwurst sausage or kielbase

Fry onions in butter and oil in a frying pan until transparent. Toss sauerkraut with fork to separate, then add to pan with apples, sugar, mustard and wine. Season with salt and pepper and caraway seeds, if using. Spread out in large greased shallow ovenproof dish. Place sausage in pan of cold water, bring to the boil, cook for 2 to 3 minutes, drain. Cut into thick diagonal slices and arrange on top of sauerkraut mixture. Cover with foil and bake in a preheated moderate oven 180C (350F) for 20 to 30 minutes or until heated through. Serve accompanied by mustard and dill pickles. Serves 6.

Shepherd's pie

A great homely dish, invented to use up leftover roast lamb but so good in its own right that it's worth making sure there's enough meat left from the roast lamb dinner. I make one every week and it's almost our favorite meal.

375g cooked boneless lamb (weight after trimming off skin, gristle and larger pieces of fat)
30g bacon dripping or butter
1 onion, chopped
1 cup leftover gravy or 1½ tablespoons flour and 1 cup warm beef stock
Salt and freshly ground black pepper
1 teaspoon worcestershire sauce
2 tablespoons tomato sauce
1 tomato, peeled, seeded and diced
500g potatoes, peeled
30g butter
2 tablespoons hot milk

Mince lamb or chop it very fine. Melt dripping or butter in a saucepan and fry onion gently until golden, about 5 minutes. Stir in gravy and bring to simmering point; or stir flour into onions, cook 1 minute, remove from heat and cool a little. Add stock, stirring until smoothly blended, then return to heat and stir until boiling. Add lamb, salt, pepper and worcestershire sauce.

Cover and simmer gently 20 minutes. Add tomato sauce and tomato and cook a further 5 minutes.

Meantime, cook potatoes until tender. Drain well, dry off over low heat and mash with butter and hot milk.

Transfer meat mixture to a pie dish. Spread potato over and rough up surface with a fork. Place under a preheated moderate grill until top is golden-brown or bake in moderate oven 180C (350F) for 45 minutes. Serves 4-6.

Turn into heated serving dish and sprinkle with grated cheese and, if liked, more parsley. Serves 4.

Lemon-ginger chops

Serve these lemony chops with creamy mashed potatoes and steamed cabbage or cauliflower for a simply delicious meal.

4 tablespoons oil
1 teaspoon grated lemon rind
1 tablespoon lemon juice
1 tablespoon brown sugar
1 teaspoon grated fresh ginger
Salt
Pepper
4 large chump chops

Mix together oil, lemon rind, lemon juice, brown sugar, ginger, salt and pepper. Put the chops in a shallow dish, in a single layer, pour the marinade over. Cover, refrigerate and leave all day or overnight.

Remove from marinade, drain and grill under preheated grill for 10-15 minutes or until tender, turning occasionally and basting with the marinade. Serves 4.

Rhubarb fool

Any family meal is the better for being finished off with a good dessert. This one is very easy to make.

1 bunch rhubarb
⅔ cup firmly packed brown sugar
Grated rind 1 orange
1 cup cream

Trim rhubarb and cut into short lengths. Place in saucepan with sugar, orange rind and ¼ cup water. Simmer gently until tender. Drain and cool.

Lightly whip cream and fold into cooled rhubarb. Serve cold, with sponge fingers or thin, crisp biscuits. Serves 4.

Pasta with mushrooms

Little white button mushrooms make a delicious, simple sauce for pasta. Try them with large shells or fuselli, the corkscrew pasta. A crisp salad and some crusty Italian bread make a satisfying main course.

2 tablespoons olive oil
2 tablespoons butter
1 clove garlic, chopped
500g button mushrooms, sliced
Salt and freshly ground black pepper
1-2 tablespoons chopped parsley
1 extra tablespoon butter
375g pasta
4 tablespoons grated parmesan cheese

Heat oil and butter in a large pan, add garlic and mushrooms and cook briskly for 3-4 minutes, turning over once or twice. Add salt, pepper, parsley and extra butter. Keep warm.

Cook pasta in a large saucepan of boiling salted water until 'al dente', 12-15 minutes. Drain well. Pour mushroom mixture over and toss lightly.

Above: For a budget meal that tastes like a million dollars, try Pasta With Mushrooms and Rhubarb Fool.

Golden sponge pudding

This family favorite is perfect for cool evenings — it is moreish, so serve something light as a main course.

125g butter
½ cup castor sugar
2 eggs
1½ cups self-raising flour
2-3 tablespoons milk
6-8 tablespoons golden syrup

Cream butter with sugar. Beat in eggs and stir in flour. Add sufficient milk to lighten mixture, which should be soft enough to drop lightly from a spoon.

Put golden syrup in the bottom of a greased 4-cup pudding basin. Spoon mixture into basin, cover and steam for 2 hours.

Turn out on to a heated serving dish and serve with thick cream and more hot syrup if you wish. Serves 6.

Glazed pork sausages

Serve these sausages with hot boiled rice mixed with chopped pepper, pineapple and shallots, heated gently by tossing in a little butter.

8 pork sausages
⅓ cup firmly packed brown sugar
2 cups water
1 tablespoon vinegar

Put all ingredients into a large frying pan and simmer gently until water has evaporated. Tilt pan back and forth to roll sausages and coat them with light glaze that has formed on bottom. Serves 4.

Spicy meat loaf with mustard sauce

Serve this deliciously tangy meat loaf with lots of creamy mashed potatoes and buttered brussels sprouts. A marvellous meal to serve on cold winter nights.

1 egg, beaten
⅓ cup evaporated milk
1 tablespoon vinegar
1 tablespoon treacle
1 tablespoon french mustard
1½ cups soft breadcrumbs
1 small onion, finely chopped
½ teaspoon salt
750g minced beef
SAUCE
1 cup beef stock
2 teaspoons vinegar
2 teaspoons dry mustard
1 teaspoon treacle
2 tablespoons cornflour
½ cup cold water

Combine egg, evaporated milk, vinegar, treacle, mustard, breadcrumbs, onion and salt. Stir in minced beef and mix well. Pack mixture lightly into a 23 x 13 x 8cm loaf tin. Bake in a preheated moderate oven 180C (350F) for 1¼ hours. Serve with mustard sauce. Serves 6.

MUSTARD SAUCE: In saucepan combine stock, vinegar, mustard and treacle and beat until smooth. Blend together the cornflour and cold water, add to stock and cook, stirring, until thickened and bubbly.

Saucisses aux tomates

You may wonder why a French name is given to what seems a simple, familiar dish — sausages with tomatoes. What makes it very French is the use of butter and olive oil, brown sugar to flavor the tomatoes, and the chopped garlic added at the end. Try it — you'll taste the difference.

750g thick beef sausages
30g butter
2 tablespoons olive oil
2 large onions, finely chopped
2 cloves garlic, crushed
500g ripe tomatoes
1 tablespoon brown sugar
Salt and freshly ground pepper
3 extra cloves garlic, coarsely chopped
Chopped parsley to garnish

Blanch sausages by poaching in a pan of water for about 5 minutes. Drain. Grill sausages until crisp and brown on all sides, 6-8 minutes altogether.

Meanwhile, heat the butter and oil in a large frying pan. Add onions and crushed garlic and cook over medium heat for aboout 4 minutes, until onions soften. Skin the tomatoes by plunging into boiling water, counting 10, then rinsing in cold water (the skins should slip off easily). Cut in half, flip out seeds and chop. Add to the pan with onions and cook gently until tomatoes are soft, about 5 minutes. Stir in brown sugar and season generously with salt and pepper. Stir in chopped garlic, but do not cook.

Spoon sauce on to a heated dish and arrange sausages on top. Sprinkle with chopped parsley and serve with toast or crusty bread. Serves 6.

Note: If you don't like biting into pieces of garlic you may omit the chopped garlic at the end — but it won't be the same dish!

Potato moussaka

A popular variation of Greek moussaka. Good eaten hot or cold.

4 tablespoons cooking oil
750g potatoes, thinly sliced
1 large onion, finely chopped
1kg minced beef or lamb
1 teaspoon worcestershire sauce
2 tablespoons tomato paste
2 cloves garlic, crushed
1 tablespoon chopped oregano or 1 teaspoon dried
Freshly ground pepper and salt

Two delectable ways with sausages are Glazed Pork Sausages (right) and Saucisses Aux Tomates (far right).

4 tablespoons grated parmesan cheese

SAUCE
30g butter
2 tablespoons plain flour
1¼ cups milk
1 egg, lightly beaten
Pepper and salt

Heat 3 tablespoons of oil in a frying pan and cook the potatoes for 2 minutes on each side; it will be necessary to cook these in two or three batches. Heat the remaining tablespoon of oil in another frying pan or a saucepan and fry the onion very slowly for about 5 minutes. Add the meat, worcestershire sauce, tomato paste, garlic, oregano, salt and pepper to the onion and cook these gently together for 15 minutes, stirring from time to time. Line a 2-litre (8-cup) casserole with the potato slices. Put half the meat mixture in the casserole, and cover this with a layer of potatoes; add the rest of the meat and sprinkle over the cheese.

Put the casserole on one side and make white sauce. Pour the sauce over the contents of the casserole, cover with a lid, and cook in a moderate oven 180C (350F) for 45 minutes. Serves 6-8.

SAUCE: Melt the butter, blend in the flour and cook for one minute. Add milk gradually, stirring over a moderate heat until sauce thickens. Add the beaten egg to the sauce, season to taste.

Mulligatawny

This golden-colored soup comes from India. Serve in wide, shallow bowls to allow room for adding cooked rice. Use canned coconut milk or make it from desiccated coconut.

30g butter
2 medium onions, chopped
8 curry leaves (optional)
1 tablespoon curry powder
6 cups chicken or beef stock
4 chicken thighs, boned
1 cup thinly sliced celery
2 cups coconut milk
Salt and freshly ground pepper
2 cups hot cooked rice
Lemon slices

Heat the butter in a large saucepan and gently fry the onions until golden. Add the curry leaves and curry powder and fry for a minute longer.

Add stock, chicken and celery and simmer for 20 minutes. Remove chicken and dice. Add chicken and coconut milk to soup and bring almost to boiling point again. Taste for seasoning and adjust.

Serve with rice and lemon slices. Coconut milk gives a lovely smooth flavor but you can substitute yogurt. Serves 8.

COCONUT MILK: Put 2 cups desiccated coconut into a saucepan with 3 cups water, bring slowly to the boil. Put into a blender and blend at high speed. Strain into a bowl.

Greek honey pie

If you bake the pie before starting on the rest of dinner, it will be cool enough to enjoy for dessert.

250g ricotta or cottage cheese
4 tablespoons clear honey
2 eggs
2 tablespoons castor sugar
1 teaspoon cinnamon
1 uncooked 18cm pie shell
A little extra cinnamon

Place cheese, honey, eggs, sugar and 1 teaspoon cinnamon in a blender and whirl until smooth. Or push cheese through a sieve, then mix thoroughly with remaining ingredients. Pour into the pastry shell and bake in a preheated hot oven 200C (400F) until pastry is cooked and filling set (about 35 minutes).

Remove from oven, sprinkle with a little extra cinnamon and leave on a wire rack in a cool place. Serve warm or cold. Serves 6.

Chili con carne

A popular Mexican-style dish, made more special when served with corn bread or muffins.

2 tablespoons bacon dripping or butter
1 onion, finely chopped
2 cloves garlic, finely chopped
750g stewing beef, minced or diced
1 x 425g can tomatoes
½ bay leaf
1 tablespoon Mexican-style chili powder
Salt
Pinch brown sugar
2 x 310g cans kidney beans, drained

Melt fat in a large, heavy saucepan and cook onion and garlic gently until golden. Add beef and brown lightly.

Chop tomatoes and add with their juice, the bay leaf, chili powder, salt and brown sugar. Stir, cover tightly and simmer very gently for about 1 hour. Add drained kidney beans and cook a further 15 minutes. Discard bay leaf.

Serve with corn bread or corn muffins. Serves 6.

Corn bread or muffins

A special accompaniment for chili con carne, good with any beef stew in place of potatoes or bread.

4 tablespoons melted butter or bacon dripping
½ cup plain flour
2½ teaspoons baking powder
1 tablespoon sugar
½ teaspoon salt
1½ cups yellow cornmeal
1 egg
¾ cup milk

Use 1½ tablespoons melted fat to grease a shallow 29 x 18cm cake tin or twelve 8cm muffin tins. Place in top half of a very hot oven 220C (425F) until sizzling hot.

Have all other ingredients at room temperature. Sift flour, baking powder, sugar and salt into a bowl and stir in cornmeal. Beat together egg, milk and remaining butter or bacon dripping, pour into dry ingredients and combine with a few rapid strokes; batter will be lumpy.

Turn batter into hot tin or muffin tins and bake in oven for about 25 minutes or until well-risen and browned. Serve immediately, cutting bread into squares. Makes 12.

Chinese steamed broccoli

Cut 1 or 2 heads broccoli into small flowerets and the stems into thick slices. Drop into boiling salted water and cook uncovered for 6-8 minutes. Drain.

Heat 3 tablespoons oil, add 1 clove garlic, sliced, 2 tablespoons chopped green shallots and 1 teaspoon chopped ginger, cook a minute, add drained broccoli and 1 tablespoon soy sauce, toss gently until broccoli is heated through.

Noodles with chicken broth

125 Chinese egg noodles, cooked
½ cup shredded cooked chicken meat
2 slices cooked ham, shredded
3 cups chicken broth or stock
½ teaspoon salt
Pinch pepper
2 teaspoons soy sauce
4 green shallots, shredded

Place cooked noodles in heated serving bowl. Arrange chicken and ham on top of noodles. Heat broth,

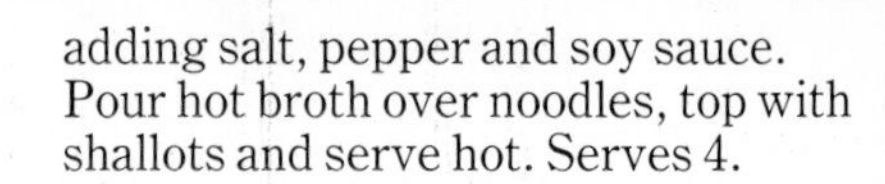
adding salt, pepper and soy sauce. Pour hot broth over noodles, top with shallots and serve hot. Serves 4.

Savory mince

This savory mince is good with mashed potatoes or with hot buttered toast. It can be varied with the addition of chopped herbs or a spoonful or two of tomato paste.

2 onions, finely chopped
1 tablespoon dripping or oil
500g minced steak
1 tablespoon plain flour
1 teaspoon salt
Pepper
1 beef stock cube
1 cup water
2 teaspoons worcestershire sauce

Fry onions in dripping or oil until soft. Add minced steak and, pressing down with a fork, fry until brown all over and separate. Add flour, salt and pepper and toss well. Dissolve stock cube in hot water with worcestershire sauce. Stir into pan, cover and bring to the boil. Reduce heat and simmer gently for 30 minutes.

Apple charlotte

Here's an old-fashioned favorite! The crumbs on top and bottom bake crisp and golden and take the place of pastry.

60g butter
2 cups soft, fresh breadcrumbs (about 6 slices white bread, crusts removed)
1 x 425g can pie apples
1 tablespoon grated lemon rind
2 tablespoons lemon juice
⅓ cup sugar
2 tablespoons brown sugar
1 teaspoon cinnamon

Grease a 20cm pie plate with half the butter, and press one cup of the crumbs on to bottom and sides. Mix apples with lemon rind, juice and sugar and spoon into the plate. Cover with rest of crumbs, dot with remaining butter and sprinkle with brown sugar and cinnamon.

Place in a preheated moderately slow oven 170C (325F) and bake until crumbs are crisp, about 40 minutes. Serve warm with cream, ice cream or custard. Serves 4-6.

Note: Crumbs are quick to make in a blender, even if the bread is fresh. Without a blender, it is easier if bread is stale. Rub it through a sieve or crumble into pieces with the fingers.

Left: For a meal as easy as it is tasty, try Noodles With Chicken Broth.

Oriental chicken legs

A quick and light meal of fried chicken with Chinese flavorings.

6 chicken legs
2 tablespoons soy sauce
1 tablespoon dry sherry
½ teaspoon black pepper
2 tablespoons cornflour
2½ cups oil for deep-frying
Coriander sprigs or shredded green shallot, to garnish

Chop knuckle joint from end of each chicken leg. Use pliers to pull out tendons between flesh and bone, if you wish, then chop leg into 2 pieces. Mix soy sauce, sherry and pepper, add chicken and leave to marinate for about 20 minutes, turning occasionally.

Coat each piece of chicken with cornflour. Heat oil to moderate (when a bread cube fries golden-brown in 45 seconds) in a wok or saucepan. Add chicken pieces and turn heat to low. Do not crowd the pan, cook in two batches if necessary.

Fry chicken pieces for about 8-10 minutes or until cooked and golden. Remove and drain on crumpled paper towels. Serve garnished with coriander or shallots and accompanied by a bowl of steaming boiled rice and, if liked, Chinese Steamed Broccoli. Serves 4.

TO CHOP CHICKEN ON THE BONE: Slice through flesh, place the blade of a heavy knife in position on bone and tap firmly with a hammer.

Above: Both grownups and kids will love Oriental Chicken Legs and Chinese Steamed Broccoli.

Fresh from the sea

Most of us eat fish because we enjoy it so much, but there are other good reasons for serving it regularly. Fish is particularly rich in vitamins A and D and in the minerals we need for good health. It is one of the best available sources of protein and a wonderful food for people who are watching or reducing their weight. In addition to being quickly cooked, fish offers you outstanding value for your housekeeping money. Most of these recipes may be adapted to different fish so don't be a snob about fish, and try some of the newer fish that fishermen are bringing to the market. When you bring your fish home, unwrap, wash in cold water, dry well with paper towels and wrap in aluminium foil or place in a covered container. Store in the refrigerator and use within 2-3 days, and remember not to overcook it. Appetites vary but here is a rule to guide you when buying fish. If you are buying a whole fish allow 500g per person but 500g of fillets will give you two large or three average servings. Combined with other food such as rice and pasta, that much will serve 4.

Baked fresh sardines

Fresh sardines and fresh garden herbs are a fitting combination.

500g fresh sardines
1 lemon
Few sprigs fresh oregano, parsley and thyme
Salt
Freshly ground black pepper
¼ cup dry white wine, optional
1 tablespoon olive oil
1 cup fresh white breadcrumbs
1 tablespoon finely chopped parsley

Slit sardines down the belly and remove intestines. Rinse under gently running water, pat dry with paper towels.

Squeeze juice from ½ lemon; cut other ½ into thin slices. Lay herbs and lemon slices on bottom of oiled shallow ovenproof dish. Arrange sardines on top and season well with salt and pepper. Sprinkle over lemon juice, white wine and oil. Combine breadcrumbs and parsley and scatter over sardines. Cook in a preheated hot oven 200C (400F) for 10-15 minutes. Serves 4.

Whole baked fish

Throughout the Mediterranean, whole fish are baked in a mixture of vegetables, mostly tomatoes and onions. Sometimes rice, sometimes potatoes are added, making the dish a complete meal. With cask wine so prevalent, make use of wine in cooking, although water is always acceptable.

1.5kg whole snapper, jewfish, mullet etc
2-3 potatoes
2 tomatoes
1 onion
2 cloves garlic
2 cups dry white wine or water
½ cup oil
Salt and pepper
2 bay leaves
1 sprig thyme
2 lemons, sliced

Clean and wipe the fish dry, remove any scales left by fish shop. Put the fish into a large shallow baking dish, large enough to let the fish lie flat.

Peel the potatoes and slice them very thin. Drop the tomatoes into boiling water, count to 10, lift out and slip off the skins, cut into thick slices or wedges. Peel the onion and garlic and chop them roughly.

Surround the fish with the vegetables. Drizzle over the wine and oil and sprinkle with salt and freshly ground pepper. Break each bay leaf in two and add dotted around with thyme. Top with sliced lemons. Cover with buttered paper or foil and bake in a moderate oven 180C (350F) for about 1 hour. Lift fish on to heated serving plate, keep warm. Place vegetables over high heat to reduce liquid and finish cooking the potatoes. Serve as an accompaniment to the fish. Serves 4.

Right: Two marvellous fish dishes of Italian origin are Baked Fresh Sardines and Prawns Di Sciullo.

Prawns di sciullo

We get such superb large prawns in Australia, it is nice to enjoy them the Italian way. Have everything ready, including the diners, before you start the actual cooking of this, as it takes only minutes. Good cold, too.

750g large raw prawns
Flour
2 eggs, beaten
90g butter
1 tablespoon oil
2 cups sliced mushrooms
½ cup dry white wine
Chopped parsley
1 cup rice, boiled, or crusty Italian bread.

Shell and devein prawns. Rinse in cold water, drain and pat dry with paper towels. Sprinkle prawns with salt and pepper and give a light dusting of flour. Dip in beaten egg.

Melt the butter and oil in a large frying pan and saute prawns over medium heat, turning often until prawns are golden. Push prawns to the side. Add mushrooms and saute for a few minutes. Add wine and cook over medium heat until wine evaporates, tossing prawns and mushrooms lightly. Sprinkle over chopped parsley.

Serve with boiled rice or crusty Italian bread to mop up the delicious juices. Serves 4.

Grilled fish

One of the simplest and best ways to cook fresh fish is to grill it. You will have tender fish every time.

The secret of success with grilling fish is to use thick, skinned fillets or steaks and to cook on one side only on a preheated grilling pan, metal tray or grilling rack covered with foil (the edges turned up to make a tray).

Heat the foil-covered pan and add 2 teaspoons butter per piece of fish. Wipe the fish with damp kitchen or paper towels, sprinkle with a little flour and season with salt and pepper. Turn in the melted butter to coat. Grill for about 8 minutes for a 2cm-thick steak, and 4 to 5 minutes for a fillet. During grilling, baste once or twice with the pan juices.

Small whole flat fish (sole or flounder) can be grilled in the same way. Other fish are grilled on both sides — if thick, slash two or three times through the thickest part. A small whole fish takes about 15 minutes.

Left, top: Grilled Fish, Fish Soup and Fish Steaks With Citrus. Left: Fritto Misto Al Pesce — fisherman's fish fry.

Fish steaks with citrus

4 fish steaks, weighing 185g each
1 tablespoon melted butter
Salt and freshly ground pepper
1 orange
1 lemon

Brush the fish with melted butter and place in a shallow flameproof dish. Season with salt and pepper. Combine the juice of half the orange and lemon with remaining butter.

Pour half the liquid over fish and slice remaining halves of fruit. Place fish under a preheated hot grill and cook for 4 minutes. Remove dish from grill, pour over remaining fruit juice, top fish with sliced fruit, return to grill and cook for a further 5 minutes or until fish is cooked through and golden. Take care not to overcook. Serve with tomato salad. Serves 4.

Fritto misto al pesce

The famous Italian fisherman's fish fry can include small whole fish or strips of fillets, plus calamari, prawns, scallops — whatever is best and freshest that day. The secret of the feather-light crispy batter in which they're enclosed is a beaten egg white folded in just before cooking.

A combination of very small fish or fish fillets and shellfish, weighing about 1kg
Juice of 1 lemon
Oil for deep-frying
Plain flour
Lemon wedges
1½ cups mayonnaise
1 tablespoon chopped capers
1 tablespoon chopped parsley
1 tablespoon chopped canned pimiento (optional)
BATTER
1 cup self-raising flour
¼ teaspoon salt
1 tablespoon brandy
1 tablespoon oil
¾ cup warm water
1 egg white

Remove heads of small whole fish, open bodies out and remove backbones. Cut fillets into 5cm long strips. Shell prawns, leaving tails on, and devein. Remove any dark beards from scallops. Wash squid under cold running water, pull off head and empty the body sac. Peel off skin, wash body again and cut it into rings.

Dry all seafood on paper towels, sprinkle with lemon juice and leave 3 minutes.

Have oil hot (a cube of bread should brown in 30 seconds) and batter made. Taking a few pieces at a time, toss seafood in flour and dip in batter. Deep-fry for about 1 minute or until golden brown. To prevent toughness, do not overcook. Drain on crumpled paper towels and keep hot in a low oven until all the pieces are fried.

Arrange on a heated serving platter and serve immediately, with lemon wedges and mayonnaise mixed with capers, parsley and pimiento if using. Serves 4.

BATTER: Sift flour and salt into a bowl, make a well in the centre and add brandy and oil. Gradually add water, stirring from the centre until mixed, then beat batter until smooth. Leave 30 minutes. Just before cooking seafood, beat egg white until it stands in soft peaks and fold gently into the batter.

Fish soup

Make this soup with a snapper head but if they are unavailable use fish stock and 250g of lightly poached gemfish.

45g butter
1 carrot, sliced
1 onion, finely chopped
1 stalk of celery, finely sliced
2 tablespoons flour
6 cups fish stock, heated
2 cups lightly cooked fish
1 bottle of oysters (optional)
Salt and pepper
Lemon juice
Cream

In a large saucepan, melt butter and saute sliced carrot, onion and celery till soft but not brown. Sprinkle the vegetables with flour and cook for 2 minutes, stirring continuously. Slowly add the heated stock, bring to the boil and simmer gently until the vegetables are tender. Add the cooked fish and cook till the fish is warm, add the drained oysters if using. Season with salt and pepper, a little lemon juice and just before serving a tablespoon of cream can be added to each plate. Serves 6.

Fish stock

750g fish bones and trimmings
1 tomato, chopped
Parsley sprigs
1 bay leaf
1 onion, sliced
1 celery stick
2 teaspoons salt
6 peppercorns
9 cups water
½ cup white wine (optional)

Wash fish bones well. Place in a large saucepan with all the other ingredients. Cover and bring to the boil. Skim the surface and simmer gently for 20 minutes. Strain the stock through a sieve, remove any fish from the bones and head and use in soup or make into fish mornay.

Mussels with herbs

When buying mussels, I select the smaller ones and check that they are live. Live mussels hold their shells together so tightly it is difficult to prise them apart. This is an excellent recipe for entertaining in that it can be prepared in advance then finished off at the last moment.

3kg mussels in the shell
1 cup wine
1 chopped onion
1 bay leaf
25g butter, softened
9 green shallots, finely chopped
4 cloves garlic, crushed
1 cup breadcrumbs (made from day-old bread)
½ cup finely chopped parsley
2 teaspoons chopped lemon thyme
Salt
Freshly ground pepper

Scrub the mussels well in several changes of water, scrape off the beards and soak in cold water to cover for several hours. Drain and rinse under cold running water. Place in a large pan with wine, chopped onion and a broken bay leaf, cover and bring wine to the boil, lower heat and allow to steam 5-6 minutes, shaking the pan once or twice until the shells have opened. Discard any unopened mussels.

Combine remaining ingredients until well blended, seasoning generously with salt and pepper.

Remove top shells from mussels, and cover each mussel with butter mixture, filling the shells to the top. Arrange in baking tins and chill, covered, for 30 minutes or until ready to cook.

Place under a preheated grill for 3 minutes, or until tops are golden and butter mixture bubbly. Serves 6 as a first course.

Oyster loaf

A sublime Sunday brunch.

1 small loaf french bread
125g butter, melted
2 jars oysters, drained, or 24 fresh
2 eggs beaten with 2 tablespoons water
1 cup dried breadrumbs
Salt and freshly ground black pepper
Paprika
Worcestershire sauce
Lemon wedges, to serve

Cut the bread in half lengthwise. Scoop out the centre and set aside (use to make breadcrumbs, which may be kept in the freezer).

Brush the inside of the bread with melted butter, place on an oven tray and toast lightly in a very hot oven 220C (425F).

While the bread is heating, dip oysters in beaten egg mixture then roll in breadcrumbs. Heat remaining butter in a frying pan and saute the oysters for 20 seconds only, just until the edges begin to curl.

Spoon oysters into one half of the toasted loaf, sprinkle with salt, pepper, a little paprika and worcestershire sauce, cover with the other half of the loaf and serve immediately, cut into chunks. Pass lemon wedges separately. Serves 4.

OYSTER CLUB SANDWICH: Follow the recipe, but add a layer of grilled bacon rashers and one of sliced tomato just before adding the top crust.

Jellied fish

This dish was part of our family fare as long as I can remember. It was made from herrings in Scotland. I find our oily but flavorsome mullet a good substitute.

6 herring or mullet
1 onion, sliced
Vinegar
Water
4 bay leaves
2 cloves
12 allspice
2 blades mace
1 teaspoon salt

Clean herrings or mullet and remove head and backbone. Large mullet should be filleted, remove any bones. Lay fish skin side down on working surface and place sliced onion on centre of each fish. Roll up from head to tail and secure with a toothpick.

Place fish in an ovenproof dish and add vinegar and water to cover in the proportion of 3 parts vinegar to 1 part water. Add herbs, spices and salt. Cover and cook in a slow oven 150C (300F) for 3 hours, or until fish is cooked.

The liquid must not boil. Transfer fish to a serving dish, spoon or strain liquid over, cool then chill in refrigerator. The liquid sets in a soft jelly.

Note: Jellied fish may be prepared in a slow cooker — allow 3 hours on low.

Whiting fillets with vermouth sauce

When you want a dinner-party dish that's glamorous but quick and easy to prepare, think of fish. Whiting (or john dory) are two of the finest, delicate in both flavor and texture. The fishmonger will skin the fillets if you ask.

90g butter, melted
8 fillets of whiting or john dory, skinned
4 tablespoons dry vermouth
1 tablespoon lemon juice
1 teaspoon tomato paste
Salt and freshly ground pepper
½ cup cream
Chopped parsley
Puff pastry fleurons

Brush a large, flameproof baking dish generously with some of the butter and lay fillets in it side by side. Blend remaining butter with vermouth, lemon juice and tomato paste. Pour over the fish, season with salt and pepper and place over high heat. Cook, basting fish with pan juices, just until flesh turns white.

Lift fish on to a heated serving dish. Add cream to the baking dish and stir until sauce thickens a little. Pour over the fish, sprinkle with chopped parsley and serve immediately, garnished with fleurons. Serves 4.

FLEURONS: Roll out puff pastry thinly — if using ready-rolled pastry, roll it a little thinner — and brush the surface with beaten egg. Cut out 8 crescent shapes 6-8cm in length. Place on a dampened baking sheet and bake in a very hot oven 230C (450F) for 6-8 minutes or until puffed and golden. Serve 2 fleurons with each portion.

Scallops in sauce verte

Scallops are lightly poached in vermouth then served on a green mayonnaise sauce.

750g scallops
⅔ cup dry vermouth
2-6 green shallots, chopped
1 sprig parsley
1 bay leaf
Salt
Freshly ground black pepper
GREEN SAUCE
3-4 spinach leaves
⅔ cup mayonnaise
¼ cup finely chopped parsley
2 tablespoons snipped chives
1 tablespoon finely chopped fresh dill, or ½ teaspoon dried
TO SERVE
8 small lettuce leaves, chopped parsley, long slivers green shallots or chives

Remove any brown parts from scallops but retain coral. Heat vermouth with shallots, parsley sprig, bay leaf, salt and pepper in a saucepan. Add scallops and simmer gently for 3-4 minutes or until tender, shaking pan occasionally. Drain and cool.

SAUCE: Wash spinach leaves, trim off whites, then steam, in a covered saucepan for 1 minute only, cool quickly in cold water. Press out water and chop spinach finely. Blend mayonnaise with parsley, spinach, chives and dill. Add extra mayonnaise to taste, if necessary. To serve, smear a little sauce in a semi-circle on 4 plates, arrange scallops on sauce. Arrange lettuce on plates. Strew parsley and slivers of shallots or chives over. Serves 4.

Curried fish in coconut cream

No curry meal is complete without curried fish. This is a very simple recipe but quite delicious. Gemfish fillets or any large firm fish is ideal.

500g firm fish fillets
Salt
2 tablespoons ghee or butter
2 slices fresh ginger, finely chopped
1 large onion, finely chopped
1 clove garlic, crushed
2 teaspoons curry powder (or to taste)
1 cup canned coconut milk
1 tablespoon tamarind juice or vinegar

Cut fish into bite-sized squares. Sprinkle with salt and allow to stand for a minute. Heat 1 tablespoon of the ghee in a heavy frying pan, and fry the fish on both sides until golden. Remove from pan and set aside.

Add remaining ghee to pan, and heat. Add ginger, onion, garlic and curry powder and stir until onion is softened, about 3 minutes.

Add coconut milk and simmer uncovered until sauce is reduced and thickened. Add fish and simmer for another minute or two, until fish is heated through.

Stir in tamarind juice or vinegar and taste for seasoning (more salt may be needed). Serve with rice and a few side dishes if desired (for instance, chopped peanuts, desiccated coconut, chutney, chopped tomato, mint). Serves 3 to 4.

Crisp-skin fish in sweet and sour vegetable sauce

This Chinese way of preparing fish gives juicy flesh sealed under a crisp outside.

1 large or 2 small whole white fish (snapper, bream, whiting, mirror dory) cleaned and scaled
1 egg white
½ teaspoon salt
1 tablespoon rice wine or dry sherry

Good grinding black pepper
1 tablespoon water
3 tablespoons cornflour
1 extra cup cornflour for coating the fish
Oil for frying

SAUCE
2 tablespoons oil
2 dried Chinese mushrooms, soaked in hot water 30 minutes, drained and cut into fine strips
1 can bamboo shoots, cut into fine strips
1 small green pepper cored, seeded and cut into fine strips
4-5 green shallots, shredded
2.5cm piece fresh ginger, peeled and finely shredded
½ small carrot, peeled and cut into fine strips
2 tablespoons sugar
2 tablespoons vinegar
1 teaspoon soy sauce
½ teaspoon salt
1 tablespoon tomato sauce
½ teaspoon cornflour

Make several deep, diagonal gashes in each side of the fish, cutting through to the bone and twisting the knife to lift flesh a little from the bone but not detaching it.

Mix egg white, salt, rice wine, pepper, water and 3 tablespoons cornflour. Rub the mixture well into the fish, inside and out and in the gashes.

Dredge the fish all over, inside and out, with the extra cornflour. Shake off excess.

Heat oil for deep-frying in a large wok or frying pan until a slice of ginger, dropped in, will sizzle briskly and move immediately to the side of the pan. Grasp fish firmly by the tail, hold over the oil and spoon the hot oil carefully into the gashes a few times to open them. Place fish in oil and fry, spooning oil over, until delicately browned and crisp. Place fish on a heated serving platter and keep hot while making sauce.

Pour off oil from wok or frying pan, add 2 tablespoons fresh oil and heat. Stir-fry vegetables for a minute or two, remove.

Add remaining sauce ingredients to the wok or pan and bring to the boil. Return vegetables to the pan, stir and pour over the fish. Serve immediately with boiled rice. Serves 4.

Fish fried in cornmeal

Cornmeal makes a crispy coating with a sweet, nutty flavor.

4 fish steaks or thick fillets (snapper, gemfish), skinned
Milk
1 cup cornmeal (polenta)
½ cup oil
90g butter
Lemon wedges, to serve

Dip the fish in milk, then coat with cornmeal. Heat oil in a frying pan, add butter and, just as the mixture changes color, add fish and cook, turning once, until delicately browned and cooked through (when a toothpick pushed into the fish slides in easily). Drain on crumpled paper towels and serve immediately with lemon wedges. Serves 4.

Above: Garlic Chili Prawns are favorites all over Australia.

Garlic chili prawns

500g large green prawns
¾ cup olive oil
4 cloves garlic, finely chopped
1-2 teaspoons chopped red chili, or ½ teaspoon chili powder
2 teaspoons salt
1 tablespoon chopped parsley
1 tablespoon snipped chives

Shell and devein prawns or leave whole, unshelled. Place in covered container with ½ cup olive oil, the garlic, chili and salt. Cover and refrigerate for at least 2 hours. When ready to serve, heat remaining oil in 4 flameproof dishes. Drain prawns, reserving marinade. Divide prawns between dishes and cook for 3-4 minutes or until prawns turn pink. Pour reserved marinade over, add parsley and chives and cook for further 1 minute. Serve with crusty french bread. Serves 4.

• *For more seafood recipes, see index.*

June

Beautiful soups

Some soups are almost a meal in themselves. Thick and hearty soups are wonderful for relaxed weekend luncheons and suppers, along with a generous sandwich — toasted seems just right. Garnishes are important — they can add tremendously to the look of the soup and take only minutes to prepare. Chopped parsley and other fresh herbs, snipped chives and dill — do these with scissors at the last minute — fried croutons of bread, a dollop of light sour cream all add color, texture and extra vitamins. Many of these soups are old, traditional recipes. I've brought them up to date and made them more in keeping with today's healthy approach to eating by using a good stock that is made in advance, then only lightly cooking the vegetables. This way you get maximum nutrition, the minerals drawn from the long slow cooking of the bones and the vitamins retained in the quickly cooked vegetables. Although soup does not necessarily need to be made from homemade stock, it is a simple matter to make a good stock and have it on hand in the refrigerator or freezer ready to turn into a lovely soup, and you certainly can tell the difference. Stock cubes can be used, but tend to be rather salty and give a sameness to soups. Canned consomme is quite expensive, whereas homemade stock is usually made from ingredients which are very cheap or would otherwise be discarded, and a homemade stock is nutritious in itself when made correctly. Canned consommes do have their place. When time is short it is a comforting thought to go to the cupboard and make a lovely soup with these as a base.

Beef stock

1kg beef bones (shank, marrow bone or rib bones or a combination)
500g chopped shin of beef
1 carrot, thickly sliced
1 onion, thickly sliced
2 teaspoons salt
About 3 litres cold water (enough to cover the bones)
1 teaspoon black peppercorns
Bouquet garni of 2 celery stalks, 4 sprigs parsley, 1 sprig thyme, 1 bay leaf

Put the bones into a large saucepan, then add the other ingredients and the bouquet garni tied together and cover with cold water. Bring slowly to the boil, skim the surface well, then simmer very gently, half-covered, for 4 to 5 hours (very slow simmering for a long time is the secret).

Strain through a fine sieve, cool, then chill in the refrigerator. Remove the surface fat before using. This stock is used in brown sauces and soups. Clarified, it is also used in clear soups and this method follows.

CHICKEN STOCK: Make as for beef stock, replacing beef bones and shin with approximately 1kg chicken bones — carcass, wings, etc, and, for good measure, 1 or 2 marylands.

TO CLARIFY STOCK: Remove all fat from the cold stock and place in a saucepan with 2 egg whites, lightly beaten, and the 2 egg shells. Bring slowly to the boil, whisking occasionally with an egg whisk. Allow the liquid to rise in the pan as it reaches boiling point, then lower the heat, and simmer very gently for 20 minutes.

You will find that as the egg whites cook they attract and hold any remaining particles of fat and residue that might cloud the stock. Strain through a colander lined with butter muslin, and you have a clear liquid which is the basis for many delicious soups.

FISH STOCK: See index.

Green velvet soup

2 large, dark green cucumbers
2½ cups chicken stock
30g butter
1½ tablespoons flour
1 cup warm milk
1 teaspoon chopped fresh dill or ¼ teaspoon dried
Salt and freshly ground pepper
¼ cup cream
Snipped fresh dill or chives

Peel cucumbers thinly, so that the green beneath the skin is left on. Halve lengthwise, scoop out seeds, and cut into pieces. Whirl in a food processor or blender until smooth, adding a little stock to help the process if necessary. Pour into a jug, add remaining stock, and set aside.

Melt butter in a large saucepan, stir in flour, and cook gently for 1 minute. Remove from heat, cool a little, and stir in milk. Blend smoothly together, return to heat and stir until boiling. Add cucumber mixture, dill and salt and pepper to taste. Stir in cream. Reheat gently until piping hot. Serve in heated bowls, garnished with dill or chives. Serves 6.

Dhall soup

Dhall, a lentil puree flavored with spices, appears at many Indian meals. The same ingredients make an interesting and nutritious soup — remember that lentils contain 25 per cent protein.

1 cup lentils
6 cups water
60g ghee or butter
1 medium onion, finely chopped
2 cloves garlic, crushed
1 tablespoon ground coriander
5cm stick cinnamon
1 teaspoon each ground turmeric and cumin
½ teaspoon ground fenugreek
¼ teaspoon chili powder (or to taste)
2 tablespoons tomato paste
Salt
Lemon juice
Croutons

Simmer lentils with water in a covered saucepan until tender, about 1½ hours. Pour into a bowl and set aside.

Heat ghee or butter in the same saucepan and gently fry onion and garlic until golden. Add spices and cook for 2 minutes, stirring constantly. Pour lentils and cooking liquid back into the saucepan and add tomato paste and salt to taste. Simmer, covered, for 30 minutes, then remove the cinnamon stick.

Above: Golden Carrot Soup, Clear Soup With Ravioli and Green Velvet Soup make a palette of flavors, textures and colors, and are perfect autumn eating.

With a wooden spoon, mash some of the lentils against the side of the saucepan, so you have a thickened soup with some whole lentils in it. Add lemon juice to taste, correct seasoning and serve with croutons. Serves 6.

CROUTONS: Remove crusts from 6-8 slices of white or wholemeal bread and cut each slice into 4. Brush both sides with oil, place in a single layer on a scone tray and bake in a slow oven 150C (300F) until crisp and golden.

Vegetable soup

Use any combination of vegetables for this soup. It is one of the simplest and quickest soups to make and you don't require stock. It is ready as soon as the vegetables are tender.

2 tablespoons oil
2 cloves garlic, crushed or finely chopped
2 onions, chopped
1 leek, sliced
3 rashers steaky bacon, rind removed and diced
½ bunch broccoli, sliced
1 carrot, diced
1 white turnip, diced
2 potatoes, peeled and diced
¼ cabbage, shredded
4 zucchini, sliced
2 tablespoons flour
6 cups hot water
1 bouillon cube
2 tomatoes, peeled, seeded and chopped, optional
Salt and freshly ground black pepper
Chopped parsley

Heat oil in a large saucepan, add garlic, onions, leek and bacon and cook very gently until onion is soft but not brown. Add remaining vegetables (except tomatoes) and cook, stirring occasionally, for 10 minutes. Sprinkle over the flour and cook a minute, stirring.

Add hot water and cube, bring to the boil, stirring lightly, then lower the heat, add tomatoes and season with salt and pepper. Simmer until vegetables are tender — about 20 minutes. Lastly add some chopped parsley. Serve with fresh crusty bread.

Borsch

There are many ways of making this famous Russian soup — in this version the vegetables are cooked for only a short time, thus retaining most of their vitamins.

500g shin of beef or chuck steak
10 cups water
2 teaspoons salt
1 bay leaf
2 beetroot
2 carrots
1 turnip or parsnip
1 onion
30g butter
2 tablespoons tomato paste
1 tablespoon vinegar
2 teaspoons sugar
½ small head cabbage
Freshly ground pepper
Light sour cream or yogurt

Cut beef into small cubes and put in a saucepan with water, salt and bay leaf. Bring to the boil, reduce heat, cover and simmer until tender, about 1½ hours.

Meanwhile, peel and shred or finely slice beetroot, carrots and turnip, and chop onion. Melt butter in a saucepan, then add vegetables, tomato paste, vinegar and sugar. Cover and cook very gently for about 15 minutes, stirring frequently to prevent sticking. Shred cabbage, add to pan and cook for a further 10 minutes. Add vegetables to meat and stock.

Adjust seasonings and add more vinegar if desired. Simmer soup for a few minutes.

Serve with light sour cream or yogurt and accompany with plain rye bread. Serves 8.

Clear soup with ravioli

For this Italian-inspired soup you can use canned beef consomme. Two cans of consomme will do, made up to 7 cups with water.

7 cups beef stock
½ cup dry white wine or vermouth
3 tablespoons tomato paste
1 bay leaf
Salt and freshly ground pepper
24-30 frozen ravioli (about 250g)
Freshly grated parmesan cheese

Place stock, wine or vermouth, tomato paste and bay leaf in a large saucepan and blend together. Heat until soup boils, taste, and season with salt and pepper. Add ravioli to pot and simmer until tender, about 20 minutes.

Remove bay leaf and ladle soup into bowls. Sprinkle with a little grated parmesan cheese and serve extra parmesan. Serves 6.

Oyster chowder

We are lucky in Australia to be able to buy superb oysters at a price most of us can afford. I love serving them this way — a most agreeable start to a casual Saturday lunch.

2 medium potatoes, diced
1 carrot, finely chopped
2 stalks celery, chopped
6 cups milk
1 tablespoon chopped onion
Salt and freshly ground black pepper
2 tablespoons plain flour
60g butter
3 dozen oysters, bottled or fresh
2 tablespoons chopped parsley

In a large saucepan, boil the potatoes, carrot and celery in a small amount of boiling salted water until tender. Drain. Add the milk, onion, salt and pepper and bring to the boil. Cream the flour with half the butter and gradually add to the boiling mixture.

Cook, stirring, until thickened. Cook the oysters with their liquid in the remaining butter until the edges curl. Add to the soup and serve immediately, sprinkled with parsley. Serves 4 to 6.

Carrot soup

30g butter
2 large carrots, peeled and grated
1 large potato, peeled and diced
1 small onion, peeled and chopped
1 teaspoon sugar
4 cups chicken stock or vegetable water
Salt and freshly ground pepper
1 tablespoon chopped parsley or mint

Melt butter in a large saucepan. Add carrots, potato, onion and sugar. Cover, and cook on very low heat for 15 minutes, stirring several times. Pour in stock or vegetable water, season to taste with salt and pepper, and simmer, covered, for 20 minutes.

Remove soup from heat and puree in batches in a food processor or blender, or rub through a sieve. Return to the rinsed-out saucepan, reheat, and add parsley or mint. Serves 6.

Pumpkin and pepper soup

A South American variation on our own popular pumpkin soup, this is full of vitamins and other valuable nutrients.

500g pumpkin or butternut squash
4 garlic cloves
3 cups chicken stock
1 red pepper, chopped, or 2 canned peppers
½ cup cream
Dash of Angostura bitters

Peel the pumpkin and cut into cubes. In a medium saucepan combine the pumpkin, garlic and chicken stock, bring to the boil, reduce heat and simmer, covered, for 10 minutes. Add the red pepper and simmer further 10 minutes. In a food processor or blender puree the mixture in batches and return to the pan. Stir in the cream, bitters and season to taste with salt and freshly ground pepper, reheat soup over low heat, stirring. Serves 6.

● *For other soup recipes, see index.*

Left: Try an all-time favorite like Vegetable Soup or an unusual spicy combination like Pumpkin And Pepper Soup.

Chicken specialities

As a child, I loved to watch my mother in the kitchen. With no mechanical food chopper to help her, she made the traditional stuffings, chopping away with her biggest knife. I once asked her why she always stuffed a chicken — I thought how much easier it would be just to cook the chicken without it. She said that with a family of six children, with the stuffing, everyone would have enough. Besides, some of them liked the stuffing better than the bird. Chickens were often pot-roasted in her big iron pot — it would take two chickens comfortably. Today chickens are not often stuffed but when they are, they are superb. I do believe we have become much more international in our approach and are cooking chickens with wine, herbs, artichokes, garlic, lemon and mushrooms among other foods.

Chicken in riesling

For this variation of the superb French Coq au Vin, we use chicken and a good Australian riesling. Serve with buttered noodles or boiled rice, and follow with a mixed salad.

8 chicken pieces
3 tablespoons oil
30g butter
3 carrots, sliced
2 tablespoons chopped spring onions
2 cloves garlic, crushed
1½ tablespoons flour
2 tablespoons brandy
½ bottle riesling or dry white wine
Bouquet garni
4 crushed peppercorns
½ teaspoon salt
Nutmeg
¾ cup cream
1 egg yolk, beaten
Juice of 1 lemon

Wipe chicken with paper towels. Heat oil in a heavy saucepan or a flameproof casserole, add butter and saute chicken pieces until golden brown. Remove pieces and drain on absorbent paper.

In the same pan, lightly brown carrots and spring onions, add crushed garlic and return chicken pieces to pan. Dust lightly with flour and cook gently for a few minutes. Remove from heat. Pour over brandy and ignite. Add wine, bouquet garni, peppercorns. Salt and a pinch of nutmeg. Return to heat and bring to boiling point, stirring constantly. Cover and simmer for 25-30 minutes, or until juices run clear, not pink, when tested with a skewer. Remove chicken pieces to a plate and keep warm.

Strain the sauce, return to pan, and thicken with a mixture of cream, egg yolk and lemon juice. Place chicken pieces in sauce, heat through, but do not allow to boil. Serves 4.

Chicken Hungarian style

Invest in a fresh packet of paprika for this dish if you've had it in your pantry for over 6 months. Like many spices it loses its pungency with age.

6-8 chicken pieces
Flour
60g butter
1½ tablespoons oil
1 onion, chopped
1 clove garlic, crushed
1½ tablespoons paprika (mild)
6 tablespoons white wine
½ cup cream
Salt and freshly ground pepper
Chopped parsley
Light sour cream, to serve

Dry chicken well, toss in flour then shake off excess. Melt butter and oil in a fry pan, add chicken pieces and saute until golden. Remove chicken to a warm plate.

Add onion and garlic and saute lightly, then stir in paprika and wine. Return chicken, cover and simmer for 30 minutes, or until chicken is tender.

Remove chicken pieces and keep warm. Stir in cream and simmer gently for 5 minutes. Season to taste with salt and pepper.

To serve, arrange chicken on a heated platter, cover with sauce and garnish with parsley. Serve with freshly boiled noodles or rice and a bowl of light sour cream to spoon over chicken. Serves 6.

Right: Fried Chicken Florentine comes with crispy fried parsley.

Chicken pilaf

4 chicken half breasts or fillets
2 onions
90g butter
1 cup long grain rice
1 red or green pepper thinly sliced
3 cups water
Chicken stock cube
Pinch each ground cloves, cinnamon
Salt and freshly ground pepper

Quarter chicken breasts, removing skin and bones if liked, and slice onions. In a heavy frying pan, fry chicken and onion in butter for a few minutes, until golden. Add rice and pepper and cook for a minute or two, stirring. Pour over stock. Add spices, season with salt and pepper and bring to boil. Cover and reduce heat, simmer gently until rice and chicken are tender, about 25 minutes. Serve with a green salad. Serves 4.

Sauteed chicken fillets

Once you discover the skinless, boneless half-breasts of chicken that are sold by the name of chicken fillets, you have the perfect answer for a quick dinner for yourself or a few friends. Serve with buttered noodles or rice and a sauce.

4 chicken fillets
3 tablespoons plain flour, mixed with a little salt and pepper
1 tablespoon butter and oil for sauteeing

Trim off any jagged edges from the chicken fillets. Cut and pull out the white tendon that runs down the underside of the meat.

Put the seasoned flour on a piece of greaseproof paper and turn the chicken about in it until lightly coated with flour. Heat the butter and oil in a frying pan until foaming, pat chicken to remove excess flour and place it in the pan.

Saute over medium heat for about 4 minutes until golden brown, then turn and cook other side for about 4 minutes more. Do not crowd the pan, saute the chicken in batches if necessary.

To check when the chicken is done press it with your finger; if it feels springy, it is ready. If still soft and yielding, cook it for a minute or two more but keep checking. If cooked until there is no springiness it is overdone and will be tough and dry.

Serve immediately, or keep warm for a minute or two while making one of the suggested sauces.

WINE AND CREAM SAUCE: Pour ¼ cup dry white wine into the pan and heat until boiling, stirring to collect all the good brown bits from the bottom. Swirl in 1 tablespoon of cream and boil, stirring for a minute. Taste, correct seasoning and spoon over chicken.

MEUNIERE: Add a piece of butter, about the size of a walnut, to the pan. Heat until foaming, stirring to collect the good brown bits from the bottom, then stir in 1 tablespoon lemon juice and 1 tablespoon chopped parsley. Taste, correct seasoning and spoon over chicken.

MUSHROOM SAUCE: Add a piece of butter, about the size of a walnut, to the pan. Heat until foaming, put in 8-10 sliced mushrooms and fry the slices briskly for a minute on each side. Add ¼ cup cream and boil, stirring, for a minute, then stir in 2 tablespoons lemon juice. Taste, correct seasoning and spoon over chicken.

Chicken chop suey

4 chicken fillets
Salt
2 teaspoons soy sauce
2 teaspoons dry sherry
2 cloves garlic
1 teaspoon cornflour
6 dried Chinese mushrooms
½ cup bamboo shoot or 2 stalks celery
6-8 green shallots, cut into short lengths
8 snow peas, tipped and tailed
2 tablespoons oil
3 teaspoons oyster sauce (optional)
Ground black pepper
½ cup chicken stock

Remove any skin and bones from chicken and shred meat finely. Sprinkle with salt. Combine soy sauce, sherry, 1 crushed garlic clove and cornflour, add chicken and stir well. Soak dried mushrooms in hot water about 15 minutes, drain. Shred mushrooms, bamboo shoot and shallots the same size as chicken.

Peel remaining garlic clove, heat oil and fry garlic until golden, discard. Add chicken mixture and fry, stirring constantly, for 2 minutes. Add mushrooms, snow peas, bamboo shoot and shallots, fry further 2 minutes. Add oyster sauce, if using, and season well with freshly ground black pepper. Cook 2 minutes, then add stock and simmer 1-2 minutes longer. Serve immediately with boiled rice. Serves 4-6.

Chicken pojarski

These little chicken patties are Russian in origin — note the vodka. Use ready-minced chicken, or buy 1kg of chicken breasts and prepare your own, using a mincer or food processor. On the bone, 1kg should yield the required 750g of meat.

750g minced chicken
Salt, nutmeg and pepper
4 slices white bread
¼ cup milk
4 tablespoons vodka or dry sherry
Flour for dusting
60g butter
8 mushroom caps, thinly sliced
1 cup cream

Place chicken mince in a bowl and season with salt, nutmeg and freshly ground pepper. Trim crusts from bread, pour the milk over, and allow to soak for a minute or two. Beat until smooth, then add to chicken with 2 tablespoons of the vodka and mix together lightly but well. Shape into 6 patties and dust lightly with flour.

Heat the butter in a large frying pan, and fry the patties over medium heat for 3 to 4 minutes each side, or until cooked through. Transfer to a heated serving plate and keep warm.

Saute the mushrooms in the same pan, adding a little more butter if necessary, until tender. Stir in remaining vodka and heat through. Add cream, and stir well to pick up the brown bits from the botton. Season with salt and pepper. When the sauce takes on body and thickens a little, spoon over patties. Serves 6.

Cock-a-leekie

One of the best-loved soups of Scotland.

1 large chicken with its giblets
10 cups water
2 teaspoons salt
4 leeks, shredded
1 onion, chopped
2 tablespoons rice
Good pinch white pepper
1 tablespoon chopped parsley

Truss chicken and put it into a large saucepan with water, salt and giblets. Bring slowly to the boil and skim well. Cover and simmer gently for 20 minutes. Add leeks, onion and rice and continue to simmer until rice and leeks are cooked, about 20 minutes. Remove chicken and giblets, and skim off any excess fat from top of soup. If serving chicken in the soup, remove meat from bones and skin and cut it into chunks. Cut giblets into pieces and return with chicken meat to the pot. Add pepper, parsley and more salt if required, and reheat soup. Serves 6-8.

Right: Four delicious chicken dishes, clockwise from top left: Chicken Pilaf; Chicken Chop Suey; Sauteed Chicken Fillets With Mushroom Sauce; Chicken Yakitori (see index for recipe).

Chicken with carrots and fluffy dumplings

Featherlight dumplings will bring the family rushing to the table. Just remember — once the dumplings have been added to the casserole, cover with a tight-fitting lid and don't peek until ready to serve.

1.5kg chicken pieces (drumsticks, thighs, etc)
Salt and pepper to taste
2 stalks celery, chopped
3 carrots, scraped and quartered
Sprigs of parsley, and thyme
Small bay leaf
1 tablespoon lemon juice
FLUFFY PARSLEY DUMPLINGS
1½ cups self-raising flour
½ teaspoon salt
2 tablespoons finely chopped parsley
1 teaspoon finely grated lemon rind
45g butter
¾ cup milk

Place chicken pieces with salt, pepper, celery, carrot and herbs in a large saucepan. Cover with water and simmer gently for 1 hour or until the bones can be removed. Remove chicken, take off skin and pull out large bones. Remove bay leaf and herbs; add lemon juice and correct seasoning if necessary. Return chicken to pot.

DUMPLINGS: Sift flour and salt into a mixing bowl. Add parsley and lemon rind then rub in butter with fingertips until the mixture resembles coarse breadcrumbs. Make a well in centre of mixture and stir in the milk quickly using a round-bladed knife. When a soft dough is formed, divide into 8 pieces and drop into the simmering chicken. Cover with a tight-fitting lid and simmer for 20 minutes. Do not lift lid until ready to serve.

Spatchcocks with macadamia stuffing and mango chutney glaze

6 spatchcocks (baby chickens weighing about 600g each)
60g butter, melted
STUFFING
1 small onion, finely chopped
125g butter
3 large mushrooms, chopped
4 cups diced day-old white bread
1 cucumber, peeled, seeded and finely chopped
½ cup chopped macadamia nuts
½ cup sultanas
¼ teaspoon ground cloves
2 teaspoons chopped fresh sage or 1 teaspoon dried
⅓ cup dry white wine
Salt and freshly ground pepper
GLAZE
¼ cup sugar
1 tablespoon white wine vinegar
¼ teaspoon cream of tartar
¾ cup orange juice
Thinly peeled rind of 1 orange, cut into fine matchstick strips
¾ cup mango chutney

To make the stuffing, cook onion gently in butter until soft. Remove from heat and mix with remaining stuffing ingredients.

To make the glaze, combine sugar, vinegar and cream of tartar in a small saucepan, bring to the boil, cover and boil gently 5 minutes.

Remove from heat, stir in orange juice and rind and cook on fairly low heat, stirring, until smooth. Stir in chutney.

Wipe chickens inside and out with damp paper towels. Stuff loosely, truss and sprinkle with salt and pepper. Place on a rack in a roasting pan, brush with butter and roast in a hot oven 200C (400F) for 30 minutes. Reduce heat to moderate 180C (350F) and roast 15 minutes more. Brush chickens with glaze and roast them, brushing them every 10 minutes with glaze, for a further 30 minutes.

Remove trussing strings, arrange chickens on a heated platter and garnish with a small bouquet of fresh sage or watercress. Serves 6.

Chicken with mango

4 chicken fillets
1 tablespoon light soy sauce
1 tablespoon shaohsing wine or dry sherry
¼ cup peanut oil
2.5cm piece fresh ginger, cut in fine matchsticks
6 shallots, cut in 2.5cm lengths
2 ripe mangos, peeled and cut in strips
2 tablespoons split almonds, toasted
Shallot brushes
SAUCE
1 tablespoon cornflour
1 tablespoon light soy sauce
2 tablespoons dry sherry or Chinese shaohsing wine
1 teaspoon sugar

Cut chicken into bite-sized cubes, marinate for 30 minutes in soy and wine, tossing to coat.

Heat a wok or frypan, then add the oil. When oil is hot add the chicken and stir-fry for 30 seconds, add the ginger and shallots and stir-fry further 30 seconds, then lastly the mango strips and stir-fry again, 30 seconds.

Mix all the sauce ingredients together in a small bowl, pour over chicken and stir-fry further 30 seconds.

Put on to heated platter, sprinkle over the toasted almonds. Garnish with shallot brushes and serve with a bowl of steamed rice. Serves 4.

SHALLOT BRUSHES: Cut 5cm pieces of shallots, then with a sharp pointed knife slash a 'brush' end, about halfway through lengthways. Drop brushes into iced water to curl.

Fried chicken florentine

Anyone who has visited lovely Florence will remember the crispy, succulent fried chicken of that city.

1.5 kg chicken or 4-6 chicken pieces
3 tablespoons olive oil
2 tablespoons lemon juice
½ teaspoon salt
Pepper to taste
1 tablespoon chopped parsley
Plain flour
1 egg
Oil for frying
TO SERVE
Lemon wedges
Fried parsley.

Cut chicken into serving pieces. Combine oil, lemon juice, salt, pepper and parsley and marinate the chicken in this mixture for 2 hours, turning pieces occasionally. Dry chicken thoroughly, and coat well with flour. Heat enough oil in a heavy frying pan to come about halfway up the sides of chicken pieces, and beat the egg lightly.

When oil is hot, dip chicken pieces in egg then place at once in the pan. Cook over medium heat, turning several times, until chicken is golden and crusty outside and juices run clear when flesh is pierced with a skewer. This will take about 15 minutes.

Drain on paper towels, and serve with wedges of lemon and fried parsley. Serves 4.

FRIED PARSLEY: Allow 2-3 sprigs of parsley per person. Wash thoroughly and allow to dry completely. Heat enough oil in a small saucepan to cover parsley sprigs, and plunge them in just long enough to turn crisp and crunchy — about 3 seconds. (This is easy to manage if you place the parsley in a sieve.) Serve at once.

Above: Chicken With Mango. Far left: Chicken With Carrots And Fluffy Dumplings.

• *For more chicken recipes, see index.*

Meringues and pavlovas

Meringues are said to have been invented in 1720 by a Swiss pastry cook who made them at Meyringen, a small town in Germany that gave them their name. Whatever their origin, meringues became fashionable. Marie Antoinette, according to court lore, made them with her own royal hands at the Trianon. I am giving the basic mixture which I use to make meringues in various shapes: egg-shaped for filling with cream and joining in pairs to be served with a fruit sauce for dessert; smaller rounds or ovals for serving, filled with cream and set in paper cups, with coffee; little baskets billowing with ice cream or cream and fruit; tiny miniature meringues to decorate ice cream deserts or cream cakes. The same mixture can also be used to make a large impressive meringue basket. The pavlova is one of the most delectable dessert cakes in the world. The inspiration for the delicate, light puff of ruffled meringue was Anna Pavlova when she toured Australia and New Zealand in 1926. Ever since it has been irrevocably linked with this part of the world and many good cooks have made it their speciality. In spite of its delicate air, a pavlova can be made two days before required and, when cool, stored in an airtight container. However, be guided by climatic conditions when making meringues of any kind. In damp weather it's safer to make them on the day you want to serve them or no more than one day in advance as the humidity will cause them to become sticky and weep syrup.

Rules for success

- Do have egg whites at room temperature.
- Don't think that the more freshly laid the eggs, the better a meringue will be. In fact, very fresh egg whites will not beat up well. The eggs should be a few days old.
- Do make sure beaters and bowl are completely clean and free of any grease.
- Don't allow any of the yolks to break into the egg whites when separating. If this does happen it is better to start again. Even the smallest trace of yolk will prevent the whites beating up well. That's why it's best to break each egg separately into a cup before adding to other egg whites.
- Do be sure to use 60g size eggs, they will whip up to greater volume than 50 or 55g.
- Don't beat egg whites and sugar and leave them standing; bake the meringues or pavlova right away.
- Don't add cream, filling or fruits until ready to serve.

Basic meringues

These are crisp and dry when cooked. Shape into miniature meringues for dessert garnishes (sprinkled over ice cream) or for Meringues Chantilly, individual meringue shells or a meringue pie crust.

3 large egg whites at room temperature
Scant 1/8 teaspoon cream of tartar
1 cup castor sugar

Beat egg whites on very low speed of electric mixer until frothy. Add cream of tartar and beat on highest speed until peaks hold their shape. Gradually beat in 2 tablespoons of the castor sugar and continue beating for 2-3 minutes. Add all the remaining sugar at once, folding it in quickly and lightly with a metal spoon.

Shape and bake as directed in recipe. Makes enough for about 50 miniature meringues or a 25cm meringue pie-crust or 20 egg-shaped meringues for Meringues Chantilly.

PINK MERINGUES: If desired, the mixture can be tinted pale pink by adding a few drops of red food coloring with the sugar beaten into the egg whites.

Meringues chantilly

A most delectable dessert, a proven favorite at dinner parties and with coffee.

1 quantity Basic Meringue
1 cup cream
Chopped walnuts or Apricot or Melba Sauce (optional)

Prepare Basic Meringue mixture. Set oven temperature at very low 120C (250F). Line baking trays with cooking parchment or with foil

sprayed with cooking spray and dusted with flour.

Take 2 dessertspoons or tablespoons (depending on the size you want the meringues) and, with one, scoop out a heaped spoonful of the meringue mixture. With the other spoon scoop the meringue out on to the baking tray to form an egg shape. If preferred, the meringue can be

shaped by piping, using a 1cm plain or star nozzle.

Bake in the coolest part of the oven for 1 hour, covering loosely with foil if coloring too much. Peel the parchment or foil off the backs of meringues and gently press the base of each meringue, while still warm, to make a hollow. Replace upside down on the tray and return to the oven for a further 30 minutes or until completely dry. Cool on a wire rack and store airtight.

An hour or so before serving, whip the cream and sandwich the meringues together in pairs. Place in the refrigerator until serving time. The meringues may be served plain, or with chopped walnuts sprinkled on the cream, or with a sauce. Makes about 20 egg shapes or about 30 smaller ones.

APRICOT SAUCE: Cover 250g dried apricots with cold water in a saucepan, add a small piece of cinnamon stick, bring to the boil, cover and simmer until soft. Remove

Above: A variety of mouthwatering meringues, all made from the same basic mixture.

cinnamon stick and puree apricots in a food processor or rub through a sieve. Return to the heat, stir in ½ cup sugar and cook until sugar is dissolved. A little more water may be added if sauce is too thick. Add 1-2 tablespoons brandy or Grand Marnier, if desired. Cool, then chill.

MELBA SAUCE: Puree 250g fresh or thawed, frozen raspberries in a food processor, then sieve to remove seeds, or rub the whole fruit through a sieve. Beat in 4-5 tablespoons icing sugar until mixture thickens and add a little lemon juice to sharpen flavor. The sauce can also be made by pureeing a 425g can of raspberries with their juice. Omit sugar and add lemon juice to taste. Serve sauce chilled.

German mocha pie

20cm baked meringue crust
FILLING
125g dark chocolate, chopped
3 tablespoons water
2 teaspoons cocoa
1 teaspoon instant coffee
1 cup cream
Chocolate curls or pastilles, to decorate

Melt chocolate with water in a small bowl over hot water, blend in cocoa and coffee. Stir until smooth, allow to cool.

Whip cream and fold chocolate mixture through. Pile into the cooled meringue crust and chill for 2 hours before serving.

Decorate with chocolate curls made by shaving thin curls from a block of milk chocolate at room temperature, or with chocolate pastilles (buttons) from good delicatessens and confectioners. Serves 6.

CHOCOLATE LIQUEUR PIE: Follow above recipe, using 1 tablespoon cognac, Grand Marnier or other liqueur instead of coffee.

Lemon cream pie

4 egg yolks
½ cup sugar
4 tablespoons lemon juice
1 teaspoon grated lemon rind
1 cup cream
Meringue crust

In top of double boiler, beat egg yolks lightly. Add sugar, lemon juice, rind and pinch of salt. Stir over boiling water until mixture is thick and coats back of spoon — about 10 minutes. Cool. Whip cream and fold into custard. Slowly pour into meringue crust. Chill at least 12 hours. Top with spoonfuls of whipped cream and decorate with strawberries or other fruits. Serves 8-10.

Pecan pavlova

This truly sumptuous pavlova, served with a Rich Chocolate Sauce, is baked in a springform tin.

4 egg whites
Pinch salt
1½ cups castor sugar
1½ teaspoons vinegar
1½ teaspoons vanilla
¾ cup chopped pecans (or walnuts)

Oil and flour a 23cm springform tin and set oven at slow 150C (300F).

Beat egg whites and salt at full speed until they stand in peaks. Sift sugar and gradually sprinkle in 1 tablespoon at a time, beating at high speed only until all sugar has been added. Lastly, fold in vinegar, vanilla and pecans. Put into prepared tin and cook in a slow oven for 1 hour. Turn off heat and leave pavlova in oven until cold. If using a gas range bake at 150C (300F) for 1 hour, turn heat to 120C (250F) for further 30 minutes and then turn oven off and leave pavolva in oven until cold.

When pavlova is cold remove from tin. Don't worry if pavlova collapses slightly. Before serving decorate with whipped cream, spoon some of the Chocolate Sauce over and sprinkle with chopped pecans. Serve remaining sauce separately.

Rich chocolate sauce

100g dark chocolate
¼ cup castor sugar
1 teaspoon cocoa
¾ cup water
Piece vanilla pod or vanilla essence to taste

Chop chocolate in small pieces, put into a clean large saucepan with the sugar, cocoa and half the water. Stir over moderate heat until boiling and the chocolate has dissolved. Simmer 2-3 minutes, then add the rest of the water and vanilla pod. Reboil and continue to simmer for 15-20 minutes or until the sauce is syrupy and rich-looking. Serve cold.

Cherry cream pie

3 egg yolks
⅓ cup castor sugar
Finely grated rind and juice of 1 lemon
1¼ cups cream
1 meringue crust
1 x 425g can pitted cherries

Cream the egg yolks and sugar in a small basin and blend in the lemon rind and juice. Place over a saucepan of very hot, but not boiling, water. Cook, whisking constantly, until the mixture forms a thick, smooth cream. Cool completely.

Whip the cream until it holds its shape; don't overbeat. Fold all except a few spoonfuls of cream into the cold lemon mixture.

Fold the drained cherries through the lemon cream, saving a few for decoration.

Fill the cooled meringue crust and decorate with the reserved whipped cream and cherries.

Meringue crust

This basic crust can be used with many luscious fillings, fruit salad and cream, chocolate cream or ice cream.

2 egg whites
Pinch of salt
Pinch of cream of tartar
½ cup sugar
½ cup finely chopped walnuts or pecans
½ teaspoon vanilla essence

Place a sheet of baking paper on baking tray. Draw an 18cm circle on paper. Beat the egg whites with the salt and cream of tartar until light and foamy. Add the sugar 2 tablespoons at a time, beating well after each addition. Continue to beat until the mixture stands in soft peaks then fold in the nuts and vanilla.

Spoon the meringue on to the paper. Make a depression in the middle and mould the edges up slightly so they come about 1cm up the sides. Bake the meringue in a preheated slow oven 150C (300F) for 50 to 55 minutes, or until crisp and a light straw color. Cool the crust before filling.

Basic pavlova

6 egg whites
Pinch salt
1¾ cups castor sugar
1½ teaspoons vinegar
1½ teaspoons vanilla essence

If using a gas range set oven at highest temperature just as you start to beat the egg whites. If using an electric oven, preheat oven to 150C (300F).

Draw an 18cm circle on baking paper or lightly greased aluminium foil and put on baking tray.

Beat egg whites and salt with a rotary beater or at full speed on an electric mixer until they stand in peaks. Sift sugar and gradually sprinkle in 1 tablespoon at a time, beating at high speed only until all sugar has been added. As soon as one spoonful is added, immediately start

sprinkling in the next. Lastly, fold in vinegar and vanilla essence.

Heap egg white mixture on the circle on paper. Mould up the sides with a spatula and make a slight depression on top to form a well-shaped pavlova when cooked.

If using a gas oven, turn heat to lowest temperature, then put pavlova in bottom of oven to cook for 1½ hours. In an electric oven preheated to a low temperature 150C (300F) bake pavlova in the coolest part of the oven for 45-60 minutes, turn off heat and leave until oven is cold.

PAVLOVA WITH ALMONDS: Before baking the pavlova, sprinkle with flaked almonds. To flake almonds blanch them first (or if using already blanched almonds, put them into hot water for 5 minutes to soften) and then cut into flakes with a sharp knife or potato peeler. Do this in advance so the pavlova doesn't stand around waiting to be baked.

TOPPINGS FOR PAVLOVA: Passionfruit and strawberries are the ideal topping for a pavlova. Pile whipped cream (unsweetened) on the pavlova just before serving and spoon passionfruit pulp and/or sliced strawberries on top.

If liked the berries can be sliced, sweetened with a little sugar and flavored with a teaspoon of kirsch.

For a tropical touch, some cooks like to add thin slices of banana. Dip in lemon juice to prevent dicoloring.

Above: Pavlova, beautifully decorated with strawberries or other fruit, is a Down Under classic.

An exotic addition and so pretty to look at, are slices of peeled kiwi fruit, when in season. The pale green flesh dotted with tiny black seeds are a decoration in themselves.

If the pavlova cracks or drops in the centre, that is to be expected. This may happen before or while getting it on to the serving plate. Simply pile cream into the centre and top with fruit just before serving. Chill in refrigerator half an hour and enjoy.

This type of pavlova is as it should be with its delectable crisp sugary crust and marshmallowy centre.

The biscuit barrel

I love homemade biscuits, the kind you used to get at fetes or at country afternoon teas. For years, a close friend has always offered a lovely little lemon butter biscuit with a cup of tea — so imagine my surprise when I was told they were one of my early recipes! I had forgotten them. If you have forgotten how homemade biscuits can lift the spirits, make a batch today — you will be pleasantly surprised at how quick and easy it is. They are a sign of hospitality.

Lemon butter biscuits

250g butter, softened
Grated rind 1 lemon
1 cup icing sugar, sifted
2 cups plain flour, sifted

Beat butter with lemon rind until creamy. Beat in icing sugar then stir in flour to make a soft dough. Cover and chill for 30 minutes.

Take teaspoonfuls of the mixture and roll lightly into balls. Place well apart on ungreased baking trays and press down with a fork which has been dipped into cold water to prevent sticking.

Bake in a moderate oven 180C (350F) for 10-12 minutes or until slightly colored. Ease biscuits with a spatula and cool 3 minutes on trays, then transfer to a wire rack until cold. Store in airtight jar. Makes about 50.

Gingernuts

1 cup plain flour
2 tablespoons sugar
1 teaspoon bicarbonate of soda
1 teaspoon mixed spice
1 teaspoon cinnamon
1 teaspoon ground ginger
60g butter
2 tablespoons golden syrup
Extra ½ cup sugar (optional)

Sift dry ingredients together. Melt butter with golden syrup and pour into dry mixture. Mix well and roll into walnut-size balls. If liked, roll balls in extra sugar for super crunchiness.

Place well apart on greased baking trays and press down lightly. Bake in a very hot oven 230C (450F) for 5 minutes, then reduce heat to moderate 180C (350F) and bake a further 7-10 minutes. Ease biscuits with a spatula and cool on trays. Makes about 20.

Coconut buttons

125g butter
1 cup castor sugar
1 egg
2 cups self-raising flour, sifted
Pinch salt
1 cup desiccated coconut
Extra castor sugar
Glace cherries, sliced (optional)

Cream butter and sugar, beat in egg and stir in flour, salt and coconut.

Take teaspoons of the mixture, roll into balls and press flat with the back of a spoon. Dip one side of each biscuit in castor sugar and place, sugar side up and well apart, on greased oven trays. Top with cherry slices if desired.

Bake in a moderately hot oven 190C (375F) 10-15 minutes or until golden. Ease biscuits with a spatula, cool 3 minutes on trays then transfer to a wire rack until cold. Store in an airtight jar. Makes about 40.

COCONUT DISCS: Follow above recipe but use only 1 cup of flour. This gives a thinner biscuit with a slightly chewy texture.

Chocolate hazelnut biscuits

1¼ cups plain flour
¾ cup icing sugar
½ teaspoon cinnamon
125g unsalted butter
⅔ cup ground hazelnuts
1 teaspoon grated lemon rind
1 egg yolk, lightly beaten
60g dark chocolate
¼ cup chopped hazelnuts or halved hazelnuts, to decorate (optional)

Sift flour, icing sugar and cinnamon together, rub in butter until mixture resembles breadcrumbs. Mix in ground hazelnuts and lemon rind, add egg yolk and combine well to make a dough (your hand is best for this). Knead dough lightly until smooth and chill 30 minutes.

Roll out dough on a lightly floured surface to 3mm thickness and cut into rounds or other shapes with a 5cm cutter. Place rounds on lightly greased oven trays and bake in a moderate oven 180C (350F) for 10-15 minutes or until lightly colored. Ease biscuits with a spatula, cool three minutes on trays then remove to a wire rack.

Melt chocolate over hot water and spread a little on each cooled biscuit. Top with a sprinkling of chopped hazelnuts or a hazelnut half if desired. Makes about 40.

Note: This is a very soft dough. If hard to handle, roll out between two sheets of plastic film and chill before cutting out biscuits.

Left: There's nothing quite like the taste of homemade biscuits. Here's a tempting selection to serve next time friends visit.

Peanut plum slices

A crunchy bar biscuit that is great for picnics, school lunch boxes and with tea or coffee. Nutritious, too, with protein-rich peanuts.

125g butter, softened
¼ cup sugar
1 egg
½ teaspoon vanilla essence
1¼ cups plain flour, sifted
Pinch of salt
¾ cup plum jam
TOPPING
2 cups finely chopped unsalted peanuts
1 cup sugar
¼ teaspoon nutmeg
½ teaspoon cinnamon
2 teaspoons grated lemon rind
4 egg whites, lightly beaten

Cream together the butter and sugar, then beat in the egg and vanilla. Sift the flour with the salt and add in three parts to the butter mixture, blending well each time. Pat the dough into a greased 23 x 33cm shallow tin. Bake in a preheated moderate oven 180C (350F) for 15 minutes, until set but not cooked.

Meanwhile, make the topping. Place all ingredients in a large saucepan and combine well. Cook over gentle heat, stirring all the time, until the sugar has dissolved. Increase the heat slightly and continue cooking and stirring until the mixture leaves the sides of the pan.

Spread the pastry with jam, then with the nut topping. Bake for a further 15 minutes, until the pastry is crisp and the topping firm.

Cut into slices when cold. Makes about 48 2.5 x 5cm slices.

Nutty caramel slice

1 cup plain flour
½ teaspoon baking powder
90g butter
1 egg, lightly beaten
1 cup pecans or walnuts
TOPPING
60g butter
⅓ cup golden syrup
⅓ cup firmly packed brown sugar
1 egg, lightly beaten
2 tablespoons self-raising flour, sifted

Sift flour and baking powder into a bowl, rub in butter, mix in egg to make a soft dough.

Press dough evenly over base of a well-greased 28 x 18cm lamington tin. Bake in a moderate oven 180C (350F) for 15 minutes, remove from oven and sprinkle nuts over.

TOPPING: Melt butter, remove from heat, stir in remaining ingredients and continue stirring until smooth.

Pour topping over the biscuit base and nuts, return to oven and bake a further 15 minutes. Leave in tin until cold then cut into fingers or squares.

Melting moments

250g butter
⅓ cup icing sugar
1½ cups plain flour
½ cup cornflour
LEMON FILLING
60g butter
½ cup icing sugar
1 teaspoon grated lemon rind
3 teaspoons lemon juice

Cream butter and icing sugar until light and fluffy. Sift flours together and mix in.

Divide mixture into eighths, then roll each part into 5 small balls. Place well apart on greased oven trays and press flat with a fork dipped in flour. Bake in a moderate oven 180C (350F) for 10-12 minutes until pale golden. Ease biscuits with spatula, cool 2 minutes on trays then remove to wire rack. When cold, join in pairs with lemon filling. Makes about 20 complete biscuits.

LEMON FILLING: Cream butter and icing sugar until light and fluffy, beat in lemon rind and juice, a little at a time.

July

Stews, casseroles, and goulashes

A robust casserole on the table is a comforting sight indeed. The rich flavor of slow-cooked food, with its own flavorsome juices and the heady smell when the lid is taken off is one of the rewards of winter, which seems to be the ideal time for a casserole. Casserole cookery is usually economical and easy, important if you are a working woman who has a family to feed or likes to entertain, for most casseroles actually taste better for having been made a day or two before required. Many types of casserole dishes are available. Cast aluminium with silverstone lining is my personal favorite, for use on top of the stove or in the oven, practical and easy to clean. Cast iron with an enamel coating is both fireproof and ovenproof, and has the advantage that it can also be used on top of the stove. There are also flameproof ceramic casseroles, but check before using on top of the stove; it usually says 'flameproof' on the bottom. Attractive earthenware and stoneware pots come in brown and terracotta shades, but most of these cook only in the oven. A flameproof casserole saves using two vessels. Pyroceram is also a durable material used for casseroles; it will never break from extremes of temperature. When selecting a casserole look for the one which is large, heavy, has a tight-fitting lid and which cooks well and looks good enough to be taken to the table. Consider also the electric slow-cookers, which, to a large extent, have taken the place of casseroles. It is easy to adapt any of these recipes to slow-cookers; allow them about 6-8 hours on slow or 4-6 hours on high.

Gulyas

Opinions vary about the exact color to which the onions should be cooked for a gulyas (Hungarian goulash). Different Hungarian cooks may recommend any shade from pale gold to rich brown, but they all agree that the initial cooking must be slow and the onions stirred frequently to color evenly and develop full flavor without scorching.

2 tablespoons lard or butter
4 onions, finely chopped
2 cloves garlic, finely chopped
1.5kg veal neck or shoulder, boned and cut into 5cm cubes
1 tablespoon paprika
2 green peppers, cored, seeded and chopped
2 tomatoes, peeled and chopped
1 large potato, peeled and diced
Salt and freshly ground black pepper
Hot buttered noodles and sour cream, to serve

Heat fat in a large flameproof casserole and add onions and garlic. Cook gently, stirring often, until onions are golden (or until browned, if desired). Push onions aside, add veal cubes and saute until golden.

Reduce heat, sprinkle with paprika and cook very gently, stirring often, for 10 minutes. Add vegetables, season lightly with salt and pepper and bring to simmering point. Cover and place in a slow oven 150C (300F) for 2 hours or until the meat is tender. Adjust seasoning and serve with buttered noodles and a bowl of sour cream handed separately. Serves 6.

Irish stew

Real Irish stew should have twice as much potato and half as much onion as meat, by weight. Though not authentic, other vegetables such as celery or carrots are good additions.

1kg lamb neck chops
2kg potatoes
500g onions
Salt and freshly ground black pepper
2½ cups water
Faggot of herbs (parsley, thyme, bay leaf, tied in a bunch)
2 tablespoons chopped parsley

Trim excess fat from chops. Peel potatoes, slice a few and halve the rest. Peel onions and slice thickly.

Put sliced potatoes in a layer in a deep, heavy saucepan. Cover with meat, then halved potatoes, then

Right: Gulyas (goulash), a Hungarian specialty, is cooked slowly to release its full flavor.

remaining ingredients except chopped parsley.

Bring to simmering point, cover tightly and simmer on very low heat for 2-2½ hours or until lamb is very tender and stew is thick and creamy. Shake pan gently from time to time to prevent sticking. Remove faggot and serve sprinkled with parsley and accompanied by a green vegetable. Serves 6-8.

VARIATION: Follow above recipe, but add 2 stalks celery, sliced, and 500g carrots, thickly sliced, in a layer on top of sliced potatoes.

Blanquette de veau

A blanquette is a 'white' stew for which the meat is not browned but is simmered to melting tenderness and bathed in a delicate, creamy sauce. A dish to please discerning diners whether family or guests.

1.5kg boneless veal, cut into large cubes
1 large onion, studded with 1 clove
3 carrots, quartered
1 stalk celery, sliced
Bouquet garni
5 cups veal or chicken stock
Salt and white pepper
20 white button onions
125g small button mushrooms
2 tablespoons flour
45g butter
3 egg yolks
½ cup cream
2 tablespoons lemon juice
Chopped parsley and croutes, to garnish

Blanch veal for 2 minutes in boiling salted water. Drain, rinse under cold running water and place in a deep, heavy saucepan. Add onion, carrot, celery and bouquet garni. Add stock and season with salt and pepper. Bring to simmering point then cover and simmer very gently 1½ hours or until veal is tender. Skim surface several times during cooking.

While veal is cooking, peel onions, leaving root ends intact. Cut a shallow cross in root end of each onion and blanch in boiling water for 5 minutes. Drain.

Remove vegetables and bouquet garni from veal with a slotted spoon. Add button onions and mushrooms to the saucepan and simmer 10 minutes.

Blend flour and butter together and whisk, a little at a time, into simmering liquid. Simmer another 10 minutes, then remove pan from heat.

Mix egg yolks and cream together. Stir in 2 tablespoons of liquid from veal, stir this mixture back into the saucepan with lemon juice and reheat gently without boiling.

Adjust seasoning. Serve blanquette sprinkled with parsley and garnished

with croutes. Serves 6. Serve with hot buttered rice or mashed potatoes.
CROUTES: Remove crusts from sliced bread and cut into small triangles. Fry in a little oil and butter until crisp and drain on crumpled paper towels.

Finnish karelian pot

This old Finnish dish is so popular it is sold in cans in Finland. The recipe couldn't be simpler; but the combination of meats and the long, slow cooking gives a unique flavor. In Finland, it would be served with boiled potatoes and tart-sweet lingonberries or cranberries — both available here from delicatessens or the gourment shelf of supermarkets.

500g lean, boneless pork
500g lean, boneless beef
500g lean, boneless lamb
½ tablespoon coarse salt (sea salt)
1 teaspoon whole peppercorns
3-4 juniper berries (optional)
1 cup water

Cut meat into bite-size cubes and combine. Arrange in layers in a deep, round casserole, sprinkling each layer with a little salt.

Add peppercorns, juniper berries and water and cover very tightly. (This amount of water seems small, but juices will come from the meat.)

Bake in a preheated slow oven 150C (300F) for 4 hours, or in a slow cooker set on low for 6-8 hours. Taste for seasoning, and serve from the pot. Serves 6-8.

Rabbit in its own juice

The rabbit is not marinated or browned in this recipe, but cooked very gently in its own juice. It's an interesting North Italian approach which emphasises the delicate flavor and fine texture of the meat.

1 rabbit, cut into serving pieces
Salt and freshly ground pepper
¾ cup olive oil
1 stalk celery, finely chopped
1 clove garlic, crushed
1 onion, finely chopped
1 cup white wine
1 teaspoon dried rosemary
2 tablespoons tomato paste
½ teaspoon sugar

Wash rabbit pieces and pat dry with paper towels. Arrange them in a single layer in a flame-proof casserole dish, and season with salt and pepper.

Pour the oil over, and sprinkle with celery, garlic and onion. Cover the casserole tightly and bake in a preheated moderately slow oven, 170C (325F) for 2 hours, turning the meat once or twice. During this time, the rabbit will produce quite a lot of juice.

Place the casserole on top of the stove over high heat, remove the cover, and cook until the liquid in the dish has almost evaporated.

Add wine, rosemary, tomato paste and sugar to the pan, and stir to combine. Reduce heat to low and cook rabbit for another 15 minutes, basting with sauce in the pan and turning the pieces over two or three times.

Season to taste with salt and pepper and serve from the casserole with crusty bread and a green vegetable. Serves 4.

Magic mustard chicken

There are moments in all our lives when we wish a main course would appear with the wave of a magic wand. This is almost that quick — 20 minutes from start to finish. Serve it with packaged potato straws crisped in the oven and green salad.

1 large cooked chicken (from the barbecue or delicatessen)
Dijon mustard
60g butter
1½ tablespoons plain flour
1 cup pouring cream
Salt to taste

Remove skin and bones from chicken, separating the meat into large pieces. (Save the wings to nibble on next day.)

Spread each piece thinly with mustard and arrange in a shallow casserole dish. Melt the butter in a small saucepan and stir in the flour over low heat. Add the cream gradually, stirring all the time, and continue stirring for a few minutes until the sauce is smooth and thick. Add salt to taste and spoon over chicken pieces. Bake in a preheated moderate oven, 180C (350F) for 15 minutes and serve from the casserole. Serves 4.

Beef and cashew casserole

This traditional beef casserole is made more interesting by the addition of butter-browned celery and cashews.

60g butter
2 tablespoons olive oil
1kg lean stewing beef, cut into cubes
2 large onions, sliced
2 cloves garlic, crushed
¾ cup red wine
1 bay leaf
1 tablespoon grated orange rind
1 cup beef stock
Salt and freshly ground pepper

Extra 30g butter
6 tender stalks celery, sliced
½ cup roasted, salted cashews

Heat oil and butter in a large, flameproof casserole and fry beef until brown, stirring to brown all sides.

Remove beef and add garlic and onions to pan, stirring until golden. Return beef to casserole with wine, bay leaf, orange rind and the stock. Season with salt and pepper, cover the casserole, and bake in a preheated moderate oven 180C (350F) for 1 hour.

Meanwhile, heat the extra 30g butter in a frying pan and toss celery and cashews over medium heat for 2-3 minutes.

Add celery and cashews to casserole, replace lid, and continue

cooking until meat is very tender — about 30 minutes longer. Serve from the casserole. Serves 6.

Lamb and haricot casserole

The French serve lamb with haricot beans. The two marry well, making a protein-rich dish which is good value for money.

1 cup dried haricot beans
2¼ cups water
1 teaspoon salt
30g butter
2 small onions, sliced
1 carrot, sliced
1.5kg boned shoulder of lamb
1 clove garlic
A few sprigs of fresh oregano
2 tablespoons olive oil
1 cup dry white wine
1 x 440g can peeled tomatoes
Bouquet garni
Salt and freshly ground pepper
2 tablespoons chopped parsley

Soak beans in water overnight. Drain. Place beans in a large saucepan with water and salt. Bring to the boil and simmer covered for 1-1½ hours or until tender. Drain and set aside.

Meanwhile, melt butter in a flameproof casserole, add sliced onions and carrot. Saute gently for about 10 minutes until light golden color. Remove vegetables from pan and set aside.

Sprinkle lamb with chopped garlic and herbs. Roll lamb and tie into a neat shape with string.

Above: Lamb And Haricot Casserole is a protein-rich dish very popular in France.

Add oil to pan and when hot add lamb, browning all over. Return vegetables to pan, pour in wine and boil rapidly until reduced by one-third. Add canned tomatoes and juice, bouquet garni, salt and pepper. Bring to a gentle boil, cover and simmer gently for about 1 hour.

Transfer lamb to a warm plate and remove string. Combine vegetables with beans.

Return lamb and beans to casserole and spoon over sauce. Heat casserole to a simmer and sprinkle with parsley. To serve, cut lamb into thick slices and spoon beans around it. Serves 6-8.

French provincial cooking

France, with Paris as its centre, has influenced the rest of the world in food, fashion and wine, but especially food. Certainly, eating is the principal pastime of many a Parisian and French provincial alike. The French have three answers to eating well; they eat out frequently, they buy outstanding ready-prepared and fresh products and when they cook they do it well. For generations, French cooks have learned to cook from their mothers or grandmothers or perhaps aunts, but as with the rest of the world, today's good home cooks are learning from excellent cookery articles in magazines and newspapers, and also from books. From the cooks of France to those of Australia, here is a sampling of dishes which may become your favorites, too.

Bouquet garni

Most French soups, stocks and casseroles owe some of their subtle flavor to a bouquet garni — the bundle or 'faggot' of herbs and aromatics which is simmered in the dish and removed at the end of cooking. A bouquet garni usually includes parsley, thyme and bay leaf, and may also have strips of carrot or celery, garlic, leek, orange or lemon rind, rosemary or other herbs. The ingredients are tied into a bundle, or tied up in a muslin bag; the string should have a long enough 'tail' to tie to the handle of the pan for easy removal when the dish is cooked.

Chicken marengo

How long since you've had this famous dish, which commemorates Napoleon's victory at Marengo? Select the chicken joints so that everyone gets their favorite part — breast, thigh, drumsticks — or offer bits of each.

6-8 chicken joints
Salt and freshly ground pepper
Flour
1 tablespoon oil
1 tablespoon butter
2 cloves garlic, crushed
1 bouquet garni (parlsey, thyme, bay leaf)
1 cup white wine
¼ cup brandy
2 large tomatoes, peeled and quartered
12 mushrooms
Chopped parsley

Sprinkle chicken with salt and pepper and coat lightly with flour. Heat oil and butter in a large frying pan and brown chicken over high heat until golden on all sides, turning frequently. Transfer to a flameproof casserole and add garlic, bouquet garni, white wine, brandy and tomatoes. Cover casserole tightly and cook gently for 30 minutes, turning chicken pieces several times with wooden spoon. Add mushrooms and cook for 10 minutes longer or until chicken is tender. Adjust seasoning and discard bouquet garni. Serve in casserole, sprinkled with chopped parsley.

The dish may be served with french bread fried in butter or with boiled rice. Serves 6.

Veal cutlets bonne femme

4 rashers bacon or 185g pickled belly pork
60g butter
12 small shallots or 4 onions peeled and quartered
12 button mushrooms
6 veal chops or cutlets
3 tablespoons flour
1 cup white wine
½ cup stock
Salt and freshly ground pepper
1 clove garlic
12 small new potatoes
1 tablespoon chopped parsley

Remove rinds of bacon and cut each rasher in 4 or slice pork. Fry bacon or pork and put in a casserole.

Add the butter to the frypan and lightly brown shallots or onions, then mushrooms, place them in the casserole.

Lightly dust cutlets with flour, brown them in a frypan, then place on top of vegetables. Stir in any remaining flour to pan, then add white wine and stock and stir until thickened, add salt, pepper and garlic and pour over veal.

Cover and bake in a moderate oven 180C (350F) for 30 minutes. Wash or scrub potatoes, add to casserole and cook further 40 minutes. Serve from the casserole or turn into heated serving dish, sprinkled with parsley. Serves 6.

Onion quiche

1 quantity Shortcrust Pastry (see index)
2 eggs plus 1 yolk, beaten
3 medium white onions
30g butter
½ cup cream
½ cup milk

Left: Succulent Chicken Marengo, redolent of wine and herbs, celebrates a Napoleonic victory.

1 teaspoon plain flour
½ teaspoon salt
Pinch each freshly grated nutmeg and pepper
30g swiss cheese
2 teaspoons extra butter

Roll pastry thin and use to line a 20cm or 23cm flan ring. Chill for 15 minutes, then prick all over. Line with greaseproof paper, then fill with dried beans and bake in a very hot oven 220C (425F) for 7-8 minutes or until just colored. Remove from oven, remove beans and immediately brush inside lightly with a little beaten egg. Set aside.

Slice onions thin or use slicing disc of food processor. Melt butter and cook onion, covered, on a low heat until soft. Remove lid, raise heat a little and cook until any liquid has evaporated. Remove from heat.

Using the steel blade, process remaining beaten egg, cream, milk, flour, seasonings and cheese together until cheese is finely chopped or combine ingredients, cutting cheese by hand.

Arrange onion in an even layer in flan case. Pour filling over, dot with extra 2 teaspoons butter and bake in a moderate oven 180C (350F) for 25-30 minutes, until filling is set and surface is golden-brown.

MUSHROOM QUICHE: Substitute 250g sliced mushrooms and 1 tablespoon chopped spring onions for the sliced onions in Onion Quiche.

CHICKEN AND ALMOND QUICHE: Substitute 1 cup chopped, cooked chicken, 2 tablespoons chopped spring onion and a few herbs, if liked, for the onions in Onion Quiche. Do not cook, simply arrange in flan case. Substitute 1 tablespoon sherry for the cheese in the custard mixture. Sprinkle quiche with slivered almonds before baking.

SEAFOOD QUICHE: Use 1 cup any flaked, cooked or canned seafood plus 1 tablespoon chopped shallots instead of onions. Do not cook; simply arrange in flan case. Add 1 tablespoon sherry to custard mixture.

Crumbed baked apples with Calvados

This dish is from Normandy, home of wonderful apples and the apple brandy called Calvados. Ordinary brandy, though not quite the same, is still excellent.

6 cooking apples
125g butter
6 teaspoons sugar
6 tablespoons apricot jam
6 to 8 macaroons, crushed
6 teaspoons Calvados or other brandy

Peel the apples, and trim and even bases if necessary, to make them stand upright. Remove the cores without piercing apples completely so that there is a base in the centre hole.

Cut the butter into 6 even pieces. Arrange the apples in a large baking dish and fill the centre of each hole with a piece of butter and a teaspoon of sugar.

Add about 1cm of water to the pan, cover it with buttered paper and bake the apples in a moderate oven 180C (350F) until they are almost tender, 30 minutes or more depending on the ripeness and type of apple.

Melt the jam and brush it on the apples. Sprinkle them with macaroon crumbs and put 1 teaspoon brandy in the centre of each. Bake 5 minutes more, or until tender. Serve hot with chilled pouring cream. Serves 6.

Omelet lorraine

Eggs, bacon and cheese, as everyone knows, go into the famous quiche from Lorraine. These same ingredients make an equally good omelet, another specialty of the province.

4 rashers bacon
4 eggs
½ teaspoon salt
Good grinding of black pepper
½ cup cream
1 tablespoon chopped fresh herbs (see note)
15g butter
60g gruyere cheese, thinly sliced

Choose a heavy, medium-size frying pan. Remove rind from bacon, cut into small strips and fry until lightly browned. Lift out with a slotted spoon and set aside.

Beat eggs and stir in salt, pepper, cream and herbs. Add the butter to the bacon fat in the pan and heat. When the foam subsides, add the egg mixture and cook briskly for 1 minute, pulling sides to centre with a spatula to let the uncooked mixture run underneath. Scatter the bacon and cheese over and continue cooking undisturbed until omelet is just set.

Serve immediately, cut into wedges. Serves 4.

Note: The traditional recipe calls for a mixture of chopped parsley, chives and chervil, but you can use other fresh herbs, or chop a tablespoon or parsley with ½ teaspoon mixed dried herbs.

Potato and chervil soup

This delicate, parsley-like plant makes the most wonderful soup. If it's unavailable, use parsley.

3 medium potatoes, peeled
45g butter
3 cups water or chicken stock
1 cup milk
Salt and nutmeg
2 tablespoons cream
2 tablespoons fresh chervil

Dice the potatoes and melt the butter in a heavy-based saucepan. Put in the potatoes and cook very gently in the butter until they begin to soften but don't allow to brown. Pour in the water, stir well, cover and simmer gently for 20 minutes. Sieve or puree the potatoes and return the puree to the rinsed out pan.

Heat the milk and add to potatoes, season to taste with salt and a grating of nutmeg. Just before serving, stir in the cream and snipped chervil. Serves 4-5.

Stuffed eggplant

2 medium-size eggplant
Salt and freshly ground pepper
2 teaspoons vinegar
250g minced pork
1 tablespoon fresh or 1 teaspoon dried tarragon
1 teaspoon grated lemon rind
1 tablespoon chopped parsley
4 tablespoons chopped spring onions or shallots
1 clove garlic, chopped
2 cups soft breadcrumbs
¼ cup milk
2 tablespoons olive oil

Slit the eggplants lengthwise and remove the pulp, taking care not to cut through the skins. Put the pulp into a bowl with salt, pepper and vinegar and let stand for 1 hour.

Meanwhile, put pork into a greased frying pan and brown, stirring and breaking down lumps with a fork.

Put pork in a bowl and add tarragon, lemon rind, parsley, spring onions and garlic. Add chopped, drained eggplant pulp.

Soften 1 cup crumbs with milk and add to the mixture. Season with salt and pepper and stuff the mixture into the eggplant skins. Sprinkle with the remaining breadcrumbs and drizzle with olive oil. Bake in a hot oven 200C (400F) for 30-40 minutes or until

eggplant is tender. Serve in the oven dish. Serves 4.

Mushrooms with garlic and parsley

This robust way of treating mushrooms is from Provence.

1kg firm white mushrooms caps
1 cup olive oil
1 fat clove garlic, finely chopped
Salt and freshly ground pepper
½ cup finely chopped parsley
An extra clove garlic, finely chopped
1 tablespoon lemon juice

Wipe the mushrooms and cut in half if large.

Heat about half the olive oil in a large frying pan until it begins to give off a haze, add half the mushrooms and saute on high heat without turning for 2 minutes. Sprinkle with ½ clove chopped garlic and toss for 2 more minutes. Turn into a heated serving dish and keep warm while you saute the remaining mushrooms in the remaining oil, sprinkling with another ½ clove garlic. Add to the first batch of mushrooms and sprinkle with salt and pepper to taste, extra chopped garlic, parsley and lemon juice. Serve immediately with plain or toasted french bread. Serves 6 as a first course.

French-roasted chicken

The French like their chicken tender and juicy, with golden-crisp skin.

1 roasting chicken, 1.5-1.75kg
90g butter
Salt and freshly ground pepper
A sprig of tarragon, rosemary or thyme
2 strips orange or lemon rind
1 slice onion
1 cup chicken stock
1 chicken liver, lightly sauteed in a little butter (optional).

Wipe the chicken inside and out with damp paper towels.Put 30g of the butter, a little salt and pepper, the herbs, rind and onion inside the bird.

Truss the chicken. Shape the bird with both hands, tucking the neck flap underneath the folded wings at the back. Take a piece of string and place the centre below the breast at the neck end. Run the string down over the wings, cross it at the back and bring the ends up to tie the legs and parson's nose together. Rub the chicken all over with the remaining butter.

Place the chicken on its side on a rack in a greased roasting pan. Add ⅓ cup stock to the pan and roast in a hot oven 200C (400F) for 20 minutes. Turn chicken on to the other side, baste with pan juices and roast a further 20 minutes. Turn chicken on to its back and continue roasting, basting every 15 minutes, for a further 35-40 minutes or until done (when juices run clear if thigh joint is pierced with a fine skewer). Add more stock as necessary — there should be just enough liquid in the pan to keep juices from scorching. Do not baste during last 20 minutes, to allow skin to crisp.

Take chicken from pan, remove trussing string and keep warm while making gravy.

Add remaining stock, or stock and water, to the pan to make about 1 cup liquid. Boil, stirring in brown bits from pan, until reduced to about ¾ cup. Season to taste and strain into a heated sauceboat. The chicken liver, lightly sauteed in a little butter, can be sliced and added to the gravy if desired. Carve chicken and serve with the gravy. Serves 6.

Far left: Omelet Lorraine, like its compatriot, the quiche, features bacon, eggs and cheese. Above: French-Roasted Chicken and Stuffed Eggplant. Both meals are served with Mushrooms With Garlic And Parsley.

Poulet basquaise

Lavish use of peppers and tomatoes is characteristic of the Basque cuisine and is a reflection of the cooking of southern France.

1.75kg chicken
2 tablespoons olive oil
Salt and pepper
Bouquet garni
½ cup dry white wine
4 medium tomatoes
3 medium onions
2 large peppers, 1 red, 1 green

Joint chicken, slowly brown pieces in olive oil in a heavy pan. When brown transfer to flameproof casserole, season with salt and pepper, add bouquet garni and wine.

Meanwhile, peel and seed tomatoes, chop onions finely and cut peppers into strips. Cook onions in same pan as chicken until soft but not brown. Add pepper strips to onions, cook about 10 minutes, then add chopped tomatoes. Season with salt and pepper and cook about 20 minutes. Add to chicken in casserole, cook on gentle heat 20 to 30 minutes. Accompany with a rice pilaf. Serves 4.

Lapin moutarde

Rabbit is not usually one of my favorites, but when cooked gently with mustard, wine and bacon, the subtle combination of flavors makes it a delicately delicious dish.

1 rabbit
2 teaspoons vinegar
1 tablespoon plain flour
1 tablespoon oil
30g butter
4 to 6 onions, peeled
125g streaky bacon, diced
1½ cups stock
¾ cup red wine
Salt and pepper
2 tablespoons french mustard
Bouquet garni (bunch of fresh herbs)
⅓ cup cream
2 teaspoons chopped parsley

Joint the rabbit and soak overnight in salted water, with vinegar, to cover. Drain and dry rabbit thoroughly, then coat with the flour. Heat oil and butter in a fireproof casserole or heavy saucepan, add onions, cut into quarters lengthwise, and cook for 3 minutes, then remove. Add rabbit and bacon and cook to a golden brown. Return onions. Pour in stock and wine, add salt, pepper, mustard and bouquet garni.

Bring slowly to the boil and simmer, covered, for 1½ hours or until rabbit is tender. If sauce is too thin, lift rabbit out of pan and boil liquid rapidly until slightly thickened.

Add cream and chopped parsley. If necessary, add more seasoning to taste. Pour over rabbit and serve with new potatoes or creamy mashed potatoes. Serves 4.

Coquilles st jacques

The lovely, creamy white scallops we get from our own coastline and New Zealand are a great delicacy. They need very little cooking and are superb with this delicate wine sauce.

500g scallops
1 cup dry white wine
Salt and pepper
2 spring onions, cut in two
45g butter
2 teaspoons flour
½ cup cream
1 cup breadcrumbs
Extra small lumps of butter

Remove any brown fibre from scallops. Put wine in saucepan with salt, pepper and spring onions. Add ½ cup water, heat, then add scallop meat including coral. Bring to the simmer and poach for 1 minute.

Drain, cut large scallops in 2 or 3 slices. Strain the cooking liquor and reduce over medium heat to ½ cup. Melt the butter in a saucepan, add flour and blend until smooth. Add the reduced poaching liquor, then cream, stirring until the sauce boils.

Spoon a little sauce over the base of 4 scallop shells or ovenproof ramekins, divide scallops among shells and cover with remaining sauce. Sprinkle with breadcrumbs. Put a lump of butter on top of each and brown quickly under the grill. Serves 4.

Zucchini with tomatoes and garlic

Tomatoes, garlic and oil indicate Provence. This is a different way of serving these delicious little marrows.

750g zucchini
750g tomatoes
15g butter
1 tablespoon olive oil
Salt
Pepper
1 teaspoon sugar
1 teaspoon finely chopped parsley
2 cloves garlic, crushed
1½ cups grated gruyere cheese

Cut zucchini into thin rounds. Peel tomatoes and slice thinly. Heat the butter and oil and brown zucchini and tomato together. Add salt and pepper to taste and stir in sugar, parsley and garlic.

Transfer to a shallow oven dish, sprinkle with grated cheese and bake in a moderate oven 180C (350F) until the cheese forms a golden crust. Serves 6 to 8.

Parisian cream

4 egg yolks
¾ cup castor sugar
3 teaspoons gelatine
¾ cup hock or chablis
1½ cups cream, whipped
Few drops almond essence
½ cup toasted slivered almonds
Raspberry sauce

Beat egg yolks until light and

Far left: Poulet Basquaise reflects the flavors of southern France. Left: Hearty Salade Nicoise is a speciality of the Nice area.

lemon colored. Gradually beat in the sugar until thick. Soak gelatine in white wine and dissolve over boiling water. Slowly pour gelatine over egg mixture, beating briskly to prevent curdling. Lightly fold in half the whipped cream, almond essence and half the toasted almonds.

Pour into pretty glass or china bowls. Spoon remaining cream over top and sprinkle with remaining almonds. Chill in refrigerator and serve with raspberry or strawberry sauce.

RASPBERRY SAUCE: Use 250g fresh or frozen berries, mash with a fork and push through a sieve, or process in blender. Mix with 2 tablespoons castor sugar and grated rind and juice of ½ orange. Place in a saucepan, heat gently. Mix 2 teaspoons arrowroot with a little cold water, add to the fruit puree and bring to the boil, stirring for a few moments. Allow to cool.

Trout chablis

4 trout
Salt and freshly ground pepper
2-3 tablespoons chopped fresh herbs (parsley, thyme and a little sage)
1 teaspoon grated lemon rind
2 teaspoons butter
1 cup chablis or other white wine
1 tablespoon tomato paste
2 teaspoons each butter and flour, blended
½ cup cream

Wash and dry and season trout. Place fish in a buttered ovenproof dish. Sprinkle over the chopped herbs and lemon rind. Pour around the wine, dot fish with nobs of butter. Cover with piece of greaseproof paper and cook in a moderate oven 180C (350F) for 15-20 minutes. Drain the trout and arrange on heated serving dish, keep hot.

Strain the liquor from the fish into a small pan. Whisk in the blended butter and flour and tomato paste, pour in the cream and cook for 2-3 minutes, stirring. Coat the fish carefully with this sauce. Serves 4.

Note: Trout are excellent cooked in a microwave oven. Follow instructions but cook in microwave for 5-6 minutes, drain and let stand while making sauce until flesh flakes easily when tested with a fork.

Salade nicoise

There are many ways of presenting this famous salad from Nice. Choose one of the soft-leaf lettuces, such as mignonette or cos, for the best effect. It makes a lovely luncheon salad.

6 medium-size ripe tomatoes
Salt
1 or 2 mignonette or cos lettuce
1 can flat anchovy fillets, drained
2 green peppers
3 hard-boiled eggs
8 to 12 black olives
1 medium-size can oil-packed tuna
¼ cup vinaigrette

Cut tomatoes into thin slices and sprinkle lightly with salt. Wash and dry the lettuce leaves and use them to line a round or oval platter.

Arrange tomato slices overlapping round the bed of lettuce; cut anchovy fillets in half lengthwise and arrange on the tomato. Cut the peppers into thin rings (removing ribs and seeds) and scatter over the salad. Decorate with quarters of hard-boiled egg and black olives and place the drained tuna in the centre. Just before serving, pour over the dressing. Serves 6.

Onion soup lyonnaise

A superb version of the famous soup that was once served at the Les Halles markets in the heart of Paris. The markets have moved but the soup lives on. This makes a wonderful weekend supper.

45g butter
1 tablespoon oil
750g onions, thinly sliced
1 teaspoon salt
2 tablespoons flour
5 cups boiling beef stock
1 cup dry white wine
Freshly ground pepper
ADDITION
4 eggs
150g swiss cheese, finely grated
2 tablespoons brandy
TO SERVE
6 slices dry, crustless toast.

Heat the butter and oil in a large heavy saucepan and cook onions slowly for 25-30 minutes, until very soft, stirring occasionally. Be careful not to let them brown. Sprinkle salt and flour into the pan and stir over medium heat for 2 minutes. Remove from heat, and blend in boiling stock. Add wine, season to taste, and strain soup into a large earthenware bowl. (Save the onions to use in a meat loaf, scrambled eggs etc.)

Tip the soup back into the pot and reheat. Beat the eggs until light in the bowl that has been heated with the soup, and stir in the cheese.

When the soup is boiling, pour slowly into the bowl, beating all the time. The boiling liquid will partially cook the eggs, and the soup will turn thick and creamy. Still beating, add the brandy and blend into the soup.

Turn the soup back into the pot and reheat gently for a minute or two, stirring. Do not allow to boil.

Arrange slices of dry toast in six deep bowls and ladle soup over. Serve at once. Serves 6.

Cooking for a crowd

My idea for party food is to buy one large expensive luxury piece of meat, like ham or fillet of beef (see index), and use skill and imagination with salads, desserts and drinks. I use fresh fruits and vegetables in season, when they are at their best and don't cost the earth. By popular demand, I am including a recipe for my super-economy meatballs. These can be made well ahead and stored frozen to be reheated in the microwave or a moderate oven when required. I have a few marvellous desserts that look, but don't cost, a million dollars. I like to decide on one dessert and make two or three, rather than offer an assortment. This lets people realise you are very sure of your choice!

Nectar-glazed ham

This makes a beautiful and exciting centrepiece for any buffet table and is one of the simplest dishes to serve. Make sure your carving knife is very sharp.

7kg cured leg of ham
GLAZE
¾ cup firmly packed brown sugar
2 teaspoons dry mustard
½ cup clear honey
Whole cloves
½ cup peach or apricot nectar

Cut a scallop or vandyke pattern around thick end of ham shank and ease skin away from fat. Turn ham over and ease away rest of skin which should come off in one piece. Place ham fat side uppermost, on a rack in a roasting tin containing 3.5cm of water. Cover tin with foil, making it as airtight as possible, and bake in a preheated moderately slow oven 160C (325F) for 2 hours. Remove from oven and pour off liquid in tin. Score fat with 5mm deep diagonal cuts, first one way, then opposite way to form a diamond pattern.

Mix sugar, mustard and honey together and using a brush spread half the mixture over ham. Stud every second diamond with a clove. Mix remaining glaze with nectar. Increase oven temperature to hot 200C (400F) and bake ham for a further 30-40 minutes, basting it every 10 minutes, adding more nectar if necessary. Serve warm.
Serves 20-25.

VARIATIONS

Apply any one of the following glazes in the same way as in the preceding recipe and continue baking.

Cider Glaze: Combine 1 cup firmly packed brown sugar with 1 cup apple cider and spread over ham. Use extra ½ cup apple juice for basting.

Marmalade Glaze: Combine 1 cup orange marmalade with ¼ cup cider vinegar and ¼ teaspoon nutmeg and spread over ham. Use ½ cup orange juice for basting.

Note: A 7.5kg ham will serve about 30 people. If you are serving other meats, take this into account so one ham is sufficient for 40 guests; however a second ham will be necessary for over 40 guests. This can be carved in the kitchen ready to be brought in arranged on platters.

Mixed green salad with croutons

Selection of salad greens (lettuce, curly endive, spinach, green shallots, parsley and watercress)
1 cucumber
2 clove garlic, crushed
4-5 tablespoons olive oil
Freshly ground black pepper
8 slices french bread, quartered
Vinaigrette dressing (see index)

Rinse, dry and chill salad greens. Tear into bite-size pieces. Peel cucumber leaving a little green color on the flesh. Cut in half lengthwise and scoop out seeds with a spoon. Cut into 5cm lengths.

Heat garlic in a frying pan with olive oil and a good grinding of black pepper. Mix well then toss with quartered slices of french bread. Place in moderate oven 180C (350F) and toast until just turning golden. Cool on crumpled kitchen paper. Add to bowl with salad greens and cucumber and, just before serving, toss with vinaigrette dressing.
Serves 8-10.

Mango and passionfruit mousse

3 teaspoons gelatine
2 tablespoons water
1½ cups fresh or canned mango pulp
½ cup passionfruit pulp
3 tablespoons creme de cacao or marsala
300ml (1¼ cups) carton of cream

Dissolve gelatine in the water over low heat. Cool and stir in the mango and passionfruit pulp. Place over ice until the mixture starts to thicken. Stir in creme de cacao. Fold in whipped cream.

Pour into a glass or china bowl. If liked decorate with rosettes of whipped cream and a few strawberries and a little passionfruit pulp. Serves 8-10.

Black forest trifle

20 coconut macaroons
¼ cup sherry
3 x 425g cans pitted cherries
2 tablespoons grated lemon rind
1 tablespoon gelatine
¼ cup water
5 eggs, separated
⅔ cup sifted icing sugar
½ cup rum
2 cups cream
200g bar dark chocolate curls
Extra whipped cream to decorate

Crush the macaroons and put them in a layer in the bottom of 1 large or 2 small glass serving bowls. Sprinkle with sherry. Cover with the cherries and ½ cup juice, reserving a few cherries for decoration. Sprinkle with lemon rind.

Soften gelatine in water and stand the container in hot water until gelatine is dissolved. Beat egg yolks with sifted icing sugar until pale and thick; stir in rum and dissolved, gelatine.

Whip cream and fold in. Add half the chocolate curls. Beat egg whites until they hold soft peaks and fold in. Pour over fruit and chill overnight. Decorate with whipped cream rosettes and reserved chocolate curls and reserved cherries. Serves 10-12.

CHOCOLATE CURLS: Have chocolate at room temperature; using a swivel-blade peeler, cut thin strips off chocolate, they should curl nicely. Store on a plate in refrigerator until required.

Left: Nectar-Glazed Ham, Greens And Avocado Salad (see index for recipe) and Persian Rice Salad are crowd-pleasers.

Galantine of veal

1.5-2kg breast of veal, boned
2 onions, quartered
2 carrots, quartered
Large bouquet garni
STUFFING
185g cooked ham, minced
250g pork, minced
1 small onion, finely chopped
30g butter
1 cup fresh white breadcrumbs
1 small egg, beaten
Salt and freshly ground pepper
8 pistachio nuts, blanched and shredded
Meat glaze

First make the stuffing. Mix ham and pork together. Cook onion in butter until soft and add to meat mixture with breadcrumbs. Add egg and seasoning, mix well and add pistachios.

Spread stuffing on cut surface of veal, roll up and tie securely or sew with strong thread. Wrap in greaseproof paper then in a scalded cloth. Tie at each end and fasten cloth in centre with a safety pin.

Put galantine into a large saucepan of boiling water with vegetables and bouquet garni. Cover and simmer for 1½ hours. Remove from liquid, cool a little and tighten cloth as much as possible. Put meat into a deep dish or loaf tin just large enough to hold it. Place a board or plate with 1kg weight (or a couple of cans) on top and leave overnight in refrigerator.

Remove board, cloth and paper, lift out galantine and brush with meat glaze. Serves 6-8.

TO BLANCH AND SHRED PISTACHIOS: Cover shelled nuts with boiling water and add a pinch of bicarbonate of soda to preserve the color. Leave until cool and slip skins off with fingers. Slice thinly with a sharp knife while still soft.

MEAT GLAZE: Boil down about ¾ cup good homemade brown stock or canned beef consomme until it is thick and syrupy. Cool a little before use. Brush meat with 2-3 coats of glaze, allowing each to set firm before applying next.

Kanimbla pudding

Every great party in the Thirties served a version of this scrumptious dessert. You can vary the fruit used — nectarines, apricots, peaches instead of strawberries — but do use passionfruit. This quantity serves 12. Make in two separate lots for a party of 24-25.

2 tablespoons gelatine
¼ cup water
3 eggs, separated
½ cup castor sugar
2 tablespoons sugar
2 teaspoons cornflour
Few drops of vanilla
1¼ cups milk
1 cup cream
½ cup passionfruit pulp (more, if plentiful)
1 cup sliced strawberries

Sprinkle gelatine over water and allow to sponge. Place over boiling water and heat until dissolved, then cool. Place egg whites in a large bowl with the gelatine mixture and castor sugar and beat with a rotary whisk or electric mixer until the mixture is thick and will hold its shape. Turn into a large serving bowl and place in the refrigerator for at least an hour to set.

Meanwhile, beat the egg yolks with the 2 tablespoons of sugar, cornflour and vanilla until thick and creamy. Scald the milk and pour on to the egg mixture to combine, then place in a saucepan and stir over a gentle heat until the mixture just comes to the boil and is thickened. Set aside and allow to cool.

When ready to serve pudding, pour custard over the set egg white mixture. Whip the cream and pile on top of the custard, then top with passionfruit and strawberries. Serve with extra whipped cream if desired.

Economical meatballs

2 large potatoes, peeled and diced
2 small tart apples or 1 large one, peeled and diced
2 large onions, peeled and chopped
2 rashers bacon, finely chopped
2 eggs
1kg hamburger mince
500g sausage mince
2 teaspoons curry powder
1 teaspoon each ground ginger and dry mustard
2 teaspoons salt
1 teaspoon freshly ground black pepper
1 tablespoon worcestershire sauce
Flour for shaping
Oil for frying
TO SERVE
Spicy Tomato Sauce

Put potato, apple and onion into a saucepan. Barely cover with cold water and simmer until tender, removing lid toward end of cooking time so that most of water evaporates. Drain and mash. Mix with remaining ingredients except flour and oil.

Form into balls, using well-floured hands to prevent sticking. Fry in shallow oil. Serve hot or cold with toothpicks for dipping in Spicy Tomato Sauce. Makes 130-150 small meatballs.

SPICY TOMATO SAUCE: Mix a little worcestershire sauce and sugar and a dash of Tabasco into tomato sauce.

Russian ham salad

500g cooked ham, thickly sliced and cubed
6 large potatoes, cooked, peeled and cubed
2 large crisp apples, cored and cubed
6 sticks celery, finely chopped
2 large dill pickles, finely chopped
1½ cups mayonnaise
4 tablespoons chopped parsley
1 teaspoon dried tarragon
Salt
1 small lettuce
GARNISH
Sliced cooked beetroot, cubes unpeeled apple, onion rings

Place ham, potatoes, apple, celery and pickles in a bowl. Mix mayonnaise with parsley and tarragon, add to bowl and toss lightly. Taste and season with salt as required. Line a large bowl with lettuce leaves and spoon salad into the middle. Garnish with beetroot, apple and onion rings and chill until serving time. Serves 10-12.

Guinness-glazed leg of ham

You may prefer this superb recipe for making a ham very special. The spices — don't forget the cardamom — plus the famous stout, give the ham an unbelievably good flavor.

7.5kg cooked leg of ham
2 cups Guinness stout
1 cup brown sugar
1 tablespoon dry mustard
1 teaspoon ground ginger
2 teaspoons ground cardamom
Watercress or parsley to garnish

Peel skin off ham, leaving portion around bone. Place ham, fat side up, in a roasting pan and pour 1¾ cups stout over. Bake in a moderately slow oven 160C (325F) for 3 hours, basting occasionally with stout.

Remove ham from oven and baste with drippings. Mix sugar, mustard, ginger and cardamom and add enough stout to moisten. Spread over ham. Increase oven temperature to hot 200C (400F) and bake ham a further 35 minutes. Serve hot, garnish with watercress.
Serves 20-30.

Left: Herbed Tomato Quiche (see index for recipe) and Mushroom Tarts are easy to make ahead. Make several to feed a large group.

Cheese and bacon pie

1 quantity Rich Shortcrust Pastry or ½ quantity Food Processor Pastry
3 rashers bacon, fried crisp and crumbled
300ml carton (1¼ cups) cream
½ medium onion, coarsely chopped
3 eggs
1 teaspoon worcestershire sauce
½ teaspoon salt
Small pinch cayenne pepper
185g swiss or gruyere cheese, cubed
¼ cup grated parmesan cheese

Roll out pastry and line a 23cm pie plate or flan ring. Chill 15-20 minutes.

Crumble bacon over bottom of pie shell. Put cream, onion, eggs, worcestershire sauce, salt and cayenne into container and beat until smooth, add cubed cheese.

Pour filling into pie shell and sprinkle with parmesan cheese. Bake at 190C (375F) for 25-30 minutes or until filling is set in centre. Let stand 10 minutes before serving. Serves 6.

Food processor pastry

Shortcrust made in the food processor is tender and light, and made in moments. Chill some diced butter in the freezer for this recipe.

2 cups flour
125g frozen butter, diced
¼ teaspoon salt
2 eggs
About 1 tablespoon cold water
Squeeze lemon juice

Place flour, butter and salt in food processor and process, turning processor rapidly on and off, until butter is cut into flour and mixture resembles coarse breadcrumbs.

Mix eggs, water and lemon juice together and, with motor running, pour liquid quickly through the feed tube. Do not use it all unless necessary — stop pouring immediately a ball of dough forms round the blade.

Wrap pastry in plastic film and chill 1 hour before rolling out and shaping. Chill again for 20 minutes before baking. Makes enough dough to line two 20-23cm flan rings or pie plates.

SWEET PASTRY: Follow above recipe, adding 2 tablespoons castor sugar to food processor with flour, butter and salt.

Rich shortcrust pastry

1½ cups plain flour
Pinch salt
¼ teaspoon baking powder
125g chilled butter, diced
1 egg yolk
2 teaspoons iced water
Squeeze lemon juice

Sift flour, salt and baking powder together, rub in butter until mixture resembles coarse breadcrumbs.

Mix egg yolk, water and lemon juice and stir in quickly with a knife to form a dough. Shape into a ball, wrap in plastic film and chill 20 minutes before rolling and shaping. Chill again before baking. Makes enough pastry to line a 20-23cm flan ring or pie plate.

SWEET PASTRY: Follow above recipe, beating 2 teaspoons castor sugar with egg and water before stirring into dry ingredients.

Mushroom tart

1 x 20cm shortcrust shell, baked
6 green shallots, chopped
250g button or cup mushrooms, trimmed (sliced if large)
45g butter
½ cup cream
1 egg yolk
2 whole eggs
60g gruyere cheese, grated
1 tablespoon salt
Freshly ground black pepper
Tiny pinch cayenne
Small pinch nutmeg

Prepare and make pastry shell (see Shortcrust Pastry) or make 4 individual cases. Bake shell in hot oven 200C (400F) 10 minutes. Flatten centre if it puffs up. Saute shallots and mushrooms in butter until golden, and remove from heat. Beat cream with egg yolk and eggs, and stir in mushrooms and butter, cheese, salt and pepper, cayenne and nutmeg. Pour into pastry shell and bake in a preheated moderate oven 180C (350F) until filling is set and delicately browned, about 20 minutes. Serve warm. Small tartlets will take about 15 minutes. Serves 4.

August

Winter puddings

At the first sign of cold weather my thoughts run to lovely old-fashioned puddings. It's true, some people just never outgrow the puddings of their childhood. If your family longs for a special sweet treat, you can go no further than relive the good old days when a pudding was considered the right and fitting way to finish a meal.

How to steam a pudding

Have the steamer or a large saucepan ready before pudding is mixed. If a proper steamer is not available an old saucer, rounded side up, can be placed on the bottom of the saucepan with just enough boiling water to reach halfway up the pudding basin. Cover the pan with a tight-fitting lid or a sheet of aluminium foil fitted over and pressed on to sides of pan and steam gently for required time; the saucepan should be topped up occasionally with boiling water.

Small cup puddings for individual serves look attractive and take a shorter time to cook. You can use old teacups, or inexpensive metal cups (castle pudding moulds) are readily available from most hardware and kitchen shops. An electric frypan, half-filled with water, makes an excellent steamer for these puddings.

Steamed jam puddings

Light and tender, one of the easiest puddings to make — always a favorite.

60g butter
¼ cup sugar
1 egg
½ teaspoon vanilla
1 cup self-raising flour
3 tablespoons milk
2 tablespoons jam (raspberry, apricot, plum, marmalade)

Cream butter with sugar. Beat in egg and vanilla, then fold in sifted flour and milk.

Place jam in a 4-5 cup pudding basin or 4 greased individual moulds and spoon in mixture. Cover with 2 layers of greaseproof paper and steam for 25 minutes.

Serve with custard or cream. Serves 4.

Nougat crumb pie

Spicy, crunchy and delicious — this old-fashioned pie is something the whole family will want on a regular basis.

PASTRY
60g butter or margarine
¼ cup castor sugar
1 egg yolk and 1 tablespoon milk
½ cup self-raising flour
½ cup plain flour
Pinch salt
FILLING
60g cake or breadcrumbs
¼ cup sugar
1 cup desiccated coconut
¼ cup finely chopped nuts
1 lemon
1 tablespoon apricot jam
1 egg white
1 teaspoon cinnamon mixed with 1 teaspoon brown sugar

Cream butter and sugar. Beat in egg yolk and milk. Add sifted flours and salt. Chill for 30 minutes.

Roll out pastry and line 18-20cm pie plate or flan ring. Combine crumbs, sugar, coconut, nuts, grated lemon rind and juice and apricot jam. Fold in stiffly beaten egg white.

Place mixture in pastry case. Sprinkle with cinnamon and brown sugar. Bake in hot oven 200C (400F) for 10 minutes. Reduce heat to moderate 180C (350F) and cook a further 10 minutes. Serve either warm or cold with cream or ice cream. Serves 6.

Right: Steamed Jam Puddings can be made in a basin or moulds, with a choice of jam or marmalade.

Canary pudding

This basic steamed pudding has been part of the winter scene for generations.

125g butter
¾ cup sugar
2 eggs
Finely grated rind of 1 lemon
1½ cups self-raising flour
3 tablespoons milk

Cream butter with sugar. Beat in eggs one at a time, stir in lemon rind. Fold in sifted flour and milk.

Turn into a greased pudding basin, cover with 2 thicknesses of greased greaseproof paper, tie with string and steam 1½ hours. Alternatively, spoon mixture into 6 individuals greased 1-cup-size moulds, cover and steam 25 minutes.

Serve with jam, golden syrup or sweet sauce. Serves 6.

FRUIT PUDDING: Add ¾ cup fruit (sultanas, chopped dates, mixed fruit). Fold in with the flour.

CHOCOLATE PUDDING: Omit lemon rind, add 2 teaspoons cocoa and sift cocoa with the flour. Cream 1 tablespoon jam, honey or golden syrup with butter and sugar.

Upside-down cake

Serve this dessert cake hot with ice cream, egg custard or a sweet sauce.

CARAMEL
75g butter
⅓ cup firmly packed brown sugar
DECORATION
2 rings canned pineapple
6 pitted prunes
6 walnut halves or glace cherries
CAKE
1 cup self-raising flour
½ teaspoon salt
1 egg, separated
½ cup castor sugar
½ cup milk
30g butter, melted

CARAMEL: Cream butter with sugar. Spread over bottom and sides of a greased and lined 20cm round cake tin.

DECORATION: Cut through pineapple rings to make 4 thin rings. Arrange these on caramel and decorate with prunes and walnuts or cherries.

CAKE: Sift flour and salt together. Beat the egg white stiffly and add the egg yolk. Beat in sugar gradually. Add the milk with sugar, then beat in egg until light and fluffy. A little at a time, gently fold in the flour and the melted butter. Spoon cake mixture carefully on top of the pineapple arrangement in the tin. Bake in a preheated moderate oven 190C (375F) for 20-25 minutes. Invert on to serving plate immediately cake is removed from oven. Leave for a few minutes then remove tin. Serves 6-8.

APRICOT AND WALNUT UPSIDE-DOWN CAKE: Make as above, using 8 soaked and drained dried apricots, 8 stoned dessert prunes and 6 walnut halves as decoration.

Steamed ginger pudding

An old English pudding. Packaged suet is available at most grocery shops, otherwise buy fresh beef suet from your butcher and grate it yourself.

2½ cups flour
1 teaspoon ground ginger
Pinch mixed spice
1 teaspoon bicarbonate of soda
155g finely grated suet
1 egg
¾ cup golden syrup
¾ cup warmed milk
3 tablespoons finely chopped preserved ginger

Sift flour, spices and bicarbonate of soda into a bowl. Add suet. Make a well in the centre and pour in beaten egg mixed with syrup and milk. Stir well to a batter that will fall easily from spoon. Spoon preserved ginger over bottom of greased 5-cup pudding basin. Pour mixture in, cover basin with a pleated piece of greased greaseproof paper and steam for 2½-3 hours. Serve with warmed golden syrup or custard. Serves 4-6.

Steamed cabinet pudding

A traditionally English pudding made of cubed bread or cake, dried fruit and custard. It may be baked or steamed in a mould. It is an economical family pudding.

30g butter
2 tablespoons sugar
4 slices white bread, crusts removed and diced
½ cup sultanas, raisins or *mixed dried fruit*
2 eggs
1 cup milk
Pinch salt
½ teaspoon vanilla

Use all butter to grease a 4-cup pudding basin and sprinkle with 1 tablespoon sugar. Put bread into a bowl with fruit. Beat eggs, add remaining ingredients, including remaining sugar, and pour over bread. Allow to soak for 30 minutes, then spoon into prepared basin. Cover with greased greaseproof paper and a snap-on lid, or tie down with 2 layers of foil. Place in a saucepan with boiling water to come halfway up sides of basin, cover with a lid and steam for 1 hour. Replenish boiling water as necessary. Unmould and serve with custard, cream or ice cream. Serves 4.

Note: Cabinet Pudding may also be baked. Grease a 4-cup ovenproof dish. Follow recipe instructions and spoon mixture into prepared dish. Cover with greased foil and bake in a pre-heated moderate oven 180C (350F) for 35-40 minutes or until the pudding is set.

Windsor pudding

Apples and rice have never tasted so good — a favorite English pudding.

2½ tablespoons rice
2 cups milk
1kg cooking apples, cored and roughly chopped
¼ cup castor sugar
Grated rind and juice ½ lemon
3-4 egg whites

Simmer rice in milk until tender and all the milk has been absorbed. Meanwhile, cook apples in as little water as possible, until soft. Sieve or puree in a blender, then stir in sugar, rice and lemon rind and juice. Whisk egg whites stiffly and fold lightly into the mixture. Put into a greased pudding basin, cover with greased greaseproof paper and steam very gently for about 40 minutes. Serve with custard sauce made from the egg yolks. Serves 6.

Magic fudge pudding

The magic is in the way a simple batter and hot water bake together to make a beautifully moist, dark chocolate pudding. It's very rich, so serve small portions.

1 cup flour
¾ cup sugar
2 tablespoons cocoa
2 teaspoons baking powder
½ teaspoon salt
½ cup milk
2 tablespoons melted butter
1 teaspoon vanilla essence
1 cup chopped walnuts
Extra ¾ cup brown sugar
Extra ¼ cup cocoa
1¾ cups hot water

Sift together the flour, sugar, cocoa, baking powder and salt. Stir in milk, melted butter and vanilla and mix until smooth. Stir in chopped walnuts.

Pour the mixture into a large, greased shallow casserole. Mix extra brown sugar and cocoa and sprinkle on top. Slowly pour the hot water over the mixture.

Bake in a moderately hot oven 190C (350F) for 30-35 minutes or until firm. Serve warm with pouring cream or ice cream. Serves 6-8.

Deep dish rhubarb and apple pie

This is my basic deep-dish fruit pie. I replace rhubarb with mulberries, blackberries, peaches or cherries when they are in season. Serve with pouring cream or whipped cream.

1 quantity Sweet Shortcrust Pastry (see index)
4 cups rhubarb, cut into short lengths
2 apples, peeled and cut into eighths
3 tablespoons plain flour
1 cup sugar
1 teaspoon cinnamon
Water and sugar to glaze

Make pastry and chill. Combine rhubarb and apple and toss with remaining ingredients except glaze. Spoon into a 23cm pie dish.

Roll out pastry to fit over fruit, flute edges if liked. Cut 4 or 5 oval or leaf shapes out of pastry and cover pie with pastry. Brush with a little water and decorate with cut-outs or pastry scraps if liked. Sprinkle with sugar.

Bake in a very hot oven 230C (450F) for 10 minutes, then reduce heat to moderately hot 190C (375F) and bake about 30 to 40 minutes longer. Cover top with foil if browning too much.

Chocolate puddings

Cook these little puddings in your electric frypan, or use any large flameproof dish; foil fitted over makes a good cover.

3 tablespoons cocoa
Boiling water
90g butter
½ cup castor sugar
1 egg
½ teaspoon vanilla essence
6 teaspoons raspberry jam
1½ cups self-raising flour
Pinch salt

Put cocoa into a cup, fill to ½-cup measure with boiling water, mix together until blended, cool. Cream butter and sugar, add egg and vanilla essence. Beat in thoroughly.

Grease six moulds, then put a slightly rounded teaspoon of jam in bottom of each. Sift flour and salt, then sift into the creamed mixture. Add the cocoa mixture and combine until blended.

Divide mixture between prepared moulds. Have frypan heated with a depth of about 2cm water. Place moulds in (no need to cover with paper), cover with frypan lid and simmer for 20 minutes.

Turn out and serve hot with cream or custard sauce.

Hot brown sugar sauce

Fine with hot puddings, waffles or pancakes, also good over ice cream. An electric hand beater is a help for this sauce.

1 cup brown sugar
60g butter
1 cup cream, heated
¼ cup whisky or brandy, optional
⅓ cup chopped nuts

Combine brown sugar and butter in small saucepan on low heat and beat using an electric hand beater. Gradually add hot cream, still beating over a low heat until it boils. Remove from heat, beat in whisky or brandy if using, and lastly add nuts.

Apple sponge

1 cup sugar
1½ cups water
Piece lemon rind
6 large cooking apples, peeled, cored and thickly sliced
SPONGE MIXTURE
60g butter
½ cup castor sugar
Grated rind of ½ lemon
2 eggs
1 cup self-raising flour
Pinch salt
⅔ cup milk

Mix the sugar, water and lemon rind in a saucepan, boil for five minutes then add the apple slices and poach over a gentle heat until tender. Drain off excess syrup and place apples in a round or oval ovenproof dish.

Make the sponge by creaming the butter, castor sugar and lemon rind. Beat in the eggs one at a time and when thoroughly incorporated fold in the flour, which has been sifted with salt, alternately with the milk.

Spoon the sponge mixture over the apples and bake in a moderate oven 180C (350F) for 40 minutes or until the sponge is risen and delicately brown. Serves 6.

Above: Apricot Upside-Down Cake, Pineapple Upside-Down Cake are favorites with every generation.

Apples and sago

Very old-fashioned and very good. May be served with pouring cream.

2½ cups water
¼ cup sago
6 cooking apples, peeled and cored
½ cup sugar
4 cloves
Pared rind and juice ½ lemon
Few drops red coloring

Bring water to the boil in a large saucepan. Sprinkle in sago and cook until mixture is clear, about 15 minutes.

Add apples, sugar, cloves, lemon rind and juice to the sago. Cover and simmer very gently 10-20 minutes or until apples are tender.

Lift apples out on to a heated serving dish. Remove cloves and lemon rind from sago mixture and add a few drops of food coloring. Pour sago over and round the apples. Serve warm. Serves 6.

A taste of Italy

Italian cooking is good cooking — and best of all it is fun cooking! Wherever you go in Italy, be it an inexpensive trattoria or a luxurious restaurant, the food and atmosphere will always be enjoyable. In homes it is the same. Even family meals take on a festive air and laughter and song seem to be part of the menu. I hope you enjoy some of my favorite Italian recipes — it's one way of capturing some of the magic of Italy.

To skin tomatoes and peppers

Tomatoes, the foundation of so much Italian cooking, are almost invariably skinned before using. Italian recipes often call for green and red peppers to be skinned also, to make the flavor more delicate and change the texture from crisp to richly soft.

To skin tomatoes, you can spear on a fork and turn over a gas flame until skin is split, then peel; or cover tomatoes with boiling water, count to 10, remove and drop into cold water, then peel.

To skin peppers, spear on a fork and turn over a gas flame or put close to a very hot grill, turning until skin is charred all over. Put peppers into a paper bag for 10 minutes to steam, then rub skins off under cold water. Ripe (red or yellow) peppers are easier to skin than green ones.

Pesto alla genovese

This is the famous sauce which is eaten by the Genoese with all kinds of pasta and gnocchi. It is often added to soups — try a tablespoon stirred into minestrone or a chicken broth at the last minute.

2-3 cloves garlic, chopped
4-6 tablespoons finely chopped fresh basil
4 tablespoons chopped parsley
1 tablespoon pine nuts
½ cup grated parmesan or romano cheese
About 1 cup olive oil
Freshly ground pepper

With a mortar and pestle, pound garlic, basil, parsley, pine nuts and cheese together until smooth. Gradually add oil, whisking between additions. Add enough oil, whisking all the time, to make sauce thick and smooth. Season with pepper.

Note: If made in large quantities, sauce can be made in a blender or food processor. Store in a jar in refrigerator, covered with a layer of oil.

Tagliatelle all' amatriciana

This is one of the great pasta dishes, originating in Amatrice, a little village in the Sabine country near Rome. The pasta used is the thin flat ribbons, tagliatelle, or bucatini, the thick hollow pasta. The sauce is based on a special type of bacon called 'guanciale' but bacon or speck may be used. Even better is pancetta, the same cut as bacon but it is not smoked, rather cured in salt and spices.

2 tablespoons oil
250g pancetta, bacon or speck
1 small dried chili or pinch cayenne pepper
1 small onion, chopped
500g tomatoes, seeded and chopped
Salt and freshly ground black pepper
500g tagliatelle
1 cup freshly grated mixed pecorino and parmesan cheese

Heat oil in a heavy frying pan. Cut bacon into 2.5cm pieces, add to pan and cook until brown and crisp. Remove from pan, drain and set aside. Soak the dried chili in hot water for 5 minutes, then remove the seeds and chop finely. Add chili and onion to the pan and saute until the onion is softened. Stir in the tomatoes, season with salt and pepper and simmer the sauce for 10 minutes. While sauce is cooking, drop the tagliatelle into plenty of rapidly boiling salted water and cook until 'al dente'. Drain. Place pasta in a large, shallow serving dish. Add reserved bacon to sauce and pour over tagliatelle. Sprinkle with the grated cheese and serve at once. Serves 4.

Right: This wide selection of pasta illustrates the versatility of Italian food.

Cannelloni

The precooked cannelloni tubes eliminate a big step in preparing cannelloni and you are assured of the pasta being just 'al dente', as it should be.

130g packet precooked cannelloni tubes
125g mozzarella cheese
SAUCE
1 onion, chopped
1 clove garlic, crushed
¼ cup oil
1 tablespoon chopped parsley
1 teaspoon salt
Pepper to taste
Medium can tomatoes
2 tablespoons tomato paste
2 cups boiling water
FILLING
500g minced steak
2 eggs, beaten
2 tablespoons oil
2 tablespoons grated parmesan cheese
1 tablespoon chopped parsley
1 teaspoon chopped oregano or basil or ¼ teaspoon dried
1 teaspoon salt
Pepper to taste

If not using precooked cannelloni, cook in boiling, salted water for 5 minutes. Rinse in cold water and drain. Cannelloni should be just flexible enough to handle.

SAUCE: Saute onion and garlic in oil until brown. Add parsley, salt and pepper. Stir in chopped tomatoes with juice and paste. Pour in boiling water slowly, simmer for 20 minutes. Pour half the sauce into a shallow baking dish.

Fill cannelloni with prepared filling. Arrange side by side in the sauce. Cover with remaining sauce and thin slices of mozzarella and cook in a moderate oven 180C (350F) for about 45 to 50 minutes. Serves 4 to 6.

FILLING: Combine steak, eggs, oil, cheese, parsley, herbs and season to taste with salt and pepper.

Saltimbocca

The name means 'jump in mouth' — perhaps because it takes so little time to cook. It's an Italian speciality made in minutes! The quantities given are for four, but it's a very easy recipe to multiply or reduce.

4 thin slices veal pounded very thin
Salt and freshly ground pepper
8 fresh sage leaves or teaspoon dried
8 thin slices leg ham or prosciutto (cured raw ham)
60g butter
¼ cup white wine
An extra knob of butter

Trim the veal steaks to make 8 small escalopes. Season the veal with salt and pepper and add sage. Place a slice of ham on each veal slice, and secure in place by threading with toothpicks.

Heat the 60g butter in a large, heavy frying pan and saute the escalopes for 2 minutes on each side, or until veal is cooked through. Remove toothpicks and arrange on a heated serving platter with ham side up.

Add the wine to the juices in the pan and bring to the boil, scraping up the brown bits on the bottom. Swirl in the extra butter, taste for seasoning, and pour the hot sauce over veal. Serves 4.

Spaghetti caruso

This sauce is also good with bucatini, the fine spaghetti with the hole in the middle.

2 cloves garlic, split
4 tablespoons olive oil
2 medium onions, chopped
250g chicken livers, chopped
250g mushrooms, sliced
2 tablespoons tomato paste
½ cup water
2 cups canned tomatoes with juice
1 teaspoon each thyme and basil or ¼ teaspoon dried
1 bay leaf
1 teaspoon salt
Pepper to taste
1 teaspoon sugar
500g spaghetti
1 cup grated parmesan cheese

Saute garlic in 3 tablespoons of oil for 2 minutes, discard garlic. Gently cook onions in oil 4 minutes, then add chicken livers and mushrooms, and brown for 5 minutes. Add tomato paste mixed with water, tomatoes and juice, thyme, basil, bay leaf, salt, pepper and sugar. Simmer, covered, 30 minutes. Cook spaghetti in boiling salted water with remaining olive oil. Drain and put on heated platter with half the cheese. Spoon over half the sauce and toss. Pass remaining sauce and cheese separately. Serves 4 to 6.

Zabaglione gelato

This delicious frozen confection is one of the most delectable desserts from Italy. A little marsala is often drizzled over the ice and it is accompanied by a crisp biscuit.

8 egg yolks
2 cups sugar
1½ cups marsala

Beat egg yolks using an electric beater until thick and lemon-colored. Place bowl over simmering water, add sugar then marsala and continue to beat until mixture resembles a fluffy custard.

Pour into ice cream trays, cover lightly with foil and freeze until firm, with freezer set to maximum for about 2 to 3 hours. Cover, reduce freeze to medium and allow gelato to ripen for several hours. Serves 6.

Salad of raw mushrooms

The Genoese like their insalata di funghi garnished with anchovy fillets — an unexpected and successful addition.

250g white button mushrooms
3 tablespoons olive oil
Juice ½ lemon
½ clove garlic, chopped
½ teaspoon salt
2-3 anchovy fillets, optional
1 tablespoon chopped parsley

Wipe over mushrooms with a damp cloth. Slice them fairly thinly and put in a bowl with oil, lemon juice and garlic. Add salt just before serving.

If using anchovy fillets, soak first in a little milk, then cut into long strips and arrange on mushrooms just before serving. Sprinkle over chopped parsley.

Serve as a first course with crusty french bread or as a salad with grilled meat. Serves 4.

Tortellini with pepperoni sauce

500g tortellini
125g pepperoni sausage, thinly sliced
4 tomatoes, peeled and seeded
1 tablespoon dijon mustard
1 clove garlic, chopped
2 teaspoons lemon juice
1 teaspoon red pepper flakes
½ cup olive oil
6 green shallots, finely chopped
A few basil leaves and slices pepperoni to garnish

Drop the tortellini into a generous saucepan of boiling salted water and cook 'al dente' — until just tender — drain and refresh under cold water.

In a food processor or blender rough chop (by switching the machine at the controls on and off) the pepperoni, the tomatoes, the mustard, the garlic, the lemon juice, and the red pepper flakes. With the motor running add the oil in a stream and blend the mixture until it is combined well. In a large bowl toss the shallots and the tortellini with the sauce until the pasta is coated well and garnish the dish with the basil and the additional pepperoni if desired. Serve the pasta at room temperature. Serves 4 to 6.

Right: Precooked cannelloni tubes make this dish easier to prepare.

thicker, richer paste, is made to
Italian recipe from 5 times its
specially-selected tomatoes.
Tomato Paste contains no artificial
only pure tomatoes
flavour, tightly reseal and
immediately after using
product within one month after
Always use clean spoon
TOMATOES, SALT

Spaghetti con vongole

If you can get fresh clams, by all means use them for this dish — about 500g. Wash and steam open in a little water; as soon as their shells have opened remove and drain. Remove clams, wash out any sand. Canned clams are very good and save a visit to the fish markets.

3 tablespoons oil
2 cloves garlic, crushed
3 tomatoes, peeled, seeded and chopped
1 tablespoon tomato paste
290g can clams
Salt and pepper
250g spaghetti
2 tablespoons chopped parsley

Melt the oil and fry the garlic a moment, add tomatoes and tomato paste, cook over a gentle heat, about 20 minutes. Add the drained clams and season to taste with salt and freshly ground pepper.

Cook the spaghetti in plenty of boiling, salted water and drain at the 'al dente' stage.

Pour sauce over spaghetti, toss to mix well and pour into heated serving bowl. Sprinkle with chopped parsley and, if liked, parmesan. Serves 3 to 4.

Bolognese sauce

The true bolognese sauce has several kinds of meat and good uncured bacon, pancetta, or prosciutto. Sometimes cream or butter is added just before it is tossed with the hot pasta.

250g lean minced steak
250g minced pork
60g bacon, chopped
1 tablespoon olive oil
1 clove garlic, peeled
1 small onion, finely chopped
1 tablespoon chopped parsley
1 bay leaf
1 x 500g can tomatoes
½ cup white wine
½ cup water
2 tablespoons tomato paste
Salt and freshly ground black pepper
Grated nutmeg
1 tablespoon chopped fresh basil or 1 teaspoon dried basil
Butter or cream (optional)

Put steak, pork and bacon or prosciutto, mixed well together, into a saucepan with oil, garlic, onion, parsley and bay leaf. Brown slowly, stirring frequently to prevent meat cooking in lumps. As soon as garlic turns golden, remove it and discard. Add tomatoes (with juice from can), wine, water, tomato paste, salt, pepper and nutmeg. Cover and simmer for 1 hour. Add basil and cook 1 minute longer. Remove from heat and discard bay leaf. If liked, add a little butter or a few spoonfuls of cream. Makes sufficient for 500g pasta.

Trout del nera

The delicious trout caught in the Nera and Sorda Rivers in the Marche region of Italy are treated very simply. Now that we can get excellent fresh and frozen trout from the Snowy Mountains, try them this way.

4 trout
2-3 tablespoons olive oil
Salt, pepper
½ cup chopped parsley
A few sprigs rosemary, chopped
Sprays of herbs for garnish
4 lemon wedges

Clean trout and wipe over with dampened kitchen paper. Arrange on a grilling rack. Brush trout with oil, season with salt and pepper. Combine herbs and sprinkle half over the fish.

Under a preheated moderate grill, cook about 5 minutes, turn, brush with oil, season with salt and pepper, sprinkle over remaining herbs and grill a further 5 minutes. Just before serving a little more olive oil is trickled over them. Garnish with herbs and serve with lemon wedges. Serves 4.

Pasta with peppers

This dish can be made using only one color pepper, but a variety of red, green and yellow ones makes it very colorful. We have grilled and peeled the peppers, which gives a special flavor to the sauce.

4 small peppers
500g tomatoes
2 tablespoons olive oil
30g butter or margarine
1 onion, thinly sliced
2-3 tablespoons chopped fresh basil or oregano or 2 teaspoons dried
Salt and pepper to taste
500g fresh pasta or 250g dried pasta
Freshly grated parmesan cheese

Halve the peppers, remove the seeds and membranes. Roast the peppers over a gas flame or under a grill until the skin blisters and blackens.

Rub skins off under cold running water, then seed peppers and cut into strips.

Drop tomatoes into boiling water for 10 seconds, then plunge into cold water.

Peel tomatoes, then quarter and remove seeds. Cut tomato flesh in dice. Heat oil and butter and cook onion gently until just colored. Add pepper strips and cook over a high heat, stirring until they begin to soften. Add tomatoes, basil and salt

Far left: Spaghetti Con Vognole. Left: Pasta With Peppers.

and pepper to taste. Cover and cook gently for 15 minutes. Remove lid and continue cooking until liquid evaporates.

Cook pasta in plenty of boiling salted water until tender. Drain well. Turn into a warm serving dish and top with pepper mixture. Toss lightly to mix, and sprinkle generously with cheese. Serve immediately. Serves 4.

Spinach with lemon dressing

In most Italian restaurants, big dishes of both fresh and cooked vegetables are on display. They are as often as not enjoyed cold — a surprise to an unsuspecting tourist, but should your taste be otherwise, a simple request for hot vegetables will soon be met. Many Italian vegetable dishes reheat very well.

1 bunch spinach or silverbeet
Salt and freshly ground pepper to taste
1/3 cup olive oil
Juice of 1 lemon

Wash spinach well to remove sand or grit. Cut off white stalks. Place spinach in a large saucepan (no water is needed) and cook, covered, for 5 to 10 minutes. Drain well, season, drizzle with oil and lemon juice and serve hot or cold. Serves 4-6.

Lasagne

When entertaining a crowd, make a large dish of lasagne. It may be made a day or two ahead and stored in the refrigerator. Reheat for about 45 minutes and serve cut in squares accompanied by a mixed, tossed salad.

750g minced steak
Salt and freshly ground black pepper
4 tablespoons olive oil
2x250g packets precooked lasagne
3 cups tomato sauce
500g ricotta or cottage cheese
500g mozzarella cheese
1 cup grated parmesan cheese

Season the meat with salt and pepper. Shape into balls a little larger than a marble. Heat the oil in a frying pan and brown the meatballs in three portions, so that the oil keeps hot and free from moisture. Then place all the meatballs back in the pan and allow them to cook gently for 5 minutes.

Note: If not using precooked lasagne, cook the pasta. It is better to boil the pasta in two lots, unless you have a very large saucepan. Stir while it is cooking, as this type of pasta has a tendency to stick. Bring a large pot of water to the boil, add salt and place half the lasagne pasta in the boiling water. Boil 10 to 12 minutes or until tender. Drain and refresh in cold water. Leave in cold water until ready to use. Repeat with remaining pasta. Make sauce (see below).

Butter a large baking dish or ovenproof casserole and spoon about one-third of the tomato sauce into it. Arrange half of the lasagne pasta on top and then a thin layer of sauce. Arrange half of the ricotta cheese. Slice the mozzarella cheese and arrange one-third in a layer and sprinkle with one-third of the parmesan cheese.

Spoon over more of the tomato sauce and then add the meatballs, one-third of the cheeses and the remaining lasagne pasta. Coat with remaining tomato sauce and then add remaining cheeses, ending with a layer of parmesan cheese. Bake in a moderate oven 180C (350F) for about 45 minutes or until the top is golden.

TOMATO SAUCE: Heat 3 tablespoons of olive oil in a saucepan, add 1/2 stick chopped celery, 1 finely chopped onion and 1 crushed clove garlic and brown lightly. Add 750g ripe tomatoes or 2 x 440g can of tomatoes, 3 tablespoons tomato paste, 1 cup wine or water. Season with salt and freshly ground black pepper, adding a bay leaf and bouquet of herbs. Cook gently for 30 minutes. Remove the bay leaf and bouquet garni and rub through a sieve. Serves 12 to 15.

Mushrooms in tarragon cream

This delectable dish from Tuscany, funghi alla crema, calls for pearly white button mushrooms which, thankfully, are available (salutations to our keen mushroom growers). This makes a superb first-course dish. Good dried tarragon is available in jars or packets.

1kg small button mushrooms
125g butter
1 teaspoon crumbled tarragon
Salt and freshly ground pepper
1 cup (or 300ml carton) cream
Chopped parsley

Wipe over mushrooms with a clean towel. In one large or 2 smaller frypans melt the butter, and over a high heat add mushrooms and tarragon; cook quickly, turning mushrooms. This should take 3 to 4 minutes. Season with salt and freshly ground pepper. Add cream — still over high heat — and let it bubble until it has thickened. Serve in 6 individual dishes and sprinkle with chopped parsley. Serve with crusty rolls or bread, to mop up the creamy gravy. Serves 6.

Linguine with clam sauce

If you have access to a good fish market you will probably find pipis or cockles, which are like little clams. Otherwise, use a can of clams.

375g hot, cooked linguine (thin flat noodles)

SAUCE
2kg fresh cockles or pipis, or 290g can baby clams (vongole)
¾-1 cup dry white wine
¼ cup olive oil
8 green shallots, finely chopped
1 clove garlic, crushed
¼ teaspoon dried red pepper flakes or finely chopped red chili
Salt and white pepper

If using fresh cockles or pipis, put them into a large saucepan with ¾ cup wine, cover and steam on high heat until the shells have opened, about 3 minutes. Reserve some of the shellfish for garnish and shell the remainder.

Strain the cooking liquid through a sieve lined with a disposable cloth into a measuring cup and add more wine if necessary to make 1 cup. If using canned clams, omit steaming and make up 1 cup liquid using the juice from the can and wine. Heat oil in a large, heavy frying pan and cook shallots, garlic and pepper flakes or chili until shallots are soft. Add wine mixture, bring to the boil and simmer 2 minutes. Add shellfish and salt and white pepper to taste. Toss linguine with clam sauce and garnish with reserved whole shellfish. Serves 4-6.

Risotto villa d'este

90g butter
1 small onion, finely chopped
2 cups Italian risotto rice or short grain rice
½ cup dry white wine
Salt and freshly ground black pepper
Boiling water
½ cup cream
90g shredded smoked salmon
3 tablespoons chopped parsley
3 tablespoons grated parmesan cheese
Parsley sprigs and curls of smoked salmon, to garnish

Heat 60g butter in a large, heavy saucepan and cook onion gently until soft. Add rice and stir until well coated with butter. Add wine and cook over medium heat until wine has nearly evaporated. Add a pinch of salt and a good grinding of pepper.

Stir in 1 cup boiling water. Cook the rice until the liquid is almost absorbed. Add 1 more cup boiling water and stir again. Continue to cook and add a further 2-3 cups boiling water gradually, allowing rice almost to absorb each addition before adding more, until the rice is tender and creamy, 15-20 minutes.

Stir in cream and let it cook down for a minute. Stir in remaining butter, shredded smoked salmon, parsley and cheese. Turn the risotto into a heated dish and garnish with parsley sprigs and smoked salmon curls. Serve immediately with crisp brown rolls. Serves 4.

RISOTTO ALLA FRUTTI DI MARE: Follow the above recipe but instead of smoked salmon add 250g small shelled prawns or other shellfish which have been heated in the last 30g of butter.

Stuffed tomatoes hassler

6 ripe tomatoes
Salt
1½ cups cooked long grain rice (½ cup uncooked)
2 tablespoons finely chopped parsley
1 cup chopped fresh basil or 2 tablespoons dried basil chopped with an extra ¾ tablespoon parsley
¼ cup olive oil
8 canned anchovy fillets, drained and chopped
4 cloves garlic, crushed
Freshly ground black pepper
Sugar

Cut a lid from each tomato and set aside. Scoop out flesh from tomatoes, leaving a wall about 1cm thick. Sprinkle salt inside tomatoes and turn upside-down to drain. Rub flesh through a sieve and discard seeds.

Measure ½ cup of the pureed flesh and mix with remaining ingredients, seasoning with salt, pepper and a touch of sugar. Stand tomatoes upright in an oiled shallow oven dish just large enough to hold them and fill with rice mixture. put lids on and bake in a moderately hot oven 190C (375F) for 10-15 minutes. Serve hot or cold as a first course or with meat, fish or poultry. Serves 6.

Right: Risotto Villa D'Este, Mixed Seafood Salad and Stuffed Tomatoes. Below: An attractive dish, Linguine With Clam Sauce.

Mixed seafood salad

1.5kg octopus, cleaned
Salt
1/3 cup vermouth
1kg mussels, scrubbed, cooked and shelled
250g cooked prawns, shelled and deveined
About 3/4 cup lemon juice
1/2-1 cup olive oil
625g squid, cleaned
250g scallops
1/2 cup orange juice
2 large red peppers, skinned
1 cup thinly sliced celery
1/4 cup chopped Italian parsley
White pepper
1 mignonette or small iceberg lettuce, washed, dried and crisped

Place octopus in a saucepan with 1 teaspoon salt, vermouth and water to cover and simmer until tender — for large octopus this may take 1 hour or more. Strip off suckers if you wish, rinse under cold water and cut into bite-size pieces. Place in a large bowl with mussels and prawns and toss with 1/2 cup olive oil and 1/4 cup lemon juice.

Cut squid bodies into rings, fins into strips and tentacles into short pieces. Marinate squid and scallops, covered and chilled, in orange juice and 1/2 cup lemon juice for at least 3 hours (the seafood will cook in the citrus juice).

Drain squid and scallop mixture and add to octopus mixture with peppers, celery and parsley. Add olive oil, lemon juice, salt and white pepper to taste. Toss gently and chill, covered, for 3 hours or overnight.

Allow seafood mixture to come to room temperature and serve mounded on a platter lined with lettuce leaves. Serves 6.

TO CLEAN OCTOPUS: Cut off heads below eyes and discard heads with ink sacs and intestines. With fingers dipped in salt, strip skin from tentacles and rinse in cold water.

TO SHELL MUSSELS: Scrub well, pulling off black beards round edges. Place in a large saucepan with 1 cup water, cover and steam on high heat until shells open. Discard any that will not open and remove meat from shells with a small knife.

TO CLEAN SQUID: Pull off heads with tentacles; intestines will come away with the heads. Cut off tentacles and discard heads and intestines. Pull fins off bodies and remove internal quill bones and any remaining yellow deposit. Rub skin off bodies, fins and tentacles with fingers dipped in salt, and rinse in cold water.

Dinner party dishes

The mark of a good hostess and cook is the ability to plan a dinner party using foods that are plentiful and in season and probably inexpensive and turn them into a superb meal. Plan some dishes to be prepared ahead, and always, have something freshly cooked, which seems to make a meal so much nicer. Food cooked too much ahead lacks that special freshness. If I am busy I like to serve a cheese tray after the main course with two cheeses and biscuits, sliced pears, apples, grapes or dates. Guests can nibble at the cheese and fruit and finish off their red wine while I clear the table and put the finishing touches to the dessert; it is hardly ever noticed that I am not at the table. Here are some dishes that have brightened up some dinner parties, including that most impressive of dishes, a light and airy souffle. Bon appetit!

Making a souffle

Success with souffles is simply a matter of knowing the rules and following them:

- A souffle does have to be eaten as soon as it's ready, so it's sensible to give everyone due warning.
- Traditional souffles are based on a thick, flavored sauce, into which stiffly beaten egg whites are folded. When the mixture is baked, the air trapped in the whites expands and the souffle puffs up.
- Eggs should be at room temperature.

The main point to watch when making a souffle is that the egg whites are beaten correctly. The whites must have no trace of yolk, and the bowl and beaters must be dry and free of grease. Beat the whites until foamy, add cream of tartar and beat to a velvety snow. Test by gathering a little mixture on the beater and holding it upright; at the right consistency, the beaten whites will stand on the beater in a firm peak with a slightly drooping top.

- Have the sauce warm. (If you have made it ahead, stand the bowl in warm water.) Stir a big spoonful of the whites into the base mixture to lighten it, then scoop the rest of the whites on to the surface and fold in by cutting down through the mixture with a large metal spoon or rubber spatula. Folding in the whites should take only a minute or so. The mixture will blend a little more as you turn it into the souffle dish.

Cheese souffle

45g butter
3 tablespoons flour
1 cup warm milk
45g freshly grated parmesan cheese
½ teaspoon salt
Freshly ground pepper
Pinch of cayenne
Pinch of nutmeg
4 egg yolks
5 egg whites
½ teaspoon cream of tartar

Butter an 18cm souffle dish, or 4 one-cup souffle dishes. Cut a doubled sheet of greaseproof paper long enough to wrap around dish and overlap by 8cm. It should be deep enough to extend 5cm above the rim. Butter the paper and tie firmly with string just under the rim of the dish. Place a baking tray on a shelf in the centre of the oven and set the oven to hot 200C (400F).

Melt the butter, stir in the flour and cook over low heat for 1 minute. Remove from heat, cool a little, and blend in milk, stirring until smooth. Return to heat and stir until boiling, then take from heat and stir in the cheese and seasonings. Beat in the egg yolks, one at a time. Whisk the egg whites with cream of tartar until firm but not brittle (see Making A Souffle) and fold into cheese mixture.

Pour the mixture into the prepared dish or dishes, tap the bottom of the dish lightly on the work surface to expel any large air pockets, and smooth the top of the souffle. Quickly run a spoon around the top of the mixture about 2.5cm from the edge to make the souffle rise evenly in a 'crown'. Immediately place the souffle dish on the baking tray in the centre of the oven, close the door gently, and turn the oven down to moderately hot 190C (375F). Do not open the oven door for the next 15 minutes. Bake the souffle until it is

Right: Sure to become favorites with guests are Mushrooms With Fresh Herbs, Cheese Souffles and Watercress And Violet Salad.

well puffed up, golden brown on top and just firm, about 24 minutes (18 minutes for individual souffles).

Have a heated serving platter (or plates) ready and a warmed serving spoon and fork. Place the souffle dish on the platter, remove the paper and take immediately to the table. To serve, pierce the top lightly with the spoon and fork held vertically, and spread the souffle apart. Include some of the outside crust and some of the creamy centre with each serving. Serves 4-5.

Mushrooms with fresh herbs

Serve as an entree, first course or as an accompaniment to grilled meat or poultry.

750g mushrooms
5 tablespoons oil
2 cloves garlic, crushed
2 tablespoons chopped fresh herbs (parsley, oregano, etc)
Pinch thyme
Salt
Freshly ground pepper
Pinch nutmeg

Wipe over the mushrooms with a damp cloth and trim the stalks, then slice. Heat the oil in a large frying pan over a fairly high heat and quickly brown the mushrooms, a few at a time. As they brown remove them to a plate and add more fresh ones. When all the mushrooms are browned, return to the pan, reduce the heat, add the garlic and herbs, and season with salt and pepper and a pinch of freshly grated nutmeg. Cook slowly for about 2 minutes longer, stirring occasionally. Spoon into a heated serving dish.

This may be served with hot buttered toast as a light luncheon dish. Serves 6.

Watercress and violet salad

The slightly sweet dressing is an interesting contrast to the peppery watercress.

1 bunch watercress
1 bunch violets
2 tablespoons olive oil
2 teaspoons wine vinegar
1 teaspoon Grand Marnier
2 tablespoons chopped pecan nuts

Pick tiny sprigs off watercress, tie into small bundles with rubber bands. Stand in water. Snip heads off violets. Shake together in a screw-top jar the olive oil, vinegar and Grand Marnier. Shake water off watercress and remove rubber bands. Place in bowl, top with violets and nuts, add dressing, toss and serve. Serves 6.

Beef wellington

Named after the Iron Duke, or was it the boots that bear his name? An imaginative chef browned a fillet of beef, flamed it with brandy, topped it with pate de foie and wrapped it in pastry.

1x1.5kg fillet of beef
Salt
Freshly ground black pepper
60g butter
¼ cup brandy
90g liver pate
60g button mushrooms
A little extra butter
250g puff pastry
1 egg, lightly beaten

Trim the beef fillet and season with plenty of salt and pepper. Heat the butter in a large frying pan and sear the fillet over a high heat turning with two spoons until brown on all sides.

Warm the brandy, set alight and pour over the beef. Shake the pan until the flames subside. Remove to a dish and allow to cool. Reserve any liquid remaining in the frying pan for the sauce.

Spread the pate on top of the beef. Slice the mushrooms and cook in a little butter for a few minutes. Arrange them on the pate.

Roll out puff pastry on lightly floured board to 3mm thickness. Trim the edges, place fillet on one side of the pastry. Brush edges with beaten egg. Fold the other half of the pastry over the fillet.

Press the edges of the pastry together and tuck underneath to form a neat parcel. Place on a baking sheet which has been dampened with water.

Cut thin strips of pastry about 5mm wide. Brush the pastry encasing the fillet with egg and then arrange pastry strips in a lattice fashion about 2.5cm apart. Brush with beaten egg.

Bake in a very hot oven 230C (450F) for 15 minutes, reduce to moderate 180C (350F) and cook for a further 15-20 minutes.

If watercress is in season serve the Beef Wellington garnished with a few sprigs. Serves 6.

Mushrooms en croute

250g mushroom cups
8 thick slices french bread
90g butter
3 tablespoons finely chopped parsley
2 cloves garlic, crushed
1 teaspoon lemon juice
Salt and freshly ground black pepper

Trim mushroom stalks and keep for another dish. Arrange bread slices side by side in a shallow dish. Place mushroom cups rounded side down on the bread slices. Melt butter, add parsley, garlic and lemon juice and season with salt and pepper. Spoon butter sauce over mushrooms and bread. Bake in a preheated moderately hot oven 190C (375F) for about 20 minutes. Serve at once. Serves 4.

Rigatoni carbonara

These fat ribbed pasta tubes done in the 'charcoal burner's style' make a delectable first course.

500g rigatoni, penne or spaghetti
1 tablespoon oil
125g bacon or speck
4 eggs
¾ cup freshly grated parmesan cheese
1 tablespoon salt
Freshly ground black pepper
¼ cup cream
60g butter

Cook pasta in plenty of rapidly boiling water until 'al dente'. Drain. Meanwhile, heat oil in a heavy frying pan, cut bacon into 2.5cm pieces and fry until crisp and brown. Remove. Beat eggs in a bowl, add cheese, salt, pepper and cream and mix well. Melt butter in frying pan, add egg mixture, stirring constantly until it begins to thicken. Add drained spaghetti and bacon, mix together quickly and serve at once.

Note: It is important to cook and drain pasta before cooking the eggs and to add it to the eggs just as they are thickening. They must not overcook and should be moist. Serves 6 to 8.

● Mushrooms En Croute.

Highland mist

Light and delicious with just a whiff of whisky to remind you of the beauty of a Highland mist.

18-20 coconut macaroons
2-3 tablespoons cream
2 tablespoons whisky
1 cup cream, whipped with vanilla
2 punnets strawberries, sliced, or blackberries in season

With a rolling pin crush the macaroons, add the 2-3 tablespoons cream and the whisky and stir the mixture to a paste. Spread a layer of the mixture in a crystal or glass bowl and cover it with a layer of vanilla whipped cream.

Repeat the layers until all the macaroon mixture is used and finish with a layer of whipped cream. Chill the mist and serve it with fresh sliced strawberries or blackberries when in season. Serves 6.

Pecan tart

At Donlevy's in Melbourne, few patrons can resist the beautiful variation on a classic walnut tart. This makes a splendid large 28-30cm tart, to serve 12 or 14 people for a dinner party, but you can halve the ingredients for a 20-23cm tart.

PASTRY
½ cup shelled pecans
150g butter
⅓ cup castor sugar
2 cups plain flour
1 egg, beaten
FILLING
175g butter
1 cup brown sugar
½ cup warmed honey
6 eggs
¾ cup shelled pecans
DECORATION
30g dark chocolate

Grind the pecans for the pastry in a nut grinder, or process to a fine meal

Left: Mushrooms En Croute make a perfect first course.

in a food processor (being careful not to over-process them to a paste). Cream butter and sugar, beat in ground pecans and flour. Beat egg and stir in with a knife to make a soft dough. Do not use all the egg unless necessary. Gather the dough into a ball with your fingertips, wrap in plastic film and chill for 20 minutes.

Roll out to line a 28-30cm shallow, fluted flan tin, and place in the refrigerator while making the filling.

Cream the butter and sugar until light and fluffy, and beat in warmed honey and eggs alternately. Spread the filling evenly in the pastry case and scatter the pecans over.

Place in a preheated hot oven, 200C (400F) and bake for 5 minutes, then turn down to moderately hot, 190C (375F) and continue baking 15 minutes or until the filling is set (protect the pastry sides of the tart with strips of aluminium foil if they are getting too brown). Remove from the oven and cool the tart.

To decorate the tart, melt chocolate in a small bowl over hot water (off the heat). Dip a fork into the chocolate and use it to drizzle fine ribbons of chocolate, in a zigzag pattern, over the tart. Allow to set, and serve the tart at room temperature. Serves 12-14.

Above: Warm Mushroom, Spinach And Chicken Liver Salad is superb.

Warm mushroom, spinach and chicken liver salad

If you can't get the true English spinach, substitute with tender watercress sprigs.

1 bunch English spinach
10 button mushrooms
2 teaspoons sugar
1 tablespoon vinegar
125g bacon
250g chicken livers
¼ cup brandy
Salt and freshly ground pepper

Wash spinach leaves and tear into large bite-size pieces. Slice mushrooms thin and toss with spinach, sugar and vinegar in a salad bowl. Remove the rind from the bacon and cut into thin strips. Cook in a frying pan in its own fat until browned and crisp. Remove bacon from the pan and set aside.

Meanwhile trim all sinew from chicken livers and separate each into 2 pieces. Pat dry and add to the hot pan. Cook in the bacon fat until brown on the outside and still slightly pink inside, shaking pan frequently, for about 2 minutes. Return the bacon to the pan and pour on the brandy, heating it then flaming it. Pour the chicken livers, still flaming, over the mushrooms and spinach. Toss and season well with salt and freshly ground pepper. Serve while still warm.

Timbales of smoked salmon

A stunning new way to present smoked salmon — expensive, but worth it for a very special dinner. Creme fraiche, one of the darlings of the new cuisine, makes a delicate filling.

125g thinly sliced smoked salmon
½ cup Creme Fraiche
2 tablespoons red caviar
Dash of cayenne or Tabasco
Fresh Tomato Puree
Snipped chives or fresh dill, and whole chives or dill sprays to garnish.

Rinse 4 individual souffle dishes or other small moulds (about ⅓ cup size) and line the bases with dampened white paper. Line with smoked salmon, trim level with the rims and chop the trimmings finely.

Have the creme fraiche well chilled. Beat it until soft peaks form and fold in chopped salmon, caviar and cayenne or Tabasco. Fill the moulds with the mixture and chill well.

Run a thin knife around the inside of each mould. Invert a serving plate over each, hold plate and mould firmly together and turn them over. Rap the plate sharply on the table to release the timbale, and lift the mould off carefully.

Spoon fresh tomato puree in a cordon around each timbale and sprinkle with snipped chives or dill. Garnish each plate with chives or dill. Serves 4.

CREME FRAICHE: Pour half a carton (150 ml) of cream into a jar. Mix in 1 tablespoon plain yogurt, cover and keep warm for 8 hours or overnight. One method of doing this is to put the jar into an electric frypan on the lowest temperature, with a few centimetres of warm water in pan; another is to wrap the jar well and leave it above — not in — an oven on a very low setting. Chill the creme well before using; it will thicken as it chills.

FRESH TOMATO PUREE: Peel, seed and chop four ripe red tomatoes. Mash the flesh with a fork or puree in a food processor fitted with the steel blade, then rub the puree through a fine sieve. Season with salt and pepper and chill.

Spinach roulade with mushroom sauce

750g spinach
Salt
3 tablespoons cream
¼ teaspoon grated nutmeg
Freshly ground black pepper
5 large eggs, separated
3 tablespoons grated parmesan cheese
FILLING
250g ricotta cheese
2 tablespoons plain yogurt
Salt and freshly ground black pepper
2 tablespoons chopped green shallots
SAUCE
250g mushrooms sliced
30g butter
1 tablespoon flour
1 cup milk
½ cup cream
Salt
Lemon juice
2 tablespoons chopped parsley

Line the base and ends of a swiss roll tin 25 x 30cm with greaseproof paper, using enough paper to overhung by 5cm at both ends. Spray with non-stick spray and dust with flour. Preheat oven to 200C (400F).

Trim thick stems from spinach and wash leaves. Pack into a heavy saucepan, add a pinch of salt, cover tightly and cook on low heat, shaking saucepan frequently, 4-5 minutes, or until spinach is wilted and tender.

Drain and, when cool enough to handle, squeeze spinach to remove as much moisture as possible and chop fine.

Put spinach into a bowl and stir in cream, nutmeg, pepper, 1 teaspoon salt and lightly beaten egg yolks. Beat the egg whites until they hold soft peaks and fold into spinach mixture.

Spread the mixture in the lined tin and sprinkle with parmesan. Bake just above the centre of the oven for 10-12 minutes or until firm.

While roulade is baking, make filling by combining all ingredients.

Remove roulade from oven and invert on to another piece of oiled greaseproof paper. Peel off the first piece of paper and spread roulade with filling. Roll up, using the paper to help, and rolling roulade on to a heatproof serving platter with the last turn. Return to oven for a few minutes to reheat. Serve with mushroom sauce. Serves 6.

SAUCE: Cook mushrooms briskly in butter until golden, then lower heat, stir in flour and cook 1 minute. Stir in milk and cream, season with salt and lemon juice and simmer 3 minutes. Stir in parsley.

Herbed rack of lamb in pastry

This dish can be prepared a day ahead and stored in the refrigerator until needed. The golden pastry looks impressive when it emerges from the oven with its pretty decoration of leaves and tassels. The lamb tastes delicious with mustard and fresh herb flavoring.

2 racks of lamb (6 cutlets each)
Salt and freshly ground black pepper
Butter
2 tablespoons dijon mustard
1 tablespoon mixed chopped fresh herbs
2 sheets ready-rolled puff pastry, or one 375g packet frozen puff pastry, thawed
1 egg yolk, beaten with a pinch of salt

Ask your butcher to trim off fat from racks of lamb, separate meat from bone at the top, and chine bone (check that bone is completely chopped through between cutlets so that racks will be easy to carve at the table).

Season lamb generously with salt and pepper; brush with softened butter and roast in a moderately hot oven 190C (375F) for 10 minutes. Allow to cool completely.

Spread lamb with mustard and chopped herbs. Wrap each rack in a sheet of puff pastry, allowing bones to protrude and trimming off surplus pastry (if using unrolled puff pastry, divide package in two, roll out each half into a thin sheet and wrap lamb). Make leaves and tassels from the surplus pastry and fix them on with a little beaten egg yolk. Chill the racks for at least 30 minutes.

Brush pastry lightly with water and cover leaves and tassels loosely with a little aluminium foil to prevent burning.

Place the racks on a baking sheet and bake in a very hot oven 230C (430F) for 15 minutes. Remove foil, brush pastry lightly with beaten egg yolk and continue baking until the crust is browned (10 to 15 minutes more). Serves 6.

TO MAKE A TASSEL: Cut a piece of pastry about 2.5cm wide and 8cm long. Cut this strip across like a fringe to about two-thirds of its width, then roll up lengthwise, pinching the base together, and open the fringe.

Grated zucchini with lime

A simple way with a lovely vegetable.

500g zucchini
1 lime or ½ lemon
60g butter

Wipe the zucchini and top and tail them. Grate them on a fine shredder or in the food processor. Mix them with the grated rind and juice of lime or lemon and leave for most of the day.

Just before using, drain zucchini and toss in melted butter over moderate heat for about 4 minutes. Serves 4.

Scallop, mushroom and snow pea tarts

For these tarts, a light, fresh filling of stir-fried scallops, snow peas and mushrooms is cooked at the last minute and spooned into the pastry shells. It's the way top restaurants are presenting entree tarts. When snow peas are out of season, use strips of lightly cooked fennel or asparagus tips.

1 quantity Food Processor Pastry (see index)
3 tablespoons peanut oil
¾ teaspoon grated fresh ginger
375g scallops
185g snow peas, topped, tailed and strings removed
125g button mushrooms, sliced
2 tablespoons dry sherry
1½ teaspoons cornflour mixed with 1 tablespoon light soy sauce in ⅓ cup water

Roll out pastry and line six 10cm tart tins. Prick bases and chill 20 minutes.

Line tart shells with crumpled greaseproof paper and fill with dry beans or race. Bake in a very hot oven 220C (425F) for 8 minutes or until pastry is beginning to color. Remove paper with filling, return shells to oven and bake about 5 minutes more. If sides are over browning, protect them with foil. Remove from oven and cool 5 minutes in the tins, then remove shells and use immediately or, of making the shells ahead of time, cool them on a rack. When needed, replace shells in the tins and warm through in the oven.

Make the filling just before serving. Heat oil in a wok or frying pan and fry ginger over high heat for 1 minute. Add scallops, stir 1 minute, add snow peas and mushrooms and toss 1 minute more. Add sherry and cornflour mixture and stir until boiling and thickened. Spoon filling into tart shells and serve immediately. Serves 6.

Above left: Colorful Spinach Roulade With Mushroom Sauce. Above: Scallop, Mushroom And Snow Pea Tarts. For Fruit Tartlets, see page 18.

September

Lebanese favorites

In cities throughout the world, Lebanese restaurants are flourishing, and no wonder. The Lebanese have always found a special relaxation and merriment at table and the rest of the world is catching on. Much of the food used in the Lebanese kitchen is an inspiration in itself. Dark purple eggplant, jewel-bright red and green tomatoes, oranges and lemons, snowy white cauliflowers, fresh herbs, young fresh garlic and golden olive oil. Perhaps the presence of so much attractive food stimulates an interest in both cooking and eating. The most typical Lebanese cooking is displayed in a mosaic of sauces — a kind of hors d'oeuvre called mezze. The concept of leisurely eating is enhanced by the mezze. You start with 3 or 4 items, see how hungry you are, then dish by dish you order more. You talk, you nibble, you drink wine or arak (a colorless eau-de-vie distilled preferably from grapes and flavored with aniseed), you tear off triangles of the puffy, round Arab bread to use as scoops or spear any of the food you fancy. If you have enjoyed a meal in a Lebanese restaurant don't let it stop there. Most Lebanese restaurant food is home cooking — it is both easy and inexpensive. *For a tabouli recipe, see page 48.*

Falafel

These fried chick pea rissoles are nourishing, cheap and tasty. They originated in Egypt where they are made with large white beans (not chick peas) and are believed to be as old as the pharaohs. Stuffed into pockets of pita bread with salad and hummus they make a good snack.

250g (1 cup) chick peas
4 tablespoons bulgur
3 cloves garlic
Salt and pepper
3 tablespoons plain flour
1 teaspoon cumin
¼ teaspoon ground chili
2 teaspoons ground coriander
½ cup chopped fresh coriander (optional)
1 egg
Oil for frying

Soak chick peas in water to cover for 12 hours, then pass drained peas through a mincer or mix to a paste in a food processor. Soak bulgur in water to cover for 1 hour, if very coarse pass through mincer. Crush garlic with salt and combine all ingredients except oil, check for seasoning.

Shape into balls the size of a small walnut. Heat oil in a saucepan to at least a depth of 2.5cm. When a haze appears above oil, fry falafel a few at a time until browned. Reheat oil before frying next lot. Serve hot, accompanied by a salad of chopped tomatoes, cucumber and cos lettuce and a bowl of hummus paste. Or pop everything into a pocket of pita bread.

Note: Batches of falafel mixture can be shaped and kept in the refrigerator for several days before frying.

Baba ghanouj

This lovely dip of eggplant and tahini (sesame seed paste available at health food shops and good delicatessens) is delicious.

500g firm eggplant
2 tablespoons lemon juice
4-5 tablespoons tahini
2 cloves garlic
1 teaspoon salt
1 tablespoon oil
2 tablespoons chopped flat-leafed parsley

Cut eggplant in two, lengthwise. Lightly oil a baking dish, place eggplant cut side down in dish and cook under a moderate grill, turning from time to time, until tender and skin is charred. Allow to cool.

Remove flesh from skin, while holding the stem. Mash the pulp thoroughly with a fork. Slowly beat in lemon juice alternately with tahini.

Crush the garlic with the salt and mix into eggplant mixture. Transfer the sauce to a serving dish, sprinkle with oil and chopped parsley.

Dolmades

These little vine-leaf bundles filled with aromatic rice are often served as part of the mezze selection. Dolmades freeze well so it is worth making a good batch at a time. Preserved vine leaves are available from good delicatessens or you can use young, fresh ones.

500g preserved vine leaves or about 80 young, fresh ones
¼ cup lemon juice
¼ cup olive oil

Left: Tabouli (see page 48), Dolmades, Baba Ghanouj, Djaajmishwi (Grilled Lemon Chicken), Garlic Sauce and Falafel, all Lebanese favorites.

2 cloves garlic, thinly sliced
1 cup water
Lemon wedges, to serve
FILLING
2 large onions, finely chopped
½ cup olive oil
½ cup short grain rice
3 tablespoons pine nuts
3 tablespoons currants
3 tablespoons chopped parsley
2 teaspoons chopped mint
¼ teaspoon cinnamon
Salt and freshly ground black pepper

Rinse fresh or preserved vine leaves and blanch, a few at a time, for 3 minutes in boiling water. Rinse in cold water and cut off stems.

To make filling, gently fry onions in oil until soft. Mix in remaining ingredients, cover and cook on low heat for 15 minutes or until water is absorbed. Season to taste.

Place a heaped teaspoon of filling on each leaf, shiny side down, and roll up, folding sides in to seal the filling. Reserve about 12 leaves unfilled.

Pack the rolls close together, seam sides down, in layers in a heavy saucepan, sprinkling each layer with lemon juice, oil and sliced garlic. Pour water over then cover with the reserved leaves. Cover the saucepan tightly and simmer very gently for 1 hour. Remove from heat and leave 1-2 hours or until liquid is absorbed. Lift rolls out carefully and chill several hours before serving with lemon wedges. Makes about 70.

Garlic sauce

This is rather like mayonnaise but without the eggs — indeed it is made like mayonnaise. Try to get young, fresh garlic for this sauce, which is a delicious accompaniment to grilled chicken or shellfish.

12 cloves garlic
1 teaspoon salt
1½ cups olive oil
2 tablespoons lemon juice

Smash each clove of garlic with the broad side of a cook's knife, remove skins. Crush the garlic with salt, this can be done in a mortar and pestle or with the broad part of a knife on a board.

Transfer to a bowl or electric blender and very gradually add oil, beating well after each addition, then beat in the lemon juice gradually.

The mixture should be light and fluffy. If it doesn't thicken a well-cooked and mashed potato or a little instant mashed potato can be added.

Djaajmishwi

My local Lebanese restaurant prepares this delicious grilled lemon chicken. This is at its best cooked over hot coals at a barbecue.

Juice 1 large lemon
4 cloves garlic, crushed with pinch salt
Freshly ground black pepper
6 chicken pieces, half-breasts or legs
1-2 tablespoons oil
1 lemon, sliced wafer-thin
Garlic sauce

Combine lemon juice, garlic and pepper. Marinate chicken pieces in this mixture for at least 1 hour, turning several times. Brush grill rack with oil and add chicken pieces, skin side down. Cook under a preheated grill for about 10 minutes, then turn over. Continue to grill for a further 5 minutes then arrange slices of lemon on top and continue to grill further few minutes, until chicken is cooked. Serve with garlic sauce and salads. Serves 6.

Basic kibbe mixture

This lamb and bulgur paste is the basis of many Lebanese dishes. Kibbe can be baked in a sheet and cut into squares or diagonals, moulded into ovals or made into a meat loaf. With a food processor it is really very easy to make.

1½ cups bulgur
1kg boneless lamb
1 onion
½ red pepper
2 teaspoons salt
½ teaspoon each ground allspice, cinnamon, nutmeg and pepper

In a bowl soak bulgur in cold water to cover for 30 minutes. Transfer the bulgur to a sieve lined with double thickness of cheesecloth (or Chux) and squeeze until it is dry.

Trim meat of any fat or gristle and cut into cubes. Grind the meat several times through the fine blade of a mincer or process until fine and almost a paste in the food processor.

Transfer to a bowl, process the onion and red pepper until very finely chopped. Work bulgur, lamb, onion, pepper, salt and spices together. If liked, this can be done in the food processor. For best results refrigerate in a covered container for 6-12 hours then knead again before cooking.

BAKED KIBBE: Oil a 30x25 cm baking dish. Put mixture in dish, pat down with wet hands. Cut into diamonds or squares, pour over about ¼ cup oil and bake at 230C (450F) for 20-25 minutes. Eat hot or cold with yogurt and a fresh green salad.

Kibbe bissaniye

These lamb and pine nut-stuffed ovals of kibbe are one of the popular dishes served as a part of the mezze or first course at a Lebanese meal.

½ quantity basic kibbe mixture
1 quantity kibbe stuffing
Oil for frying

Divide basic kibbe mixture into 8 parts and shape each into an oval about the size of an egg. Hold each oval in a wetted hand, make a deep lengthwise indentation in each with the back of a wooden spoon and fill each indentation with 1 tablespoon kibbe stuffing. Reshape the ovals to enclose the stuffing, using slightly wetted fingers. The shell should be thin and smooth, repair any breaks with wetted fingers.

In a frying pan heat about 5cm oil and fry kibbe over a moderate heat, turning them until they are well browned on all sides. Drain on paper towels.

Alternatively, ovals may be coated with butter and baked in a moderate oven 180C (350F) about 15-20 minutes. Makes 8.

Kibbe naye

These lamb and bulgur rounds are a variation on steak tartar.

1 cup bulgur
500g lean minced lamb
1 onion, finely chopped
1/8 teaspoon each allspice, nutmeg and salt
Pepper
Oil and green shallots

Make Kibbe mixture as for basic kibbe using above proportion of ingredients. Divide it into 8 parts. Shape each into rounds about 1.25cm thick and make an indentation in each with the thumb.

Transfer the rounds to a platter, pour a little oil into each indentation and garnish the dish with strips of green shallots. If liked, accompany with a small bowl of Hot Pepper And Onion Paste. Serves 8.

HOT PEPPER AND ONION PASTE: Grind together in a blender or food processor 1 quartered onion and 1 small hot red chili.

Kibbe stuffing

A spiced lamb and pine nut mixture is used as a stuffing for kibbe shells for ovals or meat loaves.

2 tablespoons pine nuts
1-2 tablespoons butter
2 tablespoons finely chopped onion
125g finely minced lamb
¼ teaspoon each cinnamon and allspice
Salt and pepper to taste

Cook pine nuts in 1 tablespoon butter until they are golden, remove nuts. Cook onion in pan, adding more butter if necessary, then lamb, and cook the mixture, stirring until lamb changes color, and breaking the meat up so that it doesn't form a clump. Combine nuts, lamb and spices, and season. Makes about ½ cup.

Mishmishieh

Dried golden apricots are used in many Middle Eastern dishes. The rosewater is available from most chemists and health food shops.

500g dried apricots
5½ cups water
1 cup sugar
2 teaspoons cornflour
Extra ½ cup water
1½-2 teaspoons rosewater
1 cup chopped or slivered blanched almonds
Cream, whipped

Bring apricots, water and sugar slowly to the boil and cook 20-25 minutes until fruit is very soft. Put the mixture through a sieve or puree in blender or food processor. Return to saucepan, blend cornflour with extra ½ cup water, add to puree and bring mixture to boil, stirring and cook for 3 mintues. Add rosewater to taste. Spoon the pudding into 6 dessert dishes and chill. Top with almonds and serve with whipped cream. Serves 6.

Cauliflower with avocado sauce

This Lebanese dish makes a delicious first course for a dinner party or as a main meal for the family.

1 small or ½ large cauliflower
1 teaspoon salt
SAUCE
1 clove garlic
½ teaspoon salt
½ cup tahini
¼ cup lemon juice
¼ cup cold water
¼ cup chopped parsley
1 avocado, peeled and mashed

Prepare sauce by peeling the clove of garlic and crushing with salt. Mix in the tahini and lemon juice, beat well and gradually add lemon juice. Then beat in the cold water until the sauce is thick. Fold in the chopped parsley and the mashed avocado. Season to taste. All this can be done in a food processor or blender. Place in bowl, cover and store in the fridge until ready to serve.

Break cauliflower into florets and trim any tough stalks. Place in saucepan with 2 cups of boiling water and salt, bring to the boil then cover with a lid. Steam for 10 minutes or until the florets are just tender. Arrange the cauliflower in a serving bowl with the stalks innermost. Spoon over the sauce and serve either hot or cold. Serves 4-8.

Hummus bi-tahini

This is one of the most widely known and appreciated of all Middle Eastern dishes. It is served as a dip with bread, fish, eggplant and can also be a salad with a main dish. Tahini is a paste made from sesame seeds and can be found in delicatessens, particularly Greek ones, and some health food stores. Hummus should have the consistency of a stiff mayonnaise and it should be well seasoned, but neither the flavor of garlic nor lemon juice should predominate.

1½ cups dried chick peas
Juice 2-3 lemons
2-3 cloves garlic
Salt
¾ cup tahini
GARNISH
1 tablespoon olive oil
1 teaspoon paprika
1 tablespoon finely chopped parsley

Soak chick peas overnight in cold water to cover. Next day drain, place in a saucepan with fresh water to cover, bring to the boil then cover with lid, reduce heat and cook until soft, about 3½ hours. Drain peas, reserving a little of the cooking liquid, and set aside about ½ cup whole chick peas to garnish.

Push peas through a sieve or puree in an electric blender or food processor, adding a little of the cooking liquid or lemon juice. Crush garlic with salt and add to puree gradually with a little lemon juice, tasting for flavor. Add tahini paste gradually with lemon juice and mix vigorously. Add more cooking liquid or water if necessary to bring the mixture to the consistency of thick mayonnaise. Check seasoning and add more lemon juice, garlic or salt if desired.

Above: A delightful first course, Cauliflower With Avocado Sauce.

Hummus is traditionally served spread on a flat plate. Make a shallow depression in the centre and pour in olive oil then sprinkle with paprika, or mix paprika with oil and drizzle over surface. Garnish with chopped parsley and reserved whole chick peas. Serve as a dip with flat lebanese bread.
Note : Canned chick peas can be substituted for cooked dried ones. Use about 3 cups canned chick peas.

The meat course

Get to know your butcher. He (or she) will cut and trim your beef, pork, lamb or veal just the way you want it. Indeed, when I give mine warning he seems to be able to do or obtain anything I need. So get to know your butcher and understand his business. It doesn't make for good relations requesting special meat to be minced at 5.15 pm on a busy Friday or after he has cleaned his mincer, or demanding two whole fillets of beef at 11.30am on Saturday morning. Let me tell you, M.F. gets results from her butcher because, as a housewife, she plans ahead for those special occasions — and that means planning with her butcher (and greengrocer and fishmonger). The point is that meat can make any meal special. Here are some recipes that prove that point! Nowhere in the world is there better — or cheaper — meat than in Australia.

Veal pojarski

Many of our fine young chefs are trained at the NSW North Ryde School of Catering. At a dinner there recently I was served these absolutely delicious veal cutlets which have become a household favorite. They are good for entertaining as they can be prepared ahead, needing only last-minute cooking.

500g veal steaks
60g butter
1½ cups soft white breadcrumbs
¼ cup cream
1 teaspoon salt
Freshly ground pepper
2 tablespoons each oil and butter
COATING
Seasoned flour
1 egg, beaten
1½ cups soft white breadcrumbs

Chop the meat very fine or process in a food processor until fairly fine. Work in the butter, breadcrumbs and cream, season with salt and pepper.

Divide mixture into 6 and reshape like a cutlet. Dust each with flour, dip in beaten egg then soft breadcrumbs, pressing on the crumbs with the flat of hand or a spatula.

Set on greaseproof paper and chill in refrigerator for 1 hour to harden the butter and egg coating, which cooks to a golden crisp, keeping the cutlet juicy.

Heat the oil and butter in a frypan and, when the foam subsides, add the cutlets and saute until golden on both sides — about 3 minutes each side. Arrange on heated platter and serve with noodles or boiled rice and Sauteed Mushrooms or Sauce Smetane. Serves 6.

SAUTEED MUSHROOMS: Wipe 250g mushroom caps with damp cloth, slice in 3 or 4. Heat 2 tablespoons oil and butter in a frypan and over medium-high heat toss mushrooms until golden, season with salt and pepper, and, if liked, stir in ½ cup sour cream.

SAUCE SMETANE: Lightly brown half an onion, chopped, in 1 tablespoon butter, add ½ cup white wine and heat until almost reduced, add 1 teaspoon paprika and ¾ cup sour cream and bring to the boil. Strain and add a squeeze of lemon juice.

Kidneys in mustard sauce

One sometimes forgets how delicious lamb kidneys can be; this simple recipe is a reminder.

6-8 lambs' kidneys, skinned and split in half
Seasoned flour
90g butter
2 teaspoons French mustard
2 tablespoons chopped green or French shallots
½ cup dry white wine
2 teaspoons lemon juice
¼ cup chopped parsley

Soak kidneys in cold water for 30 minutes. Drain, remove cores and slice thinly. Coat kidney slices in seasoned flour and brown in half the butter. Remove and keep hot. Stir mustard into fat in pan with remaining butter, add shallots, cook for 1 minute, stirring, then add wine and lemon juice. Return kidneys and cook gently for a few minutes. Add parsley and cook for 1 minute. Serve with fluffy boiled rice or noodles, or with toast. Serves 4.

Right: Golden brown Veal Pojarski, served with mushrooms and salad.

Lamb chops and green peppercorns

The green peppercorns and mustard add a French touch, so serve with sauteed potatoes and chilled rose wine. Thick-cut lamb chops are juicy and succulent. Trim off all but a thin layer of fat.

8 thick lamb loin chops
Salt
1 tablespoon butter
1 tablespoon oil
4 shallots, finely chopped
2 tablespoons dry sherry
1 tablespoon green peppercorns drained
⅔ cup cream
2 teaspoons French mustard
1 teaspoon tarragon, finely chopped

Trim excess fat from chops and season with salt. Curl tails around and secure with skewers or poultry pins. Heat butter and oil in a heavy-based frying pan, and when hot add the chops. Cook 5 minutes on each side or until chops are cooked. Remove from the pan, remove skewers and keep warm.

Add the shallots to the pan and saute for a few minutes until softened. Stir in the sherry. Reserve 1 teaspoon of the green peppercorns and crush the remainder. Mix crushed peppercorns with cream, mustard and tarragon and add to the pan. Bring the sauce to the boil and allow to thicken slightly. Stir in reserved peppercorns and spoon over chops. Serves 4.

Alsatian lamb

A recipe from the province of Alsace in France where they produce a lovely riesling of delicate flavor and bouquet. A local Australian riesling with our own good lamb responds well to this treatment.

1 small leg of lamb
½ bottle dry white wine
1 clove garlic, crushed
1 onion, peeled and stuck with 4 cloves
1 bay leaf
3 carrots, sliced
1 teaspoon chopped fresh thyme or ¼ teaspoon dried
Salt and freshly ground pepper
250g long bacon rashers
1 cup stock or vegetable water
1 teaspoon arrowroot (optional)

Remove excess fat from lamb. Combine wine, garlic, onion, bay leaf, carrots, thyme, salt and pepper. Marinate lamb in wine mixture for 12 hours. Preheat oven to very hot 230C (450F).

Wrap lamb in bacon rashers, securing with toothpicks. Place on a rack in a roasting pan with about 1 cup marinade. Reduce oven heat to moderate 180C (350F) and roast lamb for 1 to 1½ hours or until cooked, basting every 15 minutes with marinade. Remove lamb to a heated platter and leave in the turned-off oven with the door ajar while you make gravy.

Remove the rack from the roasting pan and place pan on top of stove. Add stock or vegetable water and boil rapidly, stirring often, until liquid is reduced to about 1 cup. If you like, thicken gravy slightly by stirring in 1 teaspoon arrowroot blended with a little cold water. Strain gravy into a heated sauceboat. Serve lamb with gravy, small boiled potatoes and whole green beans. Serves 4 to 6.

Note: Although white wine is used in the cooking of Alsatian lamb, you might like to drink a good red wine with the meal.

Swedish meatballs in cream sauce

Light and tender with subtle spicing, these meatballs are one of the best dishes of Sweden, and now that you can get fresh dill at many greengrocers it is worth making them.

500g lean minced steak
250g mixed lean minced pork and veal
1½ cups fresh white breadcrumbs
1 cup cream
½ cup milk
1 onion, finely chopped
90g butter
1 egg, beaten
2 teaspoons ground ginger
Salt and freshly ground black pepper
Nutmeg
1 tablespoon flour
½ cup stock
Chopped fresh dill

Mix meats together. Soak breadcrumbs in a mixture of ¼ cup cream and the milk. Cook onion in 30g butter until tender but not brown. Combine meats, breadcrumbs, egg and onion, and season with ginger, 1½ teaspoons salt, pepper and ¼ teaspoon nutmeg. Beat vigorously until very light in texture, then chill.

Form into small balls (about 50). Melt remaining butter in a large frying pan and lightly brown meatballs on all sides, a few at a time. Remove from pan and keep warm in an ovenproof dish in a preheated slow oven while making the sauce.

Stir flour into fat in frying pan and cook for 2 minutes, stirring. Remove from heat and add stock and remaining cream. Bring to the boil, stirring constantly. Season with salt, pepper and nutmeg and cook over a low heat for about 10 minutes or until sauce reduces and thickens, stirring frequently. Strain sauce and pour over meatballs and scatter with dill. Serve with boiled rice. Serves 6.

Note: The meatballs may be made and cooked the day before and then reheated in the oven, with the sauce poured over just before serving.

Left: Piquant Lamb Chops And Green Peppercorns. Right: Swedish Meatballs In Cream Sauce — a hearty family meal.

Spiced lamb with yogurt

1 boned shoulder of lamb
2 tablespoons lemon juice
1 teaspoon ground cardamom
1 teaspoon ground coriander
½ cup natural yogurt
30g butter
1 medium onion, finely chopped
½ teaspoon ground ginger
¾ cup milk
Salt and pepper

Do not have the shoulder rolled by the butcher, but ask him to score the fat side for you in a diamond pattern. (If he's busy, do this at home yourself.)

Combine the lemon juice, cardamom, coriander and yogurt. Spread the lamb out flat, and rub the yogurt mixture into it on both sides. Allow to stand for an hour or so, then form into a neat shape and secure meat with two long skewers. Place in a baking dish, and roast in a preheated moderate oven 180C (350F) for 30 minutes.

Meanwhile, heat the butter in a small frying pan and fry the onion until soft and golden, about 4 minutes. Stir in the ginger and spread this mixture over the surface of the lamb. Continue cooking until done to your liking: about an extra hour for well-done lamb and 30 minutes for lamb still pink in the middle.

Remove to a warm platter to rest for 5 minutes before carving. Blot up any fat from juices in pan, add milk and heat, scraping up the brown crusty bits from the bottom. Season with salt and pepper and serve as gravy with lamb. Serves 4.

Red wine beef loaf

Here's an economical loaf with an interesting sweet-sour glaze.

1kg lean minced beef
½ cup red wine
¼ cup milk
2 cups fresh wholemeal breadcrumbs
2 eggs, beaten
1 large onion, finely chopped
1½ teaspoons salt
Freshly ground pepper
GLAZE
1 teaspoon dry mustard
½ cup tomato sauce or ¼ cup chili sauce
2 tablespoons honey
1 tablespoon wine vinegar
2 teaspoons worcestershire sauce

Combine ingredients for meat loaf, and pack into a greased loaf tin. Bake in a preheated moderate oven, 180C (350F), for 1 hour. Drain any liquid from loaf tin, and turn loaf out on to a greased shallow baking dish. Combine ingredients for glaze, and brush over loaf. Return loaf to the oven for a further 15 minutes, brushing frequently with glaze until all is used. Serves 6-8.

Herbed lamb stew

1kg leg or shoulder of lamb, boned
2 tablespoons oil
2 rashers bacon, diced
1 onion, sliced
2 cloves garlic, crushed
Salt and freshly ground pepper
1 teaspoon chopped, fresh oregano or ¼ teaspoon dried
1 teaspoon rosemary or ¼ teaspoon dried
½ cup red wine
2 tablespoons tomato paste
1 x 400g can tomatoes
2 tablespoons red wine, extra

Trim excess fat from lamb and cut into 4cm pieces. Heat oil in a large, heavy frying pan. Add diced bacon, onion and garlic and saute until golden. Remove to a plate. Add half the meat and brown on all sides, repeat with remaining meat. Return meat to pan. Season with salt, pepper, oregano and rosemary. Stir in red wine and continue cooking until wine reduces to half its original quantity. Add bacon and onion, tomato paste and canned tomatoes.

Cover and simmer slowly about 1½ hours or until tender. Add extra red wine just before serving to deepen the flavor and serve directly from the pan. Serve with flat ribbon noodles or fluffy boiled rice. Serves 4-6.

Roast stuffed pork

Here is a roast of pork made from inexpensive pork belly — the cut often chopped into spare ribs. It might be a good idea to order it from your butcher the day before. Ask him to leave the belly in one piece, to remove the bones (which you can use for stock) and score the skin for crackling.

1.25kg piece of belly pork
Marmalade (optional)
STUFFING
250g pork and veal mince
4 cups fresh breadcrumbs
1 medium onion, finely chopped
1 beaten egg
1 tablespoon chopped parsley
2 teaspoons chopped sage, oregano or rosemary (or ½ teaspoon dried)
Salt and pepper to taste

Rub the pork skin with a little oil and salt, and if possible leave to soak overnight.

With a knife make a shallow incision down the centre of the belly, cutting towards but not through the rind, and make two pockets into which you place the stuffing (made by combining the remaining ingredients).

Roll the joint so that the two long ends meet around the stuffing, and tie firmly at 2.5cm intervals. Give the rind a second rubbing with salt and place on a rack in baking dish. (This is important if you want every square centimetre of crackling, as the rind will never become crisp at the point of contact with the baking dish.)

Bake in a very hot oven 230C (450F) for 30 minutes, then reduce to moderate 180C (350F) for a further 1-1¼ hours. Potatoes may be baked around the joint.

Remove to a heated serving dish. Pour off excess fat and make gravy. If you like, stir in one tablespoon of chunky marmalade.

Roast beef in foil

We are discovering that budget cuts of beef can make tender roasts when they are treated with care. Many butchers and supermarkets sell pieces of economical roasting beef, which might be topside, bolar blade or fresh silverside. There is no bone, little fat and no waste with such cuts. Ask the advice of your own butcher, and he will recommend the best-value beef on the day.

I find this way of cooking lean beef guards against dryness, and as a bonus, makes its own delicious gravy.

2kg fresh silverside, bolar blade or topside
1 fat clove garlic, crushed
1 packet french onion soup
½ teaspoon dried tarragon or thyme
A little dry mustard

Place meat on a double thickness of aluminium foil large enough to wrap around it. Spread top with half the garlic and sprinkle with half the soup and herbs and a little dry mustard. Pat seasonings well into beef, turn over, and repeat with the other side. Wrap the meat loosely in the foil, crimping the edges well together, and place in a baking dish. Bake in a preheated moderately hot oven 190C (375F) for 1 hour 30 minutes. (This will give you meat still a little rare in the middle. Overcooking can result in dryness.)

Carefully unwrap meat and remove to a heated serving dish. Pour juices that have collected back into the baking tin, and add enough hot water or stock to make a thin gravy. Reheat, taste for seasoning, and pour into a gravy boat. Carve the meat in fairly thin slices and serve with gravy, baked potatoes, pumpkin and a green vegetable.

Note: Peel and cut into serving

Left: New look for old favorites, Rissoles With Mushroom Gravy.

portions the potatoes and pumpkin. Parboil in boiling salted water about 15 minutes. Brush potatoes and pumpkin with a little oil or melted butter and bake in dish with beef for 1 hour.

Rissoles with mushroom gravy

4 tablespoons oil
1 onion, finely chopped
4 slices bread, cubed
4 tablespoons milk
750g minced steak
2 eggs, lightly beaten
2 tablespoons tomato paste
½ teaspoon salt
½ teaspoon white pepper
½ cup flour
GRAVY
45g butter
8-10 mushrooms, sliced
2 tablespoons flour
2 teaspoons paprika
1 cup beef stock
½ cup sour cream

Heat 2 tablespoons oil and gently fry onion until soft. Soak bread cubes in milk for 10 minutes. Put steak, 1 egg, tomato paste, salt and pepper in a bowl and blend well together. Add onion and soaked bread cubes and blend again.

Shape mixture into 8 rissoles. Dip in flour, then in remaining egg and coat with breadcrumbs. Heat remaining oil and fry rissoles until well browned on each side. Drain and keep warm.

GRAVY: Melt butter in a saucepan and gently fry mushrooms for 2 minutes. Blend in flour and paprika, then stir in stock. Cook gently until boiling, stirring constantly. Remove from heat, stir in sour cream and serve immediately with rissoles. Serves 4.

Marmalade lamb

1 boned shoulder of lamb weighing about 1.5kg
Salt and freshly ground pepper
1 cup orange juice
½ cup marmalade
STUFFING
3 cups soft white breadcrumbs
2 teaspoons finely chopped thyme or marjoram (or ½ teaspoon dried)
1 tablespoon chopped parsley
2 teaspoons grated lemon rind
Salt and freshly ground pepper
60g butter, melted
1 egg, beaten

Lay out lamb and sprinkle with salt and pepper to taste. Spread with stuffing and roll up and tie securely. Place in a baking dish just large enough to hold it comfortably.

Combine orange juice and marmalade and pour over lamb. Bake in a preheated moderate oven 180C (350F) for 1¼ hours or until done to your liking, basting often with pan juices. (If they seem to be drying out too much, add a little extra orange juice from time to time.)

Remove lamb to a warm platter and allow to rest for 15 minutes before removing strings and carving. Blot any fat from pan juices with paper towels and reheat, scraping up the brown bits from the bottom and seasoning to taste. Serve as gravy with the lamb. Serves 4-6.

STUFFING: Place the breadcrumbs, herbs, grated lemon rind and salt and seasoning in a bowl. Using a fork, stir in the melted butter and egg.

Meat pies

Individual oval meat-pie tins are available; they are inexpensive and brown the pastry beautifully. You can also get tins in a smaller round size. This quantity of pastry and savory mince will make you six pies; they can be eaten straight away or packed into bags and frozen.

1½ quantities Savory Mince (see index)
3 cups plain flour
Pinch salt
180g butter or dripping
6 tablespoons water or milk to mix
1 egg, beaten

Prepare savory mince, cook and then allow to cool. Sift flour and salt together. Cut the butter into small pieces, add to the flour and, using fingertips, rub the butter in until the mixture resembles breadcrumbs. Add the liquid all at once to the centre of the mixture. Blend, using a fork, until the mixture clings together in a ball, leaving the sides of the basin clean.

Turn the dough on to a lightly floured surface and knead lightly to make a smooth, fairly stiff, dough. Chill for about 15 minutes before using.

Divide pastry into six and grease oval pie tins lightly. Cut a third of each portion of pastry and reserve for the top. Roll out remaining two-thirds of each portion and use to line pie tins. Divide meat mixture evenly into the pastry-lined tins.

Roll out reserved pastry, cut to correct shape, brush edges with water and place on top of pies, pressing edges together well to seal. Cut two slits in top of the pastry to allow the steam to escape. Decorate tops of pies with leaves made from pastry trimmings. Chill 30 minutes. Glaze with a little beaten egg and bake in a hot oven, 200C (400F), for 25 to 30 minutes or until pastry is cooked and golden brown. Serves 6.

South-east Asian cuisine

A welcome South-East Asian influence has entered the Australian way of eating. So many of us have visited Bali, Hong Kong, Singapore, the Philippines or other holiday destinations and have returned eager to relive fascinating meals we've had there. We're now as likely to dine out in Vietnamese, Thai or Sri Lankan style as in the European way. Authentic ingredients for all these are to be found, not only in the increasing number of Asian specialty food shops but in many supermarkets, health food stores and delicatessens. Here is a sampling of dishes from South-East Asia to add to your repertoire.

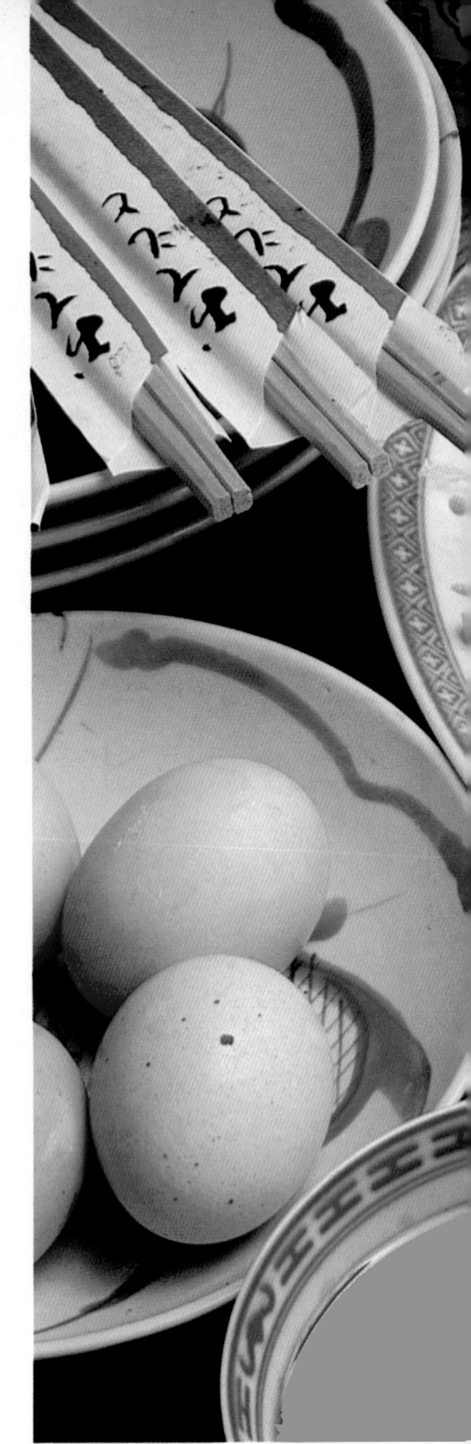

Special ingredients

GHEE is clarified butter and is widely available. To make your own, cut butter into pieces and heat slowly in a small saucepan then remove from heat. A clear yellow liquid will rise to the top as the butter stands — this is the clarified butter. Skim it off, leaving behind the whitish residue of milk solids and salt at the bottom of the saucepan.

CHINESE SESAME OIL is thick, dark and strongly flavored, quite different from the light sesame oil used for frying or for salad dressings. Chinese sesame oil is used in small quantities as a seasoning.

COCONUT MILK is a basic ingredient of South-East Asian cooking. It will keep for several days, covered, in the refrigerator.

Heat gently 1 cup desiccated coconut and 1½ cups milk. Do not boil. Pour into a blender, cover and blend for 30 seconds. Strain through a fine sieve, kneading the mixture to extract as much liquid as possible. This gives thick, creamy coconut milk.

Using same coconut, and another 1½ cups milk, repeat. This gives thin coconut milk. Unless specified otherwise, mix thick and thin coconut milk together for use.

Spicy chicken, cucumber and agar salad

This salad is an example of the way Asian cooks play different textures, colors and flavors against each other to make a perfect composition. Agar strips, made from seaweed, look like cellophane. When soaked in water, they have an interesting, chewy texture and absorb sauces and seasonings beautifully. A Chinese omelet is a cross between a French omelet and a pancake.

AGAR
30g agar strips
1 tablespoon Chinese sesame oil

CHICKEN
4 cups water
2 slices fresh ginger
1 tablespoon rice wine or dry sherry
2 whole chicken breasts

OMELETS
3 large eggs
1 tablespoon water
½ teaspoon salt
Peanut oil

SAUCE
¼ cup light soy sauce
3 tablespoons rice vinegar or white wine vinegar
2 tablespoons Chinese sesame oil
1 tablespoon rice wine or dry sherry
2 teaspoons sugar
1 teaspoon salt

CUCUMBER
1 large green cucumber, thinly peeled and cut into ribbons with a potato peeler (discard seeds)

AGAR: Cover agar strips with warm water and soak for 2 hours. Drain the strips on paper towels.

CHICKEN: Put water, ginger and wine into a saucepan, bring to the boil and add chicken. Cover and poach gently for 10 minutes then turn heat off and allow chicken to cool in the broth. Lift chicken out, remove skin and bones and cut meat into fine strips.

OMELETS: Beat eggs, water and salt together. Heat a small frying pan with just enough peanut oil to film the bottom. When pan is hot, turn heat low and pour in enough egg mixture to cover the bottom thinly. Cook until egg is just set (this will take only moments), turn omelet with a spatula and cook other side briefly, then turn omelet out on to a plate. Omelet should be pale.

Repeat with remaining egg mixture. When omelets are cool, stack them, roll up and cut into fine strips.

SAUCE: Mix all ingredients for sauce together.

ASSEMBLING THE SALAD: Choose a large platter or shallow serving dish. Put in agar, drizzle with 1 tablespoon Chinese sesame oil and toss together. Arrange cucumber in a layer on top of agar. Arrange shredded omelet in a border round the edge and mound the chicken on top of the cucumber. Pour sauce over the salad and serve immediately. Serves 6-8 as a main course.

Malayan beef satays

In Malaysia and Singapore, satay vendors and their charcoal braziers are part of the charm of the city streets. Spiced meat is threaded on bamboo or wooden skewers to make a meal. Serve with salads and spiced rice.

1kg steak, scotch fillet or rump
⅓ cup soy sauce
⅓ cup peanut oil
2 onions
2 cloves garlic
3 tablespoons toasted sesame seeds
2 teaspoons ground cumin
1 teaspoon lemon juice
Salt and pepper

Cut the steak into cubes and put into an earthenware bowl. Combine soy sauce, peanut oil, finely chopped onion, crushed garlic and sesame seeds, pour over meat and leave to marinate for 3 hours. Turn meat from time to time in the marinade. After 3 hours, or longer, drain meat, reserving marinade. Thread 4-5 meat cubes on small bamboo or wooden skewers. Wrap small pieces of aluminium foil around skewer ends to prevent burning. Mix cumin and lemon juice together and brush over meat. Grill satays over the hot coals of the barbecue or under a preheated griller, basting with marinade and turning frequently.

Above: Spicy Chicken, Cucumber And Agar Salad, a perfect combination of texture, color and flavor.

Grill satays until tender: 6-8 minutes for rare; 8-10 minutes for medium; 10-12 minutes for well done.

Season with salt and pepper before serving.

Note: Bamboo skewers can be bought in barbecue sections of large department stores. To toast sesame seeds, sprinkle into a large, heavy frying pan and cook over a medium steady heat for 2-3 minutes or until well browned. Do not use any oil. Krupek or prawn crisps are available from oriental or health food shops.

Fruit and nut compote

The combination of chilled fruit, nuts and refreshing sauce is a perfect way to end a spicy meal.

1 small fresh pineapple
2 large oranges
2 large, firm bananas
1 punnet strawberries
½ cup plain yogurt
2 tablespoons orange juice
2 tablespoons lime or lemon juice
2 teaspoons chopped blanched almonds
1 tablespoon softened butter
2 tablespoons honey
1 teaspoon grated fresh ginger
¼ cup each of stoned fresh or dried dates, walnut pieces and shelled, unsalted sunflower seeds

Prepare pineapple fans by shaving off outer skin, then cutting out eyes in the spiral pattern in which they grow. Slice across thinly, cut out core with a small scone cutter and cut each slice in half.

Peel oranges and remove skinless segments with a sharp knife. Slice bananas and brush with lemon juice. Wash and hull strawberries. Put all fruit into a bowl and chill, covered, for 2 hours.

Put yogurt, juices, almonds, butter, honey and ginger into a blender or food processor and blend until smooth. If making by hand, pound almonds, butter and ginger together until smooth then mix in yogurt, juices and honey.

Add dates, walnuts and sunflower seeds to the fruit, pour yogurt mixture over and toss lightly. Serve immediately. Serves 6-8.

Barbecued spareribs

This is a one-dish meal in Vietnam. Usually it is roasted over red-hot coals; it may also be roasted in a hot oven. Fish sauce is used in many South-East Asian dishes, it is available in most good Oriental grocery shops, sold as nam pla, nuoc cham or patis.

6 spring onions
2 cloves garlic with 2 tablespoons sugar
4 tablespoons fish sauce
Freshly ground black pepper
1kg pork spareribs
TO SERVE
Boiled rice
½ cucumber
Nuoc Cham Sauce

Finely chop the spring onions, including some of the green tops, and garlic with the sugar. Add the fish sauce and black pepper and mix well. Put the spareribs into a flat dish and spoon over the mixture, turning to coat thoroughly. Cover with plastic wrap, leave to marinate at least 2 hours.

Place on a rack in a roasting pan, spoon over the seasoning mixture and roast in a hot oven 200C (400F) for 35-40 minutes. Cut the ribs into strips. Put the rice in a serving dish, top with spareribs, decorate with sliced cucumber and sprinkle over a little of the Nuoc Cham Sauce. Accompany with the remaining sauce in a bowl. Serves 4.

Nuoc cham sauce

This hot tangy sauce accompanies most Vietnamese meals — it is sprinkled over pork, chicken and fish dishes. If you don't have a pestle and mortar, chop very finely by hand then mash with the back of a spoon.

2 garlic cloves
1 fresh red chili or 4 dried
2 tablespoons sugar
Juice of 1 lime
4 tablespoons fish sauce
1 cup water

Pound the garlic, chilis and sugar, using a pestle and mortar (or finely chop together). Add the remaining ingredients and mix well to combine. Use as required.

Prawn curry

Every South-East Asian cuisine has its version of prawn curry. This is a Sri Lankan one.

500g shelled and deveined green prawns
Juice of 1 lime or ½ lemon
¼ teaspoon saffron threads, soaked in 1 tablespoon hot water
5 garlic cloves, crushed
3 curry leaves or 1 small bay leaf
2 teaspoons grated fresh ginger
2 cloves
1 teaspoon cinnamon
½ teaspoon fenugreek
½ teaspoon crushed cardamom seed
¼ teaspoon cayenne (or to taste)
2 tablespoons peanut or coconut oil
2 large tomatoes, peeled, seeded and chopped
1 cup coconut milk
Salt

Mix prawns with lime or lemon juice, saffron and water and toss well. Add garlic, curry leaves, ginger and spices. Mix and stand, covered, at room temperature for 1 hour.

Heat oil in a frying pan, add prawn mixture and saute briskly for 2 minutes or until prawns turn pink. Lift prawns out with a slotted spoon and set them aside. Add tomato to the pan and fry gently for 3 minutes, then add coconut milk and cook until the mixture thickens a little. Add salt to taste. Return prawns to pan and heat through. Serve at once. Serves 2-3 with rice.

Sri Lankan saffron rice

A delicate golden pilau scented with ginger, coconut, precious saffron and other spices.

1 cup basmati rice
2 tablespoons ghee
2 onions, chopped
3 curry leaves or 1 small bay leaf
1 teaspoon grated fresh ginger
½ teaspoon salt
2 cups coconut milk (see special ingredients)
¼ teaspoon saffron threads, soaked in 1 tablespoon hot water
10 peppercorns, 10 cardamom pods, 8 cloves and a 5cm stick cinnamon, tied in a cheesecloth bag
TO GARNISH
Sliced hard-boiled egg
Cashew nuts, fried in a little ghee
Chopped parlsey
Lime or lemon wedges

Put rice into a sieve and rinse under cold water until water runs clear. Set aside. Heat ghee in a saucepan and add onion, curry leaves or bay leaf, ginger and salt. Saute until onion is golden. Add rice and cook briskly, stirring, until rice is translucent.

Stir in the coconut milk, saffron and water and add the bag of spices. Bring to the boil, turn heat down and cover. Simmer 10-15 minutes or until liquid is absorbed and rice is tender. Remove and discard bag of spices, fluff up the rice with a fork and turn it on to a serving platter, mounding it. Garnish with sliced hard-boiled egg, cashews, parsley and lime or lemon wedges. Serves 6.

Chicken with cellophane noodles

In Vietnam this light dish is traditionally accompanied by a salad of sliced tomatoes and onions dressed with a little white vinegar, a sprinkling of sugar, salt and pepper.

2 whole chicken breasts
4 chicken thighs
2 tablespoons oil
2 green shallots, sliced
2 tablespoons fish sauce
1 tablespoon light soy sauce
Freshly ground black pepper
½ cup water
125g cellophane noodles, soaked in hot water for 30 minutes

Remove skin and bones from breasts and thighs of chicken and cut flesh into 2.5cm pieces.

Heat a wok or frying pan, add the oil and swirl to coat the surface. Add the chicken pieces and shallots, and stir-fry for 2 to 3 minutes.

Add the fish and soy sauces, a grinding of black pepper and the water. Bring to the boil and simmer for a few minutes. Add the drained noodles, return to the boil and cook for a further 3 minutes. Serves 4-6.

Squid with vinegar and garlic

This is a variation of adobo, which is almost the Filipino national dish. Adobo may be made with meat, fowl or seafood, but is always sharp-flavored and garlicky

750g squid
MARINADE
12 cloves garlic, crushed
¼ cup white vinegar
¼ cup light soy sauce
¼ teaspoon freshly ground black pepper
SAUCE
4 cloves garlic, crushed
5 tablespoons oil
1 large onion, finely chopped
250g tomatoes, peeled, seeded and chopped
Salt and freshly ground black pepper to taste

Prepare the squid (see note at end of recipe), reserving the ink sacs. Cut bodies of squid into 4 cm squares and score with the point of the knife in a diamond pattern.

Combine marinade ingredients in a pottery, glass or enamel-lined bowl and squeeze in the ink from the reserved sacs. Add squid, cover and stand for 4 hours at room temperature or overnight in the refrigerator.

Make the sauce. Cook garlic in oil until pale gold, then add onion and cook, stirring, until onion is translucent. Add tomatoes and stir over medium heat for 3 minutes. Season with salt and pepper.

Add squid and marinade to the sauce, bring the mixture to the boil, reduce heat and simmer, covered, for 10-15 minutes or until squid is tender.

Above: A beautifully presented Asian meal — Sri Lankan Saffron Rice, Prawn Curry and Fruit And Nut Compote.

Serve with rice and chili-flavored vinegar. Serves 6-8.

TO PREPARE SQUID: Pull out the head of the squid with the tentacles from the mantle (body). Remove eyes, ink sacs and parrot-like beak at the base of the tentacles. Set ink sacs aside and discard eyes and beak. Pull the fins off the squid. Remove and discard any yellowish deposit and the long internal quill bone (which looks like hard cellophane) from the squid. Rub off the skin from the mantle and fins. Wash and dry the squid inside and out.

CHILI-FLAVORED VINEGAR: Put 1 cup palm vinegar, Japanese rice vinegar or white vinegar into a glass jar and add 2 fresh or dried chilis, slit down the sides. Stand for at least 4 hours or up to 48 hours before removing chilis. If a hotter vinegar is desired, crush chilis slightly.

Sweet mouthfuls

In Scotland one of the sweet-treats dear to every child's heart is tablet, a fudge-like confection. Tablet is made with butter, sugar and sweetened condensed milk. In Italy, lucky are the bambini who sit on their grandmother's knee and celebrate the Lord's day with ladyfingers drenched in marsala and oozing a voluptuous froth of zabaglione. A Greek sweet offered is often a lovely rich shortbread taken from a jar, drenched in icing sugar. In America you may be offered a hermit or buttery caramel. The whole world, it seems, has an answer to that age-long quest for something sweet. It's always nice to be able to produce a special something for those 'sweet tooths'.

Tablet

1¼ cups milk
1kg sugar
30g butter
1 can sweetened condensed milk
A few drops of vanilla essence

Put milk, sugar and butter in a heavy saucepan. Stir gently over a low heat until the sugar dissolves, about 20 minutes. Add condensed milk and bring to the boil. Boil over medium heat for 25 minutes or until like fudge in color. Add vanilla essence and allow to cool for a few minutes. Beat for about 10 minutes, or until mixture is thick. Pour into well-greased lamington tin 28 x 18cm. When set, cut into squares, wrap in greaseproof paper. Makes 60. Store in airtight containers.

Walnut crescents

250g butter, softened
⅓ cup castor sugar
1 egg yolk
3 cups flour, sifted
½ cup finely chopped walnuts
Sifted icing sugar

Cream butter with castor sugar until light and fluffy. Add egg yolk and beat well. Stir in flour alternately with nuts. Knead mixture lightly and form into a ball. Roll small pieces of dough into balls the size of large hazelnuts. Roll under the palm of the hand to form a small tube and then shape into crescents. Place on greased baking trays and bake in a preheated slow oven 150C (300F) for 12-15 minutes. While still warm, toss biscuits in icing sugar and place on wire racks to cool. Serve in tiny paper patty cases, if you wish. Makes 70.

GREEK SHORTBREADS: Roll dough in balls, push a whole clove in each one and bake as above.

Strawberry conserve

1kg small strawberries, hulled
1kg sugar
2 tablespoons lemon juice
Finely sliced peel of one lemon, including white pith

Layer strawberries and sugar in a large bowl, cover and leave 24 hours for sugar to extract juice. Place in a large heavy saucepan with lemon juice and peel in a muslin bag tied to saucepan handle. Bring to a rapid boil and boil 5 minutes. Remove bag of rind, reserving it and return conserve mixture to bowl. Cover and leave 8 hours, then replace in saucepan with bag of peel and boil until setting point is reached (when a little of the liquid dropped on to a cold plate and cooled appears stiff and wrinkled if pushed with the finger). Remove from heat, remove bag of peel and allow to cool slightly. Stir gently to distribute fruit evenly and pour into hot sterilised jars. Cool and seal. Makes four 500g jars.

Butter-nut caramels

Caramels should be soft and chewy; the longer you cook them, the harder they become, so be sure to stop when they are the color of milky coffee.

125g butter
2 tablespoons golden syrup
1½ cups sugar
1 x 400g can sweetened condensed milk
½ cup water
Large pinch cream of tartar
½ cup chopped walnuts
1 teaspoon vanilla

Place all ingredients except vanilla in a heavy saucepan and stir constantly over fairly low heat until mixture is pale brown — a little dropped into cold water should form a

Left: For the sweet tooth — sugar and fruit for Strawberry Conserve, Sultana Cake, Tablet, Butter-Nut Caramels and Greek Shortbreads.

firm but pliable ball. Remove from heat. Stir in vanilla and nuts and pour into a buttered 15cm square tin. When nearly set, mark into squares. Wrap squares in wax paper or cellophane when cold. Makes 36.

Sultana cake

Excellent for lunch-boxes, with tea or coffee, to take with you on a picnic, or simply to have on hand to offer guests when they drop in. A moist cake that will keep for up to 10 days when stored in an airtight container.

250g butter
1 cup sugar
3 eggs
⅔ cup milk
1½ cups sultanas
3 tablespoons almonds, blanched and chopped
3 tablespoons chopped mixed candied peel
3 cups flour
1½ teaspoons baking powder

Beat butter with sugar until light and fluffy. Add eggs and mix well. Stir in milk gradually, then add sultanas, almonds and peel. Fold in flour and baking powder sifted together. Spoon into a greased and bottom-lined 20cm round or square cake tin. Bake in a preheated moderately slow oven 160C (325F) for about 1½ hours or until a skewer inserted in centre comes out clean. Cool on a wire rack.

Chocolate truffles

Very rich, very French and very moreish. Shaped to resemble the little 'black diamond' the French worship. Make well ahead of time and store in the refrigerator, covered. Delicious with after-dinner coffee.

1 tablespoon instant coffee powder
250g dark chocolate, broken up
3 tablespoons boiling water
125g cold unsalted butter
3 tablespoons brandy or rum
Cocoa powder

Combine instant coffee, chocolate and boiling water in top of double saucepan (or heatproof bowl) over hot water. Heat until chocolate has softened. Cut butter into small pieces and beat into chocolate mixture gradually, a piece at a time. Beat in brandy or rum. Chill until firm. Break off pieces of chilled mixture and toss in cocoa powder. Place truffles in paper cases, arrange in an airtight container and store in refrigerator. Makes about 18.

Cinnamon toast

How long since you've enjoyed this childhood favorite?

4 thick slices fresh white bread
30g butter
2 tablespoons sugar
1 teaspoon cinnamon

Toast bread under a preheated hot grill. Butter each slice, then sprinkle with mixture of sugar and cinnamon. Return to grill until topping bubbles. Remove crusts and cut into fingers or triangles. Serves 2-4.

Orange french toast

This is a way of combining egg and toast in one delicious dish. Cut the toast into fingers or triangles, so it looks interesting and can be picked up in the fingers if wished.

1 egg
1 tablespoon orange juice
1 teaspoon grated orange rind
2 slices bread
Butter for frying
A little honey, jam or maple syrup for serving

Beat the egg with the orange juice and stir in the grated orange rind. Pour into a flat plate.

Soak the bread slices in the mixture, turning to soak both sides, until it is all absorbed.

Heat enough butter in a frying pan to cover the base, and brown the bread slices on both sides, turning with an egg slice. The outside should be nice and crisp, the inside soft.

Spread the toast with a little honey or jam, or pour a little maple syrup over and cut into fingers. Makes 1 generous serving.

Pecan cookies

1¼ cups flour
¼ teaspoon bicarbonate of soda
½ teaspoon salt
125g butter
¼ cup firmly packed brown sugar
¼ cup castor sugar
1 egg, beaten
1 teaspoon vanilla
1 x 100g packet Choc-Bits
½ cup chopped pecans
36 pecan halves

Sift flour, bicarbonate of soda and salt together. Cream butter with sugars until light and fluffy. Add egg and vanilla and beat well. Stir in sifted dry ingredients, Choc-Bits and nuts. Drop teaspoonfuls on to greased baking trays, leaving room for spreading, and top each with a pecan half. Bake in a preheated moderate oven 180C (350F) for 10 minutes. Cool on wire racks. Makes about 36.

Coconut cones

½ x 400g can condensed milk
1 teaspoon vanilla essence
2 cups desiccated coconut
Glace cherries for decoration (optional)

Combine the condensed milk, vanilla essence and coconut in a bowl, and mix well. Drop the mixture on to greased baking tray with a teaspoon 2.5cm apart.

Decorate with halved glaced cherries if wished. Bake in preheated moderate oven 180C (350F) for 10 minutes or until lightly tinted. Allow to cool on tray.

Pecan pralines

I became hooked on this Southern confection while visiting Louisiana.

500g light brown sugar
1/8 teaspoon salt
¾ cup evaporated milk or cream
1 tablespoon butter or margarine
2 cups pecan halves

Mix sugar, salt, evaporated milk and butter in a 10-cup heavy saucepan. Cover and stir over low heat until sugar is dissolved. Add pecans and cook over medium heat to soft ball stage, stirring constantly. Remove from heat and let cool 5 minutes. Stir rapidly until mixture begins to thicken and coat pecans

Below: Pecan Cookies (right) and Louisiana-inspired Pecan Pralines.

lightly. Drop rapidly from a teaspoon on to aluminium foil or lightly buttered baking sheet to form patties. (If the candy becomes too stiff to handle, stir in a few drops of hot water.) Let stand until cool and set. Makes about 44 small pralines.

TO TEST FOR SOFT BALL (WITHOUT THERMOMETER): Drop a small quantity of mixture into ice water. It forms a soft ball which does not disintegrate but flattens out of its own accord when picked up with the fingers.

Note: If liked, 2 tablespoons sherry, bourbon or brandy may be added in place of equal quantity of cream.

Chocolate fudge

An American confection, rich and chocolatey with just the right crunch of nuts.

1½ cups sugar
⅓ cup evaporated milk
125g cream cheese, softened and chopped
1 cup chopped marshmallows
180g dark chocolate, chopped
1 cup chopped walnuts
½ cup mixed dried fruit
½ teaspoon vanilla or 1 tablespoon brandy

Combine sugar and milk in a heavy saucepan. Stir over medium heat until boiling. Add cheese and marshmallows and cook, stirring, for 5 minutes.

Remove from heat and stir in chocolate, walnuts, dried fruit and vanilla or brandy. Pour into an oiled 18cm square cake tin. Cool, cut into squares and store in refrigerator. Makes about 24 large pieces.

Powder puffs

Speed and gentleness are essential in making powder puffs as this very light mixture quickly loses its volume if left to stand. The sponge biscuits are crisp when cooked and will keep in an airtight tin for a week.

2 eggs
½ cup castor sugar
3 tablespoons plain flour
3 tablespoons cornflour
1 teaspoon baking powder
¾ cup cream, whipped and sweetened
Raspberry jam (optional)
Icing sugar

Grease and flour 3 baking trays. Set oven temperature to hot 220C (425F). Beat eggs until light and gradually add the sugar beating until thick and creamy. Sift flour, cornflour and baking powder and fold in lightly.

Put mixture into a piping bag fitted with a 1.3cm nozzle and pipe rounds, placing them well apart on the greased trays, or you can drop the mixture from a teaspoon. Bake in hot oven until evenly but lightly colored. Lift carefully on to a wire rack to cool.

Before serving join together with whipped cream and thinly spread raspberry jam if wished. Sprinkle with icing sugar, place in covered container and store in the refrigerator for at least two hours. Makes 18.

Lemon butter

If you have a surplus of lemons, why not make this lovely lemon butter. It is excellent as a filling for tartlets, sponge cake, little cakes or as a spread.

3 lemons
6 sugar lumps
½ cup sugar
30g butter or margarine
2 teaspoons cornflour
1 tablespoon water
2 eggs

Wash and dry lemons. Rub sugar lumps over lemons until they are saturated with oil from skins. Put sugar lumps into the saucepan with sugar, butter and strained juice of lemons.

Place over low heat and stir continuously until sugar is dissolved. Add cornflour blended with water and bring to the boil. Remove from heat. Beat eggs in a china bowl on top of a double boiler and slowly add hot lemon mixture, beating continuously.

Place over simmering water and cook 10 minutes, stirring often. Lemon butter should be thick enough to coat a spoon.

Pour into hot jars and seal. This lemon butter will keep for several weeks stored in refrigerator. Makes about 1½ cups.

Hermits

These little cookies from America have a spongy cake-like texture.

¼ cup raisins
¼ cup chopped nuts
2 cups flour
60g butter
½ cup castor sugar
½ teaspoon salt
2 eggs
½ cup molasses
½ teaspoon bicarbonate of soda
¼ teaspoon cream of tartar
1 teaspoon cinnamon
½ teaspoon ground cloves
¼ teaspoon mace
¼ teaspoon nutmeg

Toss raisins and nuts in ¼ cup of the flour and set aside. Cream butter with sugar until light and fluffy. Add salt, eggs and molasses and beat well. Mix together remaining 1¾ cups flour, the bicarbonate of soda, cream of tartar, cinnamon, cloves, mace and nutmeg and add to creamed mixture. Beat thoroughly, then stir in raisin and nut mixture. Spread in a greased 25 x 30cm swiss roll tin or drop in teaspoonfuls on greased baking trays. Bake in a preheated moderate oven 180C (350F) for 15-20 minutes if using swiss roll tin or for 8-10 minutes for drop cookies. In each case, when baked the tops should be firm and golden and centres chewy. Cut mixture in swiss roll tin into 5cm squares while still warm. Makes about 30 squares or 60 drops.

CONCORD HERMITS: Substitute 1 cup firmly packed brown sugar for castor sugar and molasses and add ½ cup sour cream. You may also add 3 tablespoons chopped mixed candied peel if you wish.

Golden-shred marmalade

A special breakfast treat and an Englishman's idea of what every good breakfast table should contain — toast with marmalade.

1 grapefruit
2 lemons
1 orange
7 cups water
Approximately 1.5 kg sugar

Wash and dry fruit. Use a vegetable peeler to cut away fine outside rind. Cut into 4cm lengths, shred finely. Put into a piece of muslin and tie, leaving plenty of room.

Halve fruits, squeeze out juice, put in container, cover and refrigerate. Empty seeds into a large glass, enamel or china bowl. Chop all flesh and pith left from fruit into small pieces, and add to seeds with the water and bag of peel. Cover and stand overnight.

Next day, empty pulp into pan. Add juice and cook until pulp is very tender (about 1 hour). Remove bag of peel, retain. Strain pulp and liquid, as for a jelly, through a fine cloth. Do not disturb while draining, and do not press pulp. Leave until thoroughly drained.

Measure liquid, empty into clean pan, add the rinds, and heat gently. For each cup of pulp add a cup of sugar. Stir over low heat until sugar is dissolved, then bring to the boil and cook rapidly until setting point is reached — about 15-20 minutes.

Draw the pan off the heat and cool for about 15 minutes to distribute peel evenly, then ladle into warm, dry jars. Cover and seal.

Pancakes, crepes and fritters

Every country in the world has its own version of that good idea, the pancake. Pancakes are inexpensive, endlessly versatile — and everyone loves them. Widen your repertoire of these great basics — pancakes from Central Europe, from America and Asia — with their French cousins, crepes, which are finer than pancakes. They get their name from the delicate fabric crepe de chine. Included are some close friends like fritters and hotcakes.

Basic pancakes

1 cup flour
1 teaspoon baking powder
½ teaspoon salt
1 egg beaten
1½ cups milk
15g butter, melted
Oil for frying

Sift flour, baking powder and salt into a bowl. Make a well in the centre and add egg, milk and melted butter. Using a wooden spoon, gradually draw in flour. Beat well, cover and leave to stand for 1 hour.

Film base of pancake pan with oil, heat and pour off any surplus oil. Pour batter into a jug and pour in enough batter to coat the base of the pan, tilting pan to spread batter evenly. Cook until bubbles appear on the surface, about 1 minute, then flip over, using a metal spatula.

Drop cooked pancake on to a clean tea-towel, fold ends over to cover and continue making pancakes in the same way, stacking them with a layer of greaseproof paper between each one and folding towel over to cover again. Makes 10-12 x 18cm pancakes.

Basic crepes

1¼ cups flour
Pinch salt
3 eggs, beaten
1½ cups milk
1 tablespoon brandy
2 teaspoons melted butter
Extra butter for frying

Sift flour and salt into a bowl. Make a well in centre and add eggs and milk. Using a wooden spoon, stir from the centre, drawing in flour.

Beat well, then stir in brandy and melted butter. Cover and stand 1 hour. Strain if necessary, as the batter must be free of lumps.

To make crepes, heat a little butter in an 18cm crepe pan and pour off excess. Using a jug, pour about 1 tablespoon of batter into the pan. Rotate pan quickly to coat bottom thinly and evenly, then pour off any excess batter. Heat gently and when small bubbles appear (after about 1 minute), use a spatula to flip crepe over. Cook for about 30 seconds.

Place crepes on a clean tea-towel and fold ends over to cover. Continue making the crepes, stacking with a layer of greaseproof paper between each one. Makes 20-24.

The pancake pan

Use a heavy, flat pan, made from cast-iron or aluminium with a silverstone lining, with sides about 1cm high and about 18cm in diameter.

It should be kept only for making pancakes and their variations. Do not wash after use; simply rub it with paper towels and a few drops of oil. If the pan becomes sticky, rub with salt first and finish with oil.

TO SEASON A NEW PAN: Fill with oil and heat to smoking point. Turn off heat and stand 24 hours. Pour off oil, wipe well with paper towels.

To store pancakes and crepes

They can be made freshly each time they are required but they also freeze well. Stack groups of 8 or 10 (depending on how many you intend serving at one time), separating each with a square of greaseproof paper. Wrap in foil and place in freezer bags, then store in the freezer.

Right: Hotcakes are superb with bacon and great with maple syrup.

Hotcakes

Americans are devoted to pancakes and have invented many variations. Hotcakes are served with butter and maple syrup as an accompaniment to bacon or sausages. They're good, too, spread with butter and honey.

2 cups self-raising flour
½ teaspoon salt
2 teaspoons sugar
3 eggs
1¾ cups milk
Dash vanilla essence
3 tablespoons melted butter

Sift flour and salt together into a bowl and sprinkle sugar over. Beat eggs, milk and vanilla together and pour over flour. Stir until just blended. The batter will be lumpy. Stir in melted butter. Heat a heavy, greased frying pan or griddle until a drop of cold water, flicked on to the surface, bounces and sputters. Put batter on in spoonfuls, a little distance apart and cook until bubbles appear on the surface and the undersides are lightly browned. Turn and brown other sides. Serve in a stack with butter in between. Makes 18-20 10cm hotcakes.

Hungarian dessert cake

Marvellous for special-occasion meals. Pancakes are layered with sweet fillings and baked with a coating of meringue.

12-14 crepes or pancakes
¾ cup apricot or plum jam
125g dark chocolate, grated
1 cup cream, whipped
125g flaked almonds, toasted
1 cup chopped raisins
4 egg whites
½ cup sugar
2 tablespoons slivered or flaked almonds

Place one crepe or pancake on a greased baking tray. Spread with a little jam and sprinkle with chocolate. Place another pancake on top, spread with cream and sprinkle with toasted flaked almonds and a few raisins.

Continue with these layers until pancakes are used up, leaving the top one plain. Beat egg whites to a froth, then beat in sugar a little at a time until they form firm peaks.

Swirl egg white mixture over pancakes, making sure they are completely covered. Strew slivered or flaked almonds over the top. Bake in a preheated very hot oven 220C (425F) for 3-4 minutes or until meringue is lightly tipped with brown. Serves 6.

Sicilian pancakes

250g ricotta cheese
2 tablespoons mixed candied peel
Grated rind 1 orange
1 tablespoon castor sugar
10-12 crepes or panckes
Finely chopped walnuts
Sifted icing sugar
Whipped cream to serve

Combine ricotta, peel, orange rind and sugar. Place a spoonful of ricotta mixture into each crepe. Fold into small parcels and place in a buttered ovenproof dish. Heat in a preheated very low oven 100C (210F) for 10 minutes. Serve sprinkled with walnuts and icing sugar, with a bowl of whipped cream. Serves 5-6.

VARIATIONS: Fill crepes with sweetened stewed apple flavored with cinnamon or sweetened stewed peaches, plums or apricots, instead of ricotta mixture, then heat as above.

Fill crepes with sweetened chestnut puree flavored with a little rum, instead of ricotta mixture, then heat as above.

Crabmeat crepes

6 green shallots, finely chopped
60g butter
1 x 185g can crabmeat, drained and flaked
1 egg yolk, lightly beaten
2 teaspoons dry sherry
4 hard-boiled eggs, chopped
2 teaspoons snipped chives
2 cups cream sauce
8-12 crepes or pancakes
¾ cup grated gruyere cheese

Cook shallots gently in butter until softened. Add crab, remove from heat.

Fold egg yolk, sherry, chopped eggs, chives and crab mixture into the cream sauce. Spread on crepes, roll up and arrange in one layer in a buttered, ovenproof serving dish.

Cover dish with foil and warm in a preheated moderate oven 180C (350F) for 15 minutes.

Uncover crepes and sprinkle with grated cheese. Return to oven and bake, uncovered, 5 minutes. Serve immediately. Serves 4-6.

Cream Sauce

2 cups milk
1 bay leaf
½ onion, chopped
5 black peppercorns
60g butter
4 tablespoons flour
½ cup cream
Salt and white pepper

Heat milk slowly in a saucepan over low heat with bay leaf, onion and peppercorns. When bubbles form around edge, remove from heat, cover and stand for 10 minutes.

Melt butter over low heat, stir in flour and cook, stirring, for 1 minute. Remove from heat, cool a little, then strain in warm milk and cream. Stir until smoothly blended, then return to heat and stir until boiling. Season with salt and pepper.

Sweet batter

Use for fruit fritters.

2 egg yolks
⅔ cup milk
1 tablespoon melted butter
1 cup plain flour
1 tablespoon castor sugar
2 egg whites

Beat together egg yolks, milk and melted butter. Sift flour and sugar into a bowl, make a well in the centre, stir in egg mixture, gradually working in the flour, beating to a smooth batter. Allow to stand several hours before using. Fold in stiffly beaten egg whites just before using.

Basic fritter batter

Use for small seafood fritters. This amount will coat about two cups food.

2 cups plain flour
2 teaspoons baking powder
½ teaspoon salt
3 eggs
¼ cup milk

Sift flour, baking powder and salt into a bowl, beat eggs with milk. Make a well in centre of the flour, add egg mixture in a steady pouring stream, stirring in the flour gradually and beat to a smooth batter, or put flour in blender, add beaten eggs and milk and blend until smooth. Stand for several hours before using.

To deep fry fritters

Use an electric deep-fryer, deep wide saucepan or deep frying pan. Half-fill with oil, making sure it is deep enough to float the fritters but allowing plenty of room for the oil to boil up when the food is added. Heat oil slowly to the required temperature. At 185C (360F) a cube of day-old bread will brown in 45 seconds. At 190C (375F) the bread will brown in 30 seconds.

Place food into oil in batches of 5-6 pieces, fry until golden, turning if necessary, lift out and drain on crumpled paper towels. Use a slotted spoon, wire skimmer or tongs to lower food into the oil and remove when cooked. Remove any little bits of batter to prevent burning. After use, strain oil through a disposable cloth and store, tightly sealed, in the refrigerator or a very cool place.

Above: Melt-in-the-mouth Churros (rear) and Fruit Sauce; Beignets Souffles.

TYPES OF OIL TO USE: The most efficient oil for deep frying is the type called solid oil, which has been treated to be solid at room temperature. Solid oils can be heated to high temperatures without smoking and can usually be used 3-5 times before they begin to darken and break down.

Peanut oil is also a good oil for deep-frying as it reaches high temperatures before smoking and usually can be used several times.

Polyunsaturated oils are preferred by many people for health reasons, and can be used for deep frying but, since they break down more readily than solid or peanut oil, will probably last for only 1-2 fryings. Fritters which are twice-fried are cooked first at a slightly lower temperature, then finished in very hot oil. (see Churros and Beignets Souffles)

Churros (Spanish fritters)

In Spain these freshly fried puffy strings of light choux pastry called churros are sold by street vendors and are great favorites. In restaurants and at home a fresh fruit sauce may accompany them.

CHOUX PASTRY
60g butter
1 cup water
Pinch salt
1 cup plain flour
4 x 55g eggs
Oil for deep frying
TO FINISH
Icing sugar
Fruit sauce

Cut butter into small pieces and put into pan with water and salt. Heat until boiling and add flour all at once. Stir vigorously with wooden spoon until paste is smooth and no longer clings to the pan or spoon. Cool and gradually add slightly beaten eggs. Beat thoroughly until smooth and glossy. Put into piping bag fitted with a fine star tube.

Heat oil for deep frying and pipe mixture from bag into oil, cutting off 5cm lengths with oiled knife. Cook only a few at a time. When pale golden, drain. Reheat oil, return churros and, when cooked, drain again on absorbent paper. Serve at once, sprinkled with icing sugar and with fruit sauce.

FRUIT SAUCE: Puree lightly stewed or canned drained fruit. Flavor with brandy, rum or kirsch.

Crepes suzette

8 crepes
30g butter, melted
4 cubes sugar
2 oranges
Extra 60g butter, softened
2 tablespoons Grand Marnier, Cointreau or curacao
Sifted icing sugar for dusting
3 tablespoons brandy

Prepare and make crepes. Brush cooked crepes with melted butter and keep warm in oven.

Rub each sugar cube over skin of oranges to remove oil. This process saturates sugar with oil from the orange rind and the oranges will look as though their rinds have been grated. Crush sugar and work in softened butter and liqueur.

Spread each warm crepe with orange butter and fold into a triangle. Arrange crepes overlapping down centre of a heated serving dish and dust with icing sugar.

Heat brandy in a small saucepan, set alight and pour over the crepes. Serve at once. Serves 4.

Beignets souffles

These light and fluffy fritters of choux pastry are the French version of Spanish Churros. Fry the quantity you want to serve until pale golden, drain, then just before serving return to hot oil for a few minutes. Twice-frying helps when you want to serve a whole quantity for a dinner party.

1 quantity Choux Pastry (see Churros)
2 teaspoons grated orange rind
2 tablespoons Grand Marnier or Cointreau
Oil for deep frying
Icing sugar
Orange Sauce

Prepare choux pastry, adding orange rind and liqueur along with eggs. Heat oil for deep frying until a bread cube will brown lightly in 60 seconds. With a dessertspoon or large teaspoon take up portions of the paste. Dip another spoon in the hot fat and mould off pieces the size of a walnut into the hot fat. Cook 5 to 6 at a time, turning over in fat from time to time.

When pale golden (3-4 minutes) drain on crumpled kitchen paper. Heat oil again until a bread cube will brown lightly in 30 seconds, return beignets and fry until golden brown, about 3-4 minutes. Drain on crumpled kitchen paper.

Pile the fritters on to a serving dish and sift icing sugar over. Serve with Orange Sauce and with whipped cream, if desired. Serves 6.

ORANGE SAUCE: Mix 1 cup orange marmalade with ⅓ cup orange-flavored liqueur and 2 tablespoons lemon juice in a small saucepan. Heat gently, stirring often, until marmalade melts.

Prune fritters

This is a German speciality called Schlosser-Burben or Locksmith's Apprentices. A delicious dessert for family or friends.

1 quantity Sweet Batter
250g dessert prunes
15-20 blanched almonds
Oil for deep frying
½ cup grated dark chocolate
½ cup sifted icing sugar

Prepare the batter. Remove stones from prunes, doing as little damage to prunes as possible; they should remain in one piece. Stuff each stoned prune with a blanched almond and restore to prune shape.

Heat oil, dip prunes in batter and deep fry until golden. Drain on crumpled kitchen paper. Serve while hot, dredge with grated chocolate and icing sugar. Serves 4 to 6.

Lemon fritters

A memorable accompaniment to roast or grilled chicken or duck.

2 lemons
½ teaspoon salt
Pinch bicarbonate of soda
Oil for deep frying
1 quantity Basic Beer Batter

Place whole lemons in a saucepan with salt and soda and cover with water. Bring to the boil and boil for 30 minutes.

Drain well and cut lemons lengthwise into quarters. Cut skin and pith from quarters, remove any pips and cut each again in half.

Heat oil for deep frying to 190C (375F). Dip each piece of lemon into batter and deep-fry until golden-brown. Drain on crumpled paper towels and serve at once. Serve 2-3 fritters per person. Makes 16 fritters.

Corn fritters

2 eggs, beaten
¾ cup milk
1 teaspoon grated onion
1 tablespoon chopped parsley
2½ cups sifted plain flour
2 teaspoons baking powder
1 teaspoon salt
2 tablespoons melted butter
2 cups canned cream-style corn
Oil for deep frying

Combine eggs, milk, onion and parsley. Add sifted dry ingredients, butter and corn. Mix well. Drop batter by tablespoonfuls into deep hot fat 185C (360F). Fry for 3-4 minutes or until golden brown. Drain on kitchen paper, serve hot. Makes about 24 fritters.

Note: Fritter batter may be dropped by tablespoonfuls into 2 tablespoonfuls hot oil and shallow-fried on each side until golden brown.

Basic beer batter

Used for meat, seafood and vegetable fritters, also for some sweet fritters. Note that soda water may be used in place of beer.

1 cup plain flour
Pinch salt
2 eggs
60g butter, melted
1 cup beer or soda water

Sift flour with salt into a bowl and make well in the centre. Separate 1 egg and beat the yolk with the other whole egg. Pour into the well with the melted butter. Stir from the centre, incorporating flour gradually and adding beer or soda water little by little, until mixture is smooth. Cover and stand 1 hour.

Just before using, whisk the remaining egg white to a firm snow and fold into the batter. Makes enough to coat about 2 cups prepared food.

Fruity pikelets

You can mix and cook a pan of pikelets in about the same time it takes to perk the coffee!

1 cup self-raising flour
Pinch salt
2 tablespoons sugar
1 egg
1 cup milk
1 tablespoon mixed dried fruit, finely chopped
30g butter
1 teaspoon golden syrup
A little oil for greasing

Sift flour and salt into a bowl and add sugar. Beat egg and milk together and stir into flour with fruit. Melt butter and golden syrup together and stir over low heat until melted, then add to mixture.

Grease a griddle or shallow frying pan with a little oil, and when it is hot drop in batter in spoonfuls (about a scant tablespoon), a little apart. Cook over medium heat until the underside is browned and small bubbles appear on the surface, then turn and brown the other side.

Serve warm with butter or cold with jam and whipped cream. Makes about 20 pikelets.

Right: Beignets Souffles with Orange Sauce, a dessert to admire.

SPECIALITE
ANGERS
FRANCE

Memories of India

It is impossible to visit India and not be changed for the rest of your life. I have had three totally memorable holidays in India and for me, an Indian reminiscence includes Indian food. Indian cooking is famous the world over. It is so varied and subtle that it enjoys a reputation matched only by the Chinese and French. It was in India that I discovered that vegetarians can enjoy the best food in the world. Friends introduced me to leading Indian food writers and hostesses who shared their skills and knowledge with me. From them I learned to make many of their great dishes. They also taught me that one or two days a week on vegetarian food was not only a nutritious, healthy pattern for everyone, but because these vegetarian dishes are so delicious the family looks forward to them.

Using chili

The heat of fresh chilis and chili powder varies from one kind to another. As a general rule, the smaller the variety of chili, the hotter. The hottest parts of the pod are the seeds and veins, so if you don't like your food fiery, eliminate these.

A ripe red chili gives a different flavor from a green one of the same variety.

Personal taste for fiery flavor varies too, of course. If you don't like food with too much 'bite', use only half or less of the specified amount of chili at first. Peel fresh chilis as you would any pepper.

Spiced prawns in coconut milk

Coconut brings out the flavor of the prawns and adds creamy texture to the sauce.

3 tablespoons ghee
1 medium onion, sliced
3 garlic cloves, sliced
2 teaspoons ground coriander
1 teaspoon turmeric
1 teaspoon chili powder
½ teaspoon ground ginger
½ teaspoon salt
½ freshly ground black pepper
2 tablespoons vinegar
1 cup coconut milk
500g shelled prawns (cooked or raw)
2 tablespoons tomato paste

Melt the ghee in a heavy pan, add the onion and garlic and fry gently until soft. Mix the spices and seasoning to a paste with the vinegar, add to the pan and fry for a further 3 minutes, stirring constantly.

Stir in the coconut milk and simmer, stirring, for 5 minutes. Add the prawns and tomato paste and simmer 2 minutes until the prawns are coated with the thick sauce (if using raw prawns, cook until they become opaque). Serve immediately. Serves 4.

COCONUT MILK: For directions on how to make, see page 142.

Mixed pilau

Indian cooks consider colorful garnishes an all-important part of the presentation of a meal. This pilau is sometimes served scattered with pink rose petals.

1 tablespoon red lentils
1½ cups long grain rice
2 onions
2 large potatoes
3 tablespoons ghee
¼ cup roasted unsalted peanuts
½ cup roasted unsalted cashews
¼ cup raisins
Pinch ground cloves
¼ teaspoon ground cardamom
1 teaspoon ground cinnamon
1½ teaspoons salt
¼ teaspoon turmeric
2 cups water
1 cup cooked green peas

Soak lentils in hot water to cover for 30 minutes, drain. Rinse rice in a sieve under cold running water until water runs clear, drain. Slice onions lengthwise and separate into strips. Peel potatoes and cut into thick slices.

Heat half the ghee in a heavy pan and fry onions until golden brown. Remove them with a slotted spoon to a plate, add potato slices to the pan and fry until they are cooked through and a little crisp. Remove slices with a slotted spoon and keep warm. Fry peanuts, cashews and raisins separately in the same pan and set them aside.

Melt remaining ghee in the pan, add cloves, cardamom and cinnamon and stir 1 minute. Add lentils, fry 2 minutes, add salt, rice and turmeric and stir until rice is light brown in color.

Stir in water and half the fried onions. Cover and cook gently until liquid is absorbed and rice and lentils are tender. Add peas and mix through gently with a fork.

Turn the pilau on to a large heated serving dish and surround with fried potato. Spread nuts and raisins on top and sprinkle with remaining fried onions. Serves 6.

MIXED PILAU WITH EGGS: To make the pilau into a complete main dish, 6 eggs may be hard-boiled, halved and arranged round the edge before sprinkling the dish with fried onions.

Left: Spiced Prawns In Coconut Milk, Mixed Pilau and Hyderabad Chicken, with pappadams and tasty Sambals.

Sambals and other accompaniments

Curries should be served with plenty of boiled rice and a few other accompaniments which offer a variety of flavors and textures. Chilled plain yogurt or a fresh chutney is popular. Pappadams (crisp lentil wafers) may be eaten as an accompaniment or crumbled over the curry. They are available packaged at delicatessens, health food shops and many supermarkets; fry one at a time in about 1cm of hot oil for only a few seconds on each side, and drain on paper towels.

Sambals may be red (heating) or white (cooling) — simply add chili or leave it out, according to your preference. Offer one or two of the following, plus a choice of commercial chutneys and nuts.

APPLE SAMBAL: Shredded apple plus a little chopped onion, a touch of vinegar and salt and chopped green chili or parsley.

CUCUMBER SAMBAL: Chilled plain yogurt or sour cream with finely diced cucumber folded through. Add salt to taste and crushed garlic.

TOMATO SAMBAL: Diced or sliced tomato with chopped onion, salt and lemon juice. Sprinkle with chopped chili, mint or coriander, grated ginger or shredded coconut.

POTATO SAMBAL: Skinned and diced boiled potato lightly mixed with chopped green shallot, chopped chili if liked and a little olive oil, salt and lemon juice.

BANANA, PLUM or MANGO SAMBAL: Green mangoes, firm plums or bananas, sliced or diced and mixed with salt and lemon juice to taste, plus chili if liked.

Hyderabad chicken

Use fresh coconut for this recipe, if possible.

125g ghee
1 large onion, sliced
2 cloves garlic, peeled and sliced
4 cardamom pods
4 whole cloves
2.5cm piece of cinnamon stick
2 teaspoons Garam Masala
1 teaspoon turmeric
1 teaspoon chili powder
1 teaspoon salt
1.5kg chicken, skinned and cut into 8 pieces (or use chicken joints, halved if large)
Flesh of ½ fresh coconut, thinly sliced, or ¾ cup shredded coconut
1 tablespoon tomato paste
1¼ cups water

Melt ghee in a heavy pan, add onion and garlic and fry gently until soft. Add spices and salt and fry, stirring, a further 3 minutes. Add chicken and brown on all sides, this should take about 10 minutes. Add coconut, tomato paste and water, stir well and bring to the boil.

Reduce heat, cover with a tight-fitting lid and simmer for 45 minutes or until chicken is tender. Serve hot. Serves 4.

Mint and coriander chutney

Quickly made fresh chutneys add a refreshing note to any curry and this is one of the nicest — rather like our mint sauce, but fresher tasting.

1 cup coriander leaves
1 cup mint leaves
1 teaspoon salt
1 teaspoon sugar
1 tablespoon water
1 tablespoon vinegar or lemon juice
1 green chili, sliced
½ cup plain yogurt

Place all the ingredients except yogurt in a blender and blend until fairly smooth. If making by hand, chop the mint, coriander and chili with the sugar and salt then gradually add the vinegar and water. Fold the yogurt through. Store in an airtight jar in the refrigerator.

Eggplant with coconut

Eggplant or brinjals, as they are known in India, appear in many forms in Indian cookery.

500g eggplant
Salt
1½ tablespoons vegetable oil
5cm piece cinnamon stick
3 whole cloves
1 onion, chopped
1-2 green chilis, finely chopped
1 teaspoon chili powder
¼ teaspoon turmeric
½ packet (100g) creamed coconut, chopped
250g ripe tomatoes, peeled, seeded and coarsely chopped
2 tablespoons chopped fresh coriander

Cut the unpeeled eggplant into large cubes, place in a bowl and cover with cold salted water.

Heat oil in a frying pan, add cinnamon and cloves and fry a few moments. Add onion, chopped chili, chili powder and turmeric. Drain eggplant, pat dry with paper towels, add to the pan and fry until lightly browned.

Add half the creamed coconut, the tomatoes and ½ teaspoon salt. Stir, cover and cook 3-4 minutes until eggplant is tender. Add remaining creamed coconut, stir gently until mixed and heated through. Season to taste and serve sprinkled with chopped coriander. Serves 3-4.

Eggplant and potato curry

When buying eggplant look for firm, glossy ones with fresh green calyx. Avoid very large eggplant as they can be spongy with little flavor.

500g potatoes
500g eggplant
Salt
2 tablespoons vegetable oil
1 teaspoon mustard seed
1 teaspoon finely chopped fresh ginger
2-3 green chilis, chopped
1 clove garlic, finely chopped
4 curry leaves (optional)
½ teaspoon turmeric
Coriander sprigs to garnish

Boil potatoes and, when cool enough to handle, skin them and cut into 2.5cm cubes. Cut unpeeled eggplant into cubes of the same size, place in a bowl and cover with cold salted water.

Heat oil in a frying pan on medium heat and add mustard seed. As the seed starts spluttering, add ginger, half the chili, garlic and curry leaves if using. Fry for a minute, stir in turmeric and add drained eggplant.

Cover and cook for about 5 minutes or until eggplant is tender. Remove lid, turn up heat and add potato. Fry, turning vegetables over once or twice, for 3-4 minutes. Season to taste, adding remaining chili if liked, and serve strewn with coriander. Serves 3-4.

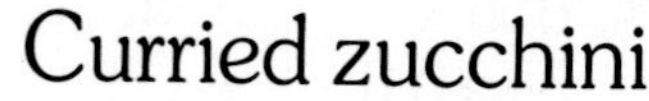

Curried zucchini

An example of Indian cooks' skill at transforming vegetables into a spicy delight.

500g small zucchini
2 tablespoons vegetable oil
½ teaspoon cumin seed
1 teaspoon finely chopped fresh ginger
1 onion, chopped
1 teaspoon chili powder
½ teaspoon turmeric
1 cup shelled fresh or frozen peas
Salt
2 tablespoons chopped fresh coriander
2 tablespoons grated fresh coconut or shredded coconut
Lime or lemon wedges, to serve

Cut zucchini into thick slices. Heat oil in a frying pan, add cumin seed and fry for a few moments, then add ginger and onion. Fry until golden, add chili powder and turmeric, stir and add peas and zucchini. Salt lightly, mix well and cover the pan tightly. Cook gently 6-8 minutes or until vegetables are tender. Remove the lid and fry until vegetables are dry.

Garnish with coriander and coconut and serve with wedges of lime or lemon. Serves 3-4.

Note: Young chokoes, sliced or cubed, may be substituted for the zucchini.

Garam masala

You can buy excellent commercial brands of this spice mix. It is often used during the last few minutes of cooking when it is sprinkled over the food.

4 tablespoons coriander seeds
2 tablespoons cumin seeds
1 tablespoon black peppercorns
2 teaspoons cardamom seeds
4 x 8cm cinnamon sticks
1 teaspoon whole cloves
1 whole nutmeg, finely grated

Over medium heat in a small pan roast separately first coriander, then cumin, peppercorns, cardamom, cinnamon and lastly cloves. Remove each spice from the pan as it begins to smell fragrant and cool it on a plate.

Put all into a blender and blend to a fine powder or pound in a mortar and pestle. Mix in nutmeg and store in an airtight jar. Will keep several months. Makes ¾ cup.

Left: Delightful vegetarian dishes — Eggplant With Coconut, Eggplant And Potato Curry, and Curried Zucchini.

Cauliflower and lentil curry

Cauliflower cheese has always been a popular vegetarian dish in Australia, so I am sure vegetarians will love this Indian curry. Lentils contain 25 per cent protein and are rich in vitamins B1 and B2 as well as being delicious and cheap.

1½ cups brown lentils
3 cups water
2 tablespoons ghee or oil
2 onions, finely chopped
½ teaspoon chili powder
1 teaspoon curry powder
½ teaspoon turmeric
2 tablespoons desiccated coconut
1 cup water
1 teaspoon salt
1 medium cauliflower
Juice of ½ lemon

Wash lentils and soak overnight in cold water. Next day, bring to the boil and simmer until amost tender.

Heat ghee in a deep saucepan and fry onions until golden.

Add spices and cook for a minute or so then add lentils, desiccated coconut, 1 cup water and salt. Bring to the boil. Break cauliflower into small pieces, and add to the saucepan.

Cover and cook until cauliflower is tender but firm, about 15-20 minutes, shaking the pan occasionally to prevent sticking. Add lemon juice and serve with rice and pickles. Serves 6.

Chicken curry

There are excellent commercial curry pastes available from health food shops and supermarkets. Try one or two, and see which suits your palate — the most expensive are not always the best. These chicken drumsticks are easy to cook and can be served hot with rice or packed cold in lunch boxes and picnic baskets.

2 tablespoons oil or ghee
3 onions, finely chopped
2 cloves garlic, finely chopped
1 tablespoon curry paste
2 tablespoons tomato paste
3 tablespoons water
1kg chicken drumsticks
Salt
Lemon juice
1 tablespoon desiccated coconut

Heat oil in a large, heavy frying pan and gently fry onions and garlic for 5 minutes. Stir in curry paste, tomato paste and water and cook gently for another 5 minutes.

Trim off shank ends of drumsticks with poultry shears if you wish (they look more attractive) and place in pan. Spoon onions over, cover tightly, and simmer very gently for 30 minutes or until chicken is tender. (Very slow cooking should prevent chicken burning, but a little extra water may be added if necessary.)

Before serving, stir in salt and lemon juice to taste, and the desiccated coconut, which will absorb any excess gravy. (Serves 6-8).

Note: This is also an excellent way to reheat cold, leftover chicken. After frying onions and pastes, stir in ½ cup water and season with salt and lemon juice. Simmer for 10 minutes before adding cold chicken pieces. Stir well, cover tightly, and cook gently for 5 minutes or until heated thoroughly.

Indian meatballs

Koftas, as meatballs are called in India, lend themselves to special spicing — these are particularly good using spices, chilis and fresh coriander or mint.

500g finely minced steak
1 onion, finely chopped
1-2 chilis, seeded and chopped
2 tablespoons chopped fresh coriander or mint
1-2 cloves garlic, crushed
½ teaspoon salt
1 tablespoon Garam Masala
1 teaspoon chili powder
Flour
Oil for frying

Above: A classic Chicken Curry, rice and Cauliflower And Lentil Curry.

SAUCE
30g butter or ghee
1 large onion, finely chopped
1 tablespoon chopped fresh ginger
½ teaspoon turmeric
¼ teaspoon salt
2 teaspoons Garam Masala
¼ teaspoon chili powder
2 large tomatoes, peeled and chopped
1 tablespoon lemon juice
½ cup water

Mix steak with onion, chilis, coriander or mint, garlic, salt, Garam Masala and chili powder. Knead mixture until stiff and smooth. Roll into walnut-sized balls and dust lightly with flour. Shallow-fry in hot oil until golden on all sides. Drain on crumpled paper towel.

SAUCE: Heat butter or ghee in a heavy saucepan and fry onion and ginger until softened. Add turmeric, salt, Garam Masala and chili powder and stir for a minute, then add tomatoes. Cook, stirring, for a few minutes. Stir in lemon juice and water.

Add meatballs and stir to coat with sauce. Cover and simmer 15-20 minutes or until sauce is thick. Serve with steamed rice, a choice of chutneys and sambals such as minted chopped tomatoes, sliced bananas, coconut and pappadams. Serves 4.

Korma kaffar shahi

Creamy 'white-cooked' meat dishes are part of India's Mogul heritage (Kaffar Shahi was a Mogul emperor). The meat in this lamb curry dish is gently cooked in a yogurt sauce which gives it melting tenderness as well as wonderful flavor. Keep the seeds from a watermelon or rock melon for this dish.

2 tablespoons melon seeds
2 tablespoons sesame seeds
60g ghee
4 large onions, chopped
1 tablespoon grated fresh ginger
4 cloves garlic, crushed
1 teaspoon salt
1 tablespoon Garam Masala
1 cup plain yogurt
1-2 green chilis, seeded and finely chopped
⅓ cup cashews
1kg lean, boneless lamb, cut into 4cm squares
½ cup cream

Process melon seeds and sesame seeds to a paste in a blender or food processor, or chop melon seeds and grind with sesame seeds in a mortar. Heat ghee in a large, heavy saucepan, add onions, ginger and garlic and fry until lightly browned.

Lower heat, add salt, Garam Masala, yogurt, chili, cashews and the ground seeds and stir until smooth. Add lamb, cover and cook very gently for 1½ hours or until lamb is tender. Stir in cream, correct seasoning and serve. Serves 4-6.

Note: Korma Kaffar Shahi should be mild-spicy but not very hot. Add the chili little by little until it is right for you.

Tandoori chicken

1.5kg chicken
Onion rings, radishes, red or green pepper, chilis and Naan (see recipe) to serve
YOGURT MASALA
3-4 garlic cloves
2.5cm piece fresh ginger
1 teaspoon cumin seeds
Pinch nutmeg
1½ teaspoons salt
¾ cup plain yogurt
1 tablespoon peanut oil
1 tablespoon tomato paste
2 teaspoons lemon juice
2-3 drops red food coloring
LEMON SPICE SAUCE
½ teaspoon freshly ground black pepper
¼ teaspoon ground cardamom
1 tablespoon peanut oil
2 teaspoons lemon juice

Remove chicken skin but leave the chicken whole. Cut 2 slits about 1cm deep in thighs and breast of chicken. *YOGURT MASALA:* Peel and finely chop garlic and ginger. Puree with remaining ingredients in an electric blender, or grind to a paste with cumin seeds, nutmeg and salt with a mortar and pestle or the end of a rolling pin in a bowl, then mix in remaining ingredients. Spread masala over the chicken, rubbing well in and refrigerate.

Next day, bring chicken to room temperature then place on a rotisserie over a pan, or on a rack in a shallow roasting pan. Pour over remaining masala. Roast in a hot oven, 200C (400F), for 15 minutes, then reduce heat to moderate, 180C (350F), and bake for 1 hour more, basting frequently with pan juices.

Mix together the ingredients for the Lemon Spice Sauce. Remove chicken from oven and cut into 6 pieces. Coat chicken pieces with any remaining masala and sprinkle with sauce. Return to a hot oven, 200C (400F), for 10 to 15 minutes, or grill under a preheated grill or over hot coals until dark reddish brown and crisp.

Serve Tandoori Chicken on a large platter with onion rings, radishes, sliced green or red pepper and for those who appreciate something hot, a few shredded fresh chilis. Pass warm Naan as an accompaniment. Serves 3 to 4.

Naan

Naan is usually baked in the wall of the tandoor, but it can be baked on foil in an ordinary oven. Naan is served warm with tandoori chicken, kebabs, korma and other tandoori dishes

¼ cup warm water
1 teaspoon sugar
2 sachets (3 teaspoons) dried yeast
5 tablespoons plain yogurt
5 tablespoons milk
½ teaspoon bicarbonate of soda
2 eggs, lightly beaten
30g ghee, melted
¼ teaspoon salt
3 cups plain flour

Combine warm water and sugar, sprinkle yeast over the top and stir to soften and dissolve. Leave in a warm place for about 10 minutes or until frothy on top.

Stir milk and yogurt together in a small saucepan and heat gently until the mixture feels comfortably warm to your fingertips. Remove from heat, cool a little and stir in soda, beaten eggs, melted ghee and the yeast mixture.

Sift salt, and half the flour into a large bowl, make a well in the centre and pour in yogurt mixture. Stir from the centre, gradually incorporating remaining flour a little at a time, working it in with your hands when mixture gets too stiff to stir. Turn dough on to a lightly floured board. Knead vigorously for about 15 minutes, until dough is smooth and elastic. If dough is still sticky knead in extra flour.

Place dough in a large, greased bowl, turn over so that the top is lightly greased and cover the bowl with greased plastic film and a cloth. Leave in a warm place until dough is doubled in bulk (or when a fingertip pushed into the dough leaves an impression that does not smooth out). Dust hands with flour and divide dough into 6 even pieces. Shape each piece into a ball, then flatten it into a circle about 4mm thick, making it a little thinner in the centre than around the edge. Pull one end outward to make a teardrop shape.

Brush one side of the dough with melted ghee and the other with water. Place wet side down on baking trays lined with foil and bake in a preheated very hot oven, 230C (450F), for about 10 minutes or until puffed and pale gold, then place under a preheated grill for a minute or two until brown spots appear on the upper side. Makes 6.

Shah jahani kebabs

A dish of grilled spiced beef, named for the Mogul emperor who built the Taj Mahal. At Sydney's Mayur Restaurant it is skewered and cooked in the tandoori oven, but excellent results can be achieved at home with a good hot grill or over hot coals.

1 green chili, seeded (or to taste)
1kg rump steak, cut into 4cm cubes
1 teaspoon salt
1 tablespoon grated fresh ginger
4 cloves garlic, crushed
¾ cup plain yogurt
1 tablespoon Garam Masala

Process chili to a paste in a blender or food processor, or chop it finely and grind with a pestle and mortar. Put beef into a bowl, add salt, ginger, garlic and chili and mix well. Leave covered for 1 hour. Add yogurt and Garam Masala and leave covered for 2 hours longer.

Thread beef cubes, not too close together, on 4 skewers. Grill close to a very hot griller or over hot coals for 5 to 7 minutes, turning to brown the beef on all sides and brushing once or twice with yogurt mixture. Arrange the skewers on a bed of hot, fluffy rice and surround the rice with Kachumbar Salad (see recipe). Serves 4.

Kachumbar salad

This salad of bright-colored vegetables is often used to garnish a dish.

1 small onion
2 large tomatoes
1 green pepper
2 tablespoons lemon juice
Salt

Peel onion and cut it downward into quarters, then into thin strips. Cut tomatoes in half, shake out seeds and cut flesh into matchstick strips. Remove seeds and inner ribs of green pepper and cut flesh into matchstick strips.

Place all vegetables in a bowl, sprinkle with lemon juice and salt and mix lightly. Chill until serving time.

Above: Colorful and creative — Shahjahani Kebabs surrounded by Kachumbar Salad and Tandoori Chicken with freshly made Naan.

Pakoras

Serve these spiced vegetable fritters with fresh mint or coriander chutney as a first course or snack.

VEGETABLES
1 small eggplant
Salt
1 small green pepper
125g spinach leaves
1 medium potato
BATTER
2 cups besan (chick-pea) flour (from health-food shops)
About 1¾ cups water
½ teaspoon each salt, turmeric, ground cumin and bicarbonate of soda
¼ cup teaspoon black pepper
Small pinch cayenne

Trim eggplant and cut lengthwise into 5mm slices. Sprinkle with salt, stand 30 minutes then pat dry with paper towels, pressing out any remaining moisture. Cut seeded pepper into 2cm strips. Wash and dry spinach and tear into 8-10cm pieces. Peel potato and slice thin.

Sift flour into a bowl and stir in enough water to make a thick batter. Stir in remaining ingredients for batter, beat until smooth, cover and stand 30 minutes.

Heat oil for deep-frying to 180C (350F), or when a cube of day-old bread will turn crisp and golden in 1 minute.

Stir batter well. Holding each piece of vegetable on a fork, dip into batter and deep-fry in batches for about 8 minutes or until browned.

Keep cooked pakoras hot on a baking tray lined with paper towels in a low oven until all are done, then sprinkle with salt and serve immediately with fresh mint or coriander chutney. Serves 4.

Puris

The dough for these light, golden breads can be made up to 48 hours ahead and kept chilled until ready to cook.

½ cup each atta, roti flour and unbleached white flour
½ teaspoon each celery seed and salt
1 tablespoon softened butter
1 tablespoon plain yogurt
About ½ cup lukewarm water
½ teaspoon vegetable oil
Oil for frying

Sift flours together into a bowl and return particles from the sifter to them. Add celery seed and salt and rub in butter. Add yogurt and combine well.

Blend in ½ cup lukewarm water or enough to make a firm dough. Knead dough for at least 10 minutes. Shape into a ball, rub all over with oil, wrap in plastic and chill for at least 2 hours (dough can be kept in a plastic bag for as long as 48 hours, chilled).

Shape the dough into 18 balls and roll on a lightly floured surface into thin rounds about 9cm diameter. Keep all dough except the piece with which you are working covered, to prevent drying out.

Heat about 4cm oil in a wok or deep frying pan until it gives off a faint haze. Fry Puris one at a time, pressing on the edges with an egg slice to encourage them to puff. When risen, turn over to cook the other side. Drain on crumpled paper towels and serve hot. Makes 18.

Note: Atta is a fine-ground wholemeal flour. Roti flour has a granular texture and is made from part of the wheat grain. These and unbleached white flour are available from health food shops.

Fish in curry sauce

A good way of cooking fillets of fish and particularly suitable for those on a low-cholesterol diet.

2 tablespoons oil
2 onions, finely chopped
2 cloves garlic, crushed
1-2 teaspoons curry powder
1 tablespoon tomato paste
¾ cup water
Salt to taste
4 fillets of fish

Heat oil in a frying pan and lightly fry the chopped onion and garlic until golden. Add the curry powder and stir over a fairly high heat for a minute or two. Stir in the tomato paste and water and cook for a few more minutes. Season to taste with salt. Slide the fillets of fish into the sauce and cook gently until the fish is done. This will depend on the thickness of the fillets. Baste the fish occasionally with the sauce but take care not to stir, just agitate the pan gently to prevent the fish sticking to the bottom.

Lime pickles are particularly nice with fish, or sliced tomatoes sprinkled with fresh coriander or mint, and of course, boiled rice. Serves 4.

Super snacks

There are times when you want something good to eat without fuss — just a quick snack. Quick and easy cooking can still be the sort of cooking we all look forward to. It's great fun preparing snacks and little dishes that are nourishing, interesting and of course appetising. We should not neglect today's convenience foods like bacon, eggs, cheese, ham and sausages. Canned and frozen foods have a place: baked beans, frozen peas. Noodles and other pastas too, and the fresh foods we always have on hand: tomatoes, lettuce, onions. And don't forget the instant flavor of commercial sauces and mustards. Breads can make a great difference to snack food. Change your bread regularly and buy different rolls and pita. Bread freezes well so keep a stock in the freezer.

Steamed vegetables with kranzsky

A couple of continental smoked sausages are a good standby in the refrigerator. They can be lightly boiled and served in a roll, with grain bread or, steamed with shredded cabbage, they make a more substantial snack.

1 kranzsky or other cooked continental sausage
1 tablespoon butter
2 cups finely shredded cabbage
½ small green pepper finely shredded
3 slices onion
Salt and freshly ground black pepper
Crusty roll or pocket bread and butter to serve

Slice kranzsky. Heat butter in small saucepan, add vegetables and toss to coat with butter. Add sliced kranzsky, cover tightly, reduce heat and steam for 5 minutes. Season with salt and pepper.

Serve with a crusty wholemeal roll or spooned into small pocket breads (pita) which have been spread outside with butter and toasted under the griller until puffed up. Serves 2.

Avocado and bacon sandwich

A personal favorite, nutritious and delicious.

1 ripe avocado
1 tomato
2 slices buttered wholegrain bread
5-6 small lettuce leaves
Salt and freshly ground black pepper
1½ tablespoons vinaigrette (optional)
2 large rashers bacon, rind removed

Halve and stone avocado, peel and cut into thick slices. Slice tomato.

Place each slice of buttered bread on a plate and arrange lettuce, tomato and avocado on top, seasoning lightly with salt and pepper and a little vinaigrette.

Cut bacon into wide strips, place in a dry frying pan, and cook on moderate heat until lightly browned. Tip bacon, including the hot drippings, over the sandwiches and serve immediately. Serves 2.

Miniature pork or chicken satays

What do you do with 1 pork chop, or 1 chicken fillet that was meant for 1 person and now there are two? You can make lovely little satays and serve them on lettuce leaves as a salad or with quick-cooking Chinese noodles.

1 small pork chop or piece pork fillet or chicken fillet
½ small onion
½ a small green pepper
4 sage leaves
1 teaspoon soy sauce
1 tablespoon oil
Freshly ground black pepper
Chinese noodles, to serve (optional)

Soak 2 small bamboo skewers in hot water. Preheat grill.

Trim fat and gristle from meat and cut into small squares. Cut onion downward into quarters and separate into petals. Cut green pepper into squares about same size as meat.

Thread meat, sage leaves and vegetables on to skewers, brush with mixture of soy sauce, oil and pepper and grill, turning and brushing again 2 or 3 times, until meat is lightly browned. If desired, serve on freshly cooked Chinese noodles (drop into boiling salted water and cook about 5 minutes, then drain) or crisp, shredded lettuce. Serves 2.

Croque monsieur

This French favorite, often made with crusty french bread, is sold in almost all pavement cafes in France, and is delicious with a glass of wine or hot coffee. Use crusty bread or a sandwich loaf.

8 slices white bread
Butter
4 slices lean ham
1 cup grated cheddar or swiss cheese
Freshly ground black pepper
Oil for frying

Spread bread generously with butter and make into sandwiches with ham, cheese and a grinding of black pepper. Press firmly together and trim crusts.

Fry in shallow hot oil until golden-brown on both sides. Drain on crumpled paper towels and serve hot, garnishing the plate with a sprig of watercress or parsley, or with a few shallots. Cut each sandwich in two or into 3 fingers.

Mushrooms nicoise

500g mushrooms
Juice of 1 lemon
Salt and freshly ground pepper
3 tablespoons olive oil
30g butter
2-3 tomatoes, peeled, seeded and chopped
2 teaspoons each chopped parsley and tarragon
8 black olives, stoned

Wipe mushrooms and trim. If they are large, quarter them. Put into a bowl and mix with lemon juice. Season with salt and freshly ground pepper. Heat 2 tablespoons oil in a frying pan, add butter and when melted add mushrooms. Cook over moderate heat about 3 to 4 minutes

tossing with a spoon. Put into heated dish, keep warm.

Heat remaining oil and cook tomatoes with salt, pepper and herbs until heated through. Stir in olives and spoon over mushrooms.

Scrambled eggs provencal

In France scrambled eggs are often served as the first course or a light luncheon dish. In Provence they are topped with anchovy fillets and black olives; it is a dramatic-looking dish, perfect for your next brunch.

12 eggs
Salt and freshly ground black pepper
Pinch of cayenne
6 slices white bread, french or italian
60g butter
1 tablespoon olive oil
6 anchovy fillets, sliced in half lengthwise
Black olives, stoned
3 tablespoons finely chopped parsley

Combine eggs, salt, pepper and cayenne and beat lightly with a fork. Remove crusts from bread and trim into rounds, if liked.

Heat half the butter and 2 teaspoons of the oil in a heavy frying pan and saute bread until very lightly browned on both sides. Remove from fat, drain on kitchen paper and keep warm.

Melt remaining butter and oil in a shallow saucepan, pour in eggs and cook over medium heat stirring occasionally until soft and creamy. Spoon on to the sauteed bread.

Arrange sliced anchovy fillets in a cross over the top and garnish with half a black olive. Sprinkle with finely chopped parsley and serve immediately. Serves 6.

Left: Meals made in minutes — Avocado And Bacon Sandwich, Steamed Vegetables With Kranzksy and Miniature Pork Satays.

Chicken brochettes

4 boneless chicken breasts
1 teaspoon french mustard
2 tablespoons olive oil
1 tablespoon lemon or lime juice
1 clove garlic, sliced
2 teaspoons fresh, chopped mixed herbs or 1 teaspoon dried
Salt and pepper
4 rashers streaky bacon, derinded and halved
Sage leaves
GARNISH
Lemon or lime slices
A few sage sprigs

Cut the chicken into 3cm cubes. Put the mustard, oil, lemon or lime juice and garlic in a bowl and mix well. Stir in the herbs, and season with salt and pepper to taste. Add the chicken, stir well and leave to marinate for 20 to 30 minutes.

Roll up the bacon pieces. Thread the chicken and bacon alternately on 4 skewers, interspersing with sage leaves to taste. Cook under a preheated hot grill for 5 to 7 minutes on each side, until golden and tender; spoon over the marinade during cooking.

Garnish with lemon or lime slices and sage and serve immediately, with buttered noodles, green salad or vegetables. Serves 4.

Spiced kebabs

Spiced minced meat is moulded on to wooden butchers' skewers or metal skewers, grilled and served on shredded lettuce

500g good quality minced beef
1 small onion, grated
2 cloves garlic, crushed
Juice of ½ lemon or 1 lime
1 tablespoon plain flour
½ teaspoon each ground cumin, chili powder and coriander
Pinch each ground cinnamon and ginger
TO SERVE
Few lettuce leaves, shredded
Cherry tomatoes
Mint sprigs
4 pita breads (optional)

Put the meat, onion, garlic, lemon or lime juice and flour in a bowl and mix well. Stir in all the spices and mix thoroughly. Season well with salt and pepper and mix until smooth.

Divide the n.ixture into 4 portions and shape around 4 skewers to make long, thin rissoles. Refrigerate if possible for 1 to 2 hours until firm.

Place under a preheated hot grill and cook for 15 minutes, turning occasionally, until well browned.

Arrange the kebabs on a bed of lettuce, garnish with cherry tomatoes and mint, and serve hot, with rice or pita breads, brushed with oil and toasted. Serves 4.

French bread pizzas

An easy and quick way to make a crunchy, delicious snack.

1 small french bread stick
2 tablespoons tomato paste
2 tablespoons mixed herbs or 2 teaspoons dried
1-2 cloves garlic, crushed (optional)
TOPPING
2 tomatoes, sliced
60g salami
2 tablespoons capers
⅔ cup grated gruyere cheese

Cut the bread in half lengthways and spread the tomato paste over the cut surfaces. Sprinkle with the herbs and garlic, if using.

Arrange the sliced tomatoes and salami on each piece of french bread. Sprinkle with the capers and top with the cheese.

Cut each piece of bread in two. Place on lightly oiled baking trays and bake in a preheated moderately hot oven, 200C (400F), for 15 minutes. Serve hot. Serves 4.

Creamed mushrooms on toast

30g butter
½ small onion, chopped
500g small button mushrooms, sliced
1 tablespoon plain flour
1 cup milk
Dash of worcestershire sauce
2 tablespoons cream (optional)
Salt and pepper
Juice of ½ lemon
2 tablespoons chopped parsley or chives
4 slices hot buttered toast
Parsley sprigs to garnish

Melt the butter in a pan, add the onion and cook for 5 to 7 minutes, without browning, until tender. Stir in the mushrooms and cook for 1 minute, stirring well. Sprinkle over flour and blend in. Gradually add the milk, stirring constantly. Bring to the boil, then simmer for 2 minutes. Add the worcestershire sauce, cream, if using, and salt and pepper to taste. Remove from the heat and stir in the lemon juice and herbs.

Put the toast on 2 warmed individual plates and spoon the mushrooms on top. Garnish with parsley and serve immediately. Serves 2.

November

Greek favorites

The Greek people are home lovers and have strong family ties. They love food and a party and are most hospitable. Having been included on many wonderful celebrations — weddings, christenings and Easter festivities — I have come to associate happy occasions and enjoyable food with friendly Greeks. Greek cooking is neither oily nor hotly seasoned as some people who are not familiar with good Greek food would have you believe. Olive oil is used to a great extent, so is butter. Mint and oregano are two herbs frequently used with meats, casseroles, vegetables and salads. Cinnamon often flavors meat dishes as well as pastries and puddings. Because sheep and goats flourish in the rocky hills of Greece, lamb is the meat most often used, and cheese from goats' milk is a staple food. Three kinds of Greek cheese most often used are: feta, a soft, salty, white goats' cheese; kaseric, creamy colored and similar to cheddar; and kefaloteri, a hard cheese rather like parmesan. These are available in most Greek delicatessens in Australia. Pasta is popular in Greece and rice is a staple, too. Eggplant also is enjoyed; it is stuffed, fried and used in many ways, including in salad. The famous Avgolemono Sauce of eggs and lemon is one of the loveliest additions to soups and meat dishes. The pastries are rich and flaky and often soaked in honey syrup, for which the Greeks are so justly famous. It all seems to add up to plenty of reasons for encouraging you to try some of the great dishes of Greece.

Bourekakia

This Turkish/Greek dish may also be made into Tiropetes. Cigar-shaped rolls can be made into small cocktail savories, served with soup or made into larger ones for snack meals.

250g filo pastry
1 bunch spinach
2 onions
30g butter
3 eggs, beaten
½ cup finely chopped shallots including a little green end
250g feta cheese, chopped
1 teaspoon ground nutmeg
½ cup finely chopped parsley
Salt and freshly ground black pepper
125g unsalted butter

Lay filo pastry flat on a dry tea towel and cover with a second dry then a damp tea towel so pastry will not dry out. Steam spinach about 5 minutes, drain, then chop. Finely chop onions and fry in butter until golden brown. Combine eggs, shallots, cheese, nutmeg and parsley. Add onions, spinach and season with salt and pepper to taste.

Melt unsalted butter and brush a little over two shallow 20cm square or one lamington tin. Fold one sheet of the filo pastry in half and place in the tin. Trim pastry to fit. Brush with butter. Repeat this process in tins until half pastry is used. Spread filling over the pastry and cover with remaining filo pastry, each layer folded and brushed with butter as before. Trim pastry edges to fit tin neatly. Cut into 4cm squares. Bake in a moderately hot oven 190C (375F) for about 1 hour or until pastry is golden brown and puffed. Cut through squares while still hot and serve immediately. Makes about 40.

Tiropetes

The ingredients for this recipe are exactly the same as for Bourekakia. Use recipe for filling as for Bourekakia.

Lay filo pastry flat on a damp tea towel and cover with a second dry then a damp tea towel so pastry will not dry out. Cut each sheet of filo pastry in half lengthwise. Fold each piece in two lengthwise. Brush with melted butter. Place a teaspoonful of the filling in one corner of the pastry strip. Fold corner of pastry over filling until it meets the folded edge of pastry, forming a triangle. Continue to fold pastry over in triangles until you come to the end of the pastry strip. Brush top with melted butter. Place on an ungreased baking tray

Left: Filo pastry is popular in Greek cuisine and is used for such favorites as Almond Cigars, Tiropetes, Cheese Puffs and Bourekakia.

and bake in a moderately hot oven 190C (375F) for 45 minutes or until puffed and golden brown.

Cheese puffs

500g feta cheese
375g ricotta cheese
5 eggs
½ cup finely chopped parsley or mint
20 sheets filo pastry
250g melted butter

Crumble feta cheese, add ricotta and mix together well. Add eggs, beat thoroughly and fold in parsley or mint. Brush a sheet of filo with melted butter and fold in 3 lengthwise. Cut the folded filo into 2 equal portions. Place one strip on a flat surface, brush with melted butter, fold in half lengthways making a strip about 5cm wide. Brush with butter.

Place 2 teaspoons of cheese mixture in the bottom righthand corner of strip and fold corner over into a triangle. Continue folding to the end of the strip making sure that you retain a triangle shape with each fold. Lightly butter the finished triangles and place on a baking tray. Bake in a hot oven 200C (400F) for 30 minutes or until golden. Turn after 10 minutes.

Almond cigars

These are delicious with coffee.

20 sheets filo pastry
250g ground almonds (or walnuts)
½ cup sugar
2 teaspoons cinnamon
250g melted butter
SYRUP
2⅓ cups sugar
1⅔ cups water
1 cinnamon stick
1 teaspoon lemon juice

Fold pastry in two lengthwise. Cut the folded filo pastry in two, across the length. Mix together the nuts, sugar and cinnamon. Brush each strip of pastry with melted butter and place 2 teaspoons of the nut mixture at the end of each strip. Roll up like a cigar and brush with butter.

Place on a baking sheet and bake in a moderate oven 180C (350F) for 20-30 minutes or until golden brown.

Remove to a rack and pour the cold syrup over the warm cigars.

SYRUP: Place all ingredients in a saucepan. Bring to the boil over a low heat and then simmer for 10 minutes. Cool.

Avgolemono

This egg lemon sauce is always made from the liquid in which meats or vegetables have been cooked, then thickened with beaten egg and fresh lemon juice. The mixture is also used to thicken soups.

2 eggs
Juice of 1 lemon
1 cup stock or broth

Beat the eggs and add lemon juice. Slowly add some of the hot broth to egg yolks while continuing to beat. Stir egg-yolk mixture into remaining broth. Remove from heat. Cover and let stand for 5 minutes to thicken.

Serve at once. Do not reheat.

Spanakoryzo

1 cup uncooked rice
1 medium onion, finely chopped
⅓ cup olive oil
2 cups boiling water
1½ teaspoons salt
500g fresh spinach

Saute rice and onion in olive oil, stirring occasionally, for 15 minutes. Add boiling water and salt. Simmer, covered, for 10 minutes.

Meanwhile, wash spinach and cut into strips with scissors. Add to rice and mix thoroughly. Cover and continue to simmer, stirring occasionally, for 15 minutes longer. Makes 4 servings.

Kotopoulo kapama

The success of this chicken and tomato casserole depends on using the rich, fleshy egg tomatoes (canned Italian tomatoes makes a good substitute) and the tangy lemon-spice seasoning of the chicken.

Juice of 1 lemon
Pinch of ground cloves
½ teaspoon ground cinnamon
Salt and pepper
A large chicken, jointed, or 6-8 chicken pieces
½ cup olive oil
6 tomatoes, peeled and chopped
2 tablespoons tomato paste
2½ cups hot water.

Mix together the lemon juice, cloves, cinnamon, salt and pepper and rub well into the chicken pieces. Heat the oil in a large saucepan and fry the chicken in it until golden brown.

Lift out and keep hot while you stir the tomatoes and paste into oil; gradually stir in the hot water and cook over a gentle heat until the tomatoes are mushy and the sauce thick.

Return the chicken pieces to the pan, turn each piece over and over until coated with the sauce and then cover the pan. Cook over a very low heat for about 30 minutes. Serve with plain boiled rice. Serves 4 to 6.

Meatballs with avgolemono

Avgolemono is delicious over Greek meatballs.

500g lean, minced beef
1 small onion, chopped
1 teaspoon chopped fresh mint
1 tablespoon chopped parsley
1 tablespoon cooked rice
Salt and pepper
1½ cups beef stock or water and stock cube
Avgolemono

Mix together the beef, onion, mint, parsley and rice, season with salt and pepper and add ¼ cup of beef stock. Mix well and form into balls the size of a walnut. Bring remaining stock and water to boil and drop in meatballs. Simmer for 35 minutes.

Drain off hot stock. Makes up to 1½ cups. Use to make Avgolemono. Spoon sauce over the meatballs. Serves 4.

Kotta pilaf

6 half chicken breasts (fillets)
¼ cup butter
1 medium onion, finely chopped
1½ cups canned tomatoes
2 cups water
1 teaspoon ground cinnamon
Salt and pepper
1 cup uncooked rice
Light sour cream

Saute chicken breasts in butter until golden brown. Add onion, tomatoes, water, cinnamon and salt and pepper to taste. Cover and simmer for 30 minutes.

Add rice and stir to mix evenly. Cover and simmer for an additional 20 minutes, or until rice is tender, adding more water if necessary. Serve with a bowl of cold sour cream, to be spooned over the hot pilaf. Makes 6 servings.

Pura

These delectable nut rolls are a typical Greek confection.

¾ cup finely chopped walnuts
½ cup finely chopped almonds
1 teaspoon sugar
¼ teaspoon ground cinnamon
½ teaspoon ground nutmeg
10 sheets filo pastry
250g butter, melted
CINNAMON HONEY SYRUP
1 cup sugar
⅔ cup water
¼ cup honey
Small cinnamon stick
1 teaspoon fresh lemon juice

Mix together nuts, sugar and spices. Brush half of a sheet of filo with melted butter, fold other half over and brush with butter so that you have a piece of filo 18cm x 30cm.

Sprinkle with 1 tablespoon of nut mixture. Beginning at one end, roll filo as you would a jam roll. Cut into three. Place on greased baking sheet with smooth side of pastry up and brush with melted butter. Repeat rolling.

Bake in preheated moderate oven 180C (350F) for 20 minutes, or until golden brown. While hot, dip into warm Cinnamon Honey Syrup and drain.

SYRUP: Mix all ingredients together and simmer for 30 minutes. Cook only until light brown.

Skordalia

This wonderfully pungent and aromatic sauce is served with meat or fish.

1 small potato
3 garlic cloves, minced
1 teaspoon salt
1 cup olive oil
⅓ cup vinegar

Peel potato and boil until tender. Put through a ricer or sieve. Measure ½ cup potato and place in a bowl; mix in garlic and salt. Gradually add olive oil and vinegar alternately while beating with a spoon. Chill. Makes about 1¼ cups.

Pasticcio

I've been told by countless Greeks that this is just the way mother used to make it.

125g butter
2 medium-sized onions, finely chopped
500g minced steak
2 tomatoes, peeled and chopped
1 tablespoon tomato paste
Salt and pepper
½ cup grated cheese
250g packet lasagne noodles, the precooked variety
Cream Sauce
1 beaten egg
¼ cup grated cheese

Melt butter in pan and cook finely chopped onions and minced steak for 2-3 minutes, stirring constantly. Add tomatoes, tomato paste and salt and pepper to taste. Continue to cook over low heat until meat is tender. Cover pan if mixture is too dry. Blend with ½ cup grated cheese.

Place half the lasagne in a greased casserole and cover with meat

mixture, then remaining lasagne. Blend cream sauce with beaten egg and 1/4 cup grated cheese. Season and pour over the lasagne.

Bake in a moderate oven for 40 to 50 minutes or until top is nicely browned. Serve hot. Serves 6.

CREAM SAUCE: Melt 60g butter, blend in 3 tablespoons flour and cook gently for 2 minutes. Add 2½ cups milk gradually, stirring over a low heat until boiling. Add 3 tablespoons cream (optional) and season to taste with salt, pepper and nutmeg.

Greek semolina cake

125g butter
½ cup castor sugar
1 tablespoon grated orange rind
2 eggs
2 tablespoons brandy
1 cup semolina
1 teaspoon baking powder
125g ground almonds
SYRUP
1¼ cups orange juice
½ cup sugar
3 tablespoons Grand Marnier, Cointreau or brandy

Grease a 20cm round or square cake tin with butter, then line with buttered greaseproof paper — a circle or square for the base and a strip for the sides. Set the oven temperature at hot 200C (400F).

Cream the butter, sugar and orange rind together until light and fluffy. Beat in the eggs one at a time, beating thoroughly after each addition, then stir in the brandy.

Stir the semolina, baking powder and almonds together and fold lightly into the mixture. Turn into the prepared tin and place on the centre shelf of the oven, lowering the temperature to moderate 180C (350F) as you do so.

Bake for 30 minutes or until golden on top and risen. (A skewer inserted in the middle should come out clean.)

While the cake is cooking, make the orange syrup. Place the juice and sugar in a saucepan, bring to the boil and boil briskly for 5 minutes. Cool slightly and add the spirits.

Take the cake from the oven, pour the syrup over, then return to the oven and cook for a further 15 minutes. Allow to cool in the tin, and turn out carefully on to a plate to serve.

Above: A great Greek main course, Kotopoulo Kapama, a chicken and tomato casserole, with Spanakoryzo, which combines rice and spinach.

• *For other Greek recipes, see index.*

Meals on a stick

Skewered foods have great appeal. They can be quick, interesting, economical for everyday meals, they dress up beautifully for entertaining and take just as easily to grilling in the kitchen as outside on the barbecue. Cooking on a stick is a popular form of cookery throughout the Middle East, Japan, Malaysia, India, Greece, Italy, Indonesia, the United States, France and of course Australia. 'Kebabs', also spelled "kebobs", from the Middle East, means small pieces of roasted meat. The addition of the word 'shish' (skewer) means the food is threaded on a skewer and then roasted. Shashlik is Russian and consists of small pieces of meat (usually lamb or mutton) which are threaded on to skewers or swords and grilled. The French serve many foods 'en brochette' 'broche' is the French word for skewer. In Japan morsels of food are threaded on small, sticks for a form of 'teriyaki' and there is the vast assortment of satays from Indonesia and Malaysia.
The secret of all skewer cookery is the seasonings or marinades used to flavor the foods. Meats are well seasoned and often marinated beforehand and may be combined with onions, peppers and so on threaded on the same skewers. Foods on skewers seem to have more fascination when presented to the diner on their skewers. It is a simple matter for each guest to remove the skewered ingredients in one graceful stroke with the push of a fork either on to a mound of rice on or into pita bread (which should be toasted lightly over the charcoal or under the grill before filling) or over a pool of luscious sauce. I have also had them served on a bed of watercress or broad-leafed parsley which is a particularly attractive form of presentation.

Cooking skewered food

Metal skewers used for grilling should be flat so that the food won't slip round on them as they are turned. Soak bamboo or wooden skewers in water for 2 hours before using so that they don't burn.

Place the skewers about 8-10 cm from the heat over glowing coals or under a preheated griller. Brush with oil or marinade and turn several times while cooking.

Lamb or beef should be well browned on the outside but still pink and juicy on the inside. For rare skewered meat, push the pieces tightly together so that the inside is protected while the outside grills brown and crusty. Pork is usually preferred well done, so space the pieces a little apart to brown well on all sides.

Moroccan kebabs

The fresh lemon flavor of cumin gives an intriguing taste to these kebabs. The other spice is ground ginger. If you want to be a little more exotic, use 1 tablespoon of grated fresh ginger instead of ground ginger, and add 3 tablespoons of natural yogurt to the marinade.

1.5kg boneless lamb, cut from leg, chump or shoulder
2 small green peppers
1 small onion
Saffron Rice or Tabouli to serve (see index)

MARINADE
1 small onion, finely chopped
1¼ teaspoons salt
1 teaspoon each powdered cumin and ginger
½ teaspoon black pepper
4 tablespoons olive oil
1 teaspoon paprika
Dash cayenne pepper

Trim excess fat and gristle from meat and then cut into bite-size cubes. Cut peppers into squares. Cut onion into quarters, then separate into petals.

Combine marinade ingredients in a glass or pottery dish, add meat, and leave for 2 hours, turning meat now and again. Thread meat, peppers and onion alternately on to 6 metal skewers, not too close together. Brush grill rack with oil and cook skewers over hot coals or under a preheated grill for 8-10 minutes, or until brown outside and still a little pink inside. Turn skewers as they cook, and brush with marinade from time to time. Serve with rice, or push skewers into pockets of pita bread with Tabouli. Serves 6.

Sosaties

A wonderful African way with cubes of pork or lamb, which are marinated overnight in a spicy apricot mixture before grilling.

1kg lean, boneless pork or lamb
MARINADE
1½ cups dried apricots
1¾ cups water
2 large onions, finely chopped
2 tablespoons curry powder
¼ cup peanut oil
60g butter
¼ cup wine vinegar
1 red chili, seeded and finely chopped
1½ teaspoons salt

Cut meat into 2cm cubes.

Cook apricots in water until very soft and puree with their cooking

liquid in a food processor or blender, or rub through a sieve.

Cook onions and curry powder in oil and butter until onions are soft. Combine with the apricot puree and remaining marinade ingredients in a large bowl. Add cubed meat and mix gently. Cover and refrigerate overnight.

Drain meat and thread on to bamboo skewers which have been soaked in water for 2 hours. Grill over hot coals or under a preheated griller until meat is crispy and well-cooked, turning and brushing with marinade once or twice while cooking.

Serve the Sosaties on a bed of rice or with an interesting pilaf. Check in the index under Rice and Pilaf for suggested recipes.

Warm the remaining marinade and serve in a separate bowl. Serves 6.

Orange lamb kebabs

The flavor of orange with soy may seem unusual, but the finished kebabs, served with a good rice pilaf followed by a tossed green salad, make an excellent meal.

1kg shoulder of lamb, boned
1 clove garlic
Large pinch salt
½ cup orange juice
2 tablespoons soy sauce
2 oranges
2 green peppers

Trim excess fat from lamb and cut into large cubes. Peel garlic and crush with salt to a smooth paste. Combine with orange juice and soy sauce in a bowl and marinate lamb cubes in this mixture for at least 2 hours or overnight, covering with plastic wrap.

Peel oranges, removing all pith, halve and cut across into thick slices. Halve peppers, remove seeds and cut into squares the same size as meat cubes.

Drain lamb cubes, reserving marinade. Arrange lamb, orange slices and pepper squares alternately on skewers. Brush with marinade and place under a preheated grill. Turn kebabs frequently and brush with marinade every few minutes. Cook for about 10 minutes or until meat is tender. Serve with rice pilaf or plain boiled rice. Serves 4-6.

Above: Orange and soy combine temptingly in Orange Lamb Kebabs.

Yakitori

For this Japanese speciality squares of boneless chicken are beautifully seasoned, then grilled on skewers.

MARINADE
2½ tablespoons sake or sherry
2½ teaspoons soy sauce
1 clove garlic, crushed
1½ teaspoons sugar
4 thin slices fresh ginger, finely shredded
SAUCE
½ cup bottled teriyaki sauce
2 tablespoons sake or sherry
½ cup chicken stock
1 tablespoon oil
FOR SKEWERS
4 half chicken breasts or chicken fillets
8 spring onions, or shallots cut in short lengths
Small bamboo skewers

Combine ingredients for marinade in a bowl. Combine ingredients for sauce in another bowl. Bone and skin the breasts of chicken and cut into bite-size squares. Cover and refrigerate. Coat with marinade and leave about 6 hours.

Thread chicken pieces and lengths of spring onion alternately on to 4 skewers, beginning and ending with chicken, brush with marinade.

Brush filled skewers with sauce mixture turning around to coat thoroughly.

Preheat the griller and line the grill rack with foil. Grill the Yakitori for 3 minutes on one side, brushing twice with sauce. Turn over and grill the other side for 3 minutes, again brushing twice with sauce.

Serve at once on individual plates. Garnish with shredded spring onion if desired, or a pretty garden leaf. Serves 4.

Bacon and prawn skewers

Brilliant for a first course or on the barbecue. The bacon protects the prawns, keeping them juicy and tender.

24 green king prawns
2 tablespoons lemon juice
6 tablespoons oil
Freshly ground black pepper
8 rashers bacon
1 red pepper

Shell prawns, leaving tail segments on, and devein them. Place in a dish, drizzle with lemon juice and oil and grind black pepper over. Turn prawns about to coat them with the mixture and leave 20 minutes. Soak bamboo skewers in hot water.

Remove rind from bacon, cut each rasher into 3 pieces. Remove ribs and seeds from pepper and cut into squares.

Take a prawn, wrap bacon round and thread on to a skewer. Repeat with remaining prawns and bacon, including a piece of pepper with every second or third prawn.

Grill at medium heat under a preheated griller or over coals for 2-3 minutes on each side. Serve immediately. Serves 8 as a first course, 4 as a meal.

Skewered prawns

For a delicious smoky flavor, grill prawns before peeling.

500g raw prawns
¼ cup olive oil
¼ cup dry sherry
1 teaspoon grated fresh ginger
2 cloves garlic, crushed with 1 teaspoon salt
Freshly ground pepper
4 green shallots, finely shredded

Wash prawns, remove heads if preferred, leave shell intact. Make a slit along the back of each prawn and devein. Pat prawns with paper towels; mix together remaining ingredients except shallots, pour over prawns, cover and let stand for 1-2 hours in the refrigerator.

Thread prawns on to individual bamboo skewers and grill on hibachi or preheated grill turning and brushing with marinade several times. They will take 7-10 minutes depending on size of prawns. They should turn pink and be easily pierced with a fine skewer.

Serve hot from the grill with a garnish of shredded shallots. For a very pretty look, shred the shallots in long thin strips and drop into a bowl of iced water. They will curl up in the most delightful way. Drain before using. Serves 4.

Turkish lamb and eggplant kebabs

This aromatic mixture of grilled meat and vegetables is good pushed off the skewer into pocket bread and topped with sliced radish or a spoonful of tomato salad.

1 large or 2 small eggplant
Salt
2 onions
2 green peppers
1kg boneless lamb from the leg
MARINADE
½ cup olive oil
¼ cup lemon juice
½ cup red wine
½ cup chopped mint
3 cloves garlic, finely chopped
Salt and freshly ground black pepper

Cut unpeeled eggplant into 4cm cubes, sprinkle with salt and leave in a colander for 30 minutes to drain. Pat dry with paper towels.

Cut onions downward into quarters and separate into petals. Cut green pepper into squares. Trim gristle and most of the fat from the lamb and cut the meat into 4cm cubes.

Combine marinade ingredients in a large bowl, add meat and eggplant and marinate, turning over several times, for 3-4 hours. Drain, reserving marinade, and thread the lamb and eggplant cubes on skewers alternately with onion and green pepper.

Grill under a preheated griller or over hot coals, turning and brushing several times with reserved marinade, for 8-10 minutes. Serves 6.

Moslem kebabs

500g minced steak
1 small onion, chopped
2 tablespoons yogurt
1½ teaspoon curry powder
½ teaspoon salt
½ teaspoon ground ginger
Freshly ground pepper
½ teaspoon Garam Masala or pinch nutmeg
1 teaspoon lemon juice
½ teaspoon grated lemon rind

Mix all ingredients, beating thoroughly so the meat absorbs the yogurt. Divide into 6 portions and shape each around a thick skewer, in a long cigar shape.

Heat grill, place kebabs on a sheet of aluminium foil and place under grill, cook for 6-10 minutes, turning regularly, until brown all over.

Serve with a rice pilaf or boiled rice and a green salad or tomatoes. Offer a bowl of yogurt to spoon over kebabs. Serves 4-6.

Delicious basic kebabs

This is one of the simplest but best marinades I know. Use it for lamb, beef, pork or chicken. It is also good with scallops, green prawns or other seafood.

1½kg boneless lamb, tender steak, or other meat
MARINADE
4 tablespoons oil
4 tablespoons lemon juice
2 tablespoons chopped parsley
2 bay leaves, crumbled
1 clove garlic, finely chopped
Salt and freshly ground pepper

Trim excess fat and gristle from meat and cut into bite-size cubes. Combine marinade ingredients and place in a glass or pottery dish with meat. Marinate for 2 hours, turning now and again.

Thread cubes on to 6 metal skewers, spacing them a little apart. Reserve marinade. Brush grill rack with oil and cook skewers over hot coals or under a preheated grill for 4-5 minutes each side. They should be brown outside but still pink inside for beef or lamb — pork is usually preferred cooked through. Brush with marinade several times as they cook. Serve with rice or noodles, or inside soft buns or pita bread with salads. Serves 6.

Spiced chicken livers, Peru-style

In Peru in South America, spicy little tidbits called anticuchos are grilled over glowing coals by street vendors. They are usually prepared with beef heart, but chicken livers are delicious spiced the same way. Pass them around with predinner drinks, or serve as a first course.

500g chicken livers
MARINADE
½ cup wine vinegar
1 clove garlic, crushed
1 small, dried red chili, seeded and finely chopped
1 teaspoon powdered cumin
½ teaspoon salt
Freshly ground black pepper to taste
1 teaspoon ground coriander
SAUCE
¼ cup reserved marinade
1 tablespoon tomato paste
1 tablespoon oil
2 teaspoons worcestershire sauce

Pick over chicken livers, removing any membranes or discolored bits, and cut each in half. Combine marinade ingredients in a glass or pottery bowl, add livers, cover and chill for 2-3 hours.

Remove livers, reserving marinade, and thread 4-5 pieces on small, presoaked bamboo skewers. Mix ¼ cup of marinade with other sauce ingredients.

Grill livers under a hot grill for 5-6 minutes, turning often and brushing with the sauce. They should be crusty brown outside and still a little pink inside. Serves 4.

Pork satay

500g pork fillet, cut into 2cm cubes
MARINADE
1 tablespoon peanut oil
2 tablespoons lemon juice
1 clove garlic, crushed
1 tablespoon soy sauce
PEANUT SAUCE
3 tablespoons peanut butter
½ teaspoon sugar
½ teaspoon Tabasco
30g butter
1 clove garlic, crushed
1 tablespoon lemon juice
1½ tablespoons soy sauce
¼ cup cream

Combine marinade ingredients and pour over pork in a bowl. Mix gently, cover and marinate 2-4 hours. Drain, reserving marinade.

Thread cocktail sticks or bamboo skewers, previously soaked in water 2 hours, with 3-5 cubes of pork each. Grill over hibachi or under a preheated grill for 10-15 minutes or until well done, turning and brushing several times with reserved marinade. Arrange skewers on a bed of rice and pour warm peanut sauce over, or serve on cocktail sticks as party savories, with sauce in a bowl for dipping.

PEANUT SAUCE: Combine all ingredients except cream in a small saucepan. Cook over low heat, stirring constantly, until smooth. Remove from heat and stir in cream.

Oriental lamb kebabs

1kg (trimmed weight) lean lamb, cut from leg
Salt and freshly ground black pepper
2 teaspoons ground coriander
2 teaspoons cumin seed
1 onion, finely chopped
2 teaspoons brown sugar
3 tablespoons soy sauce
3 tablespoons lemon juice
1 teaspoon grated fresh ginger

Cut lamb into 2.5cm cubes and combine in a glass or pottery bowl with the remaining ingredients. Mix well and marinate at least 4 hours, or in the refrigerator overnight, turning the lamb from time to time.

Drain, reserving the marinade, and thread meat on to skewers, 4 to 6 cubes on each (if using wooden skewers, soak 30 minutes in hot water first, to prevent burning). Brush lamb with marinade and grill about 8cm from hot coals or a hot, preheated grill. Grill for 5 minutes, turn and baste with marinade, and repeat this every 5 minutes until done, 10 to 15 minutes. Serves 6.

Below: Moslem Kebabs served with rice are quick and easy to prepare.

Cool cooking

One of the exciting developments in today's shopping centres and main streets is the new style delis that specialise in their own home cooking. This is a world-wide trend. I have found people flocking to deli bars buying salads to take home and use supplemented with their own salad greens — obviously a quick and easy meal on the way. During summer and holidays its a good idea to make up a few salads to have on hand for meals when time is short. Many of the salads will keep a few days — some with tomatoes are best eaten on the day they are made, but those in dressings often seem better the next day. And what better way to start a meal on a warm day than with a chilled soup? These lovely soups are almost like liquid salads.

Four-bean salad

1 cup red kidney beans
1 cup haricot beans
Salt
125g green beans
1 cup frozen broad beans
6 tablespoons vinaigrette
2 tablespoons chopped parsley
1 tablespoon chopped mixed herbs (such as oregano, thyme, marjoram).

Soak kidney and haricot beans separately in water to cover overnight. Drain the beans. Place in separate pans, cover with cold water, bring to the boil and simmer for 1 to 1½ hours, until tender, adding a little salt towards the end of cooking. Drain and place in a bowl.

Cut the green beans into 2.5cm lengths. Cook the broad beans and green beans in boiling salted water for 7 to 8 minutes, until just tender. Drain and add to the bowl. Pour over the dressing while still warm. Cool, then stir in the herbs. Transfer to a serving dish. Serves 8.

Curried chicken and pineapple salad

3 celery sticks
4 cooked chicken fillets, cut into strips
1 cup pineapple pieces, drained
½ cup split almonds, browned
6 tablespoons mayonnaise
4 tablespoons natural yogurt
1-2 teaspoons curry paste
1 tablespoon tomato ketchup
Few lettuce leaves

Cut the celery into match-size strips. Place in a bowl with the chicken, pineapple and almonds. Toss the ingredients together.

Mix the mayonnaise, yogurt, curry paste and tomato ketchup together, pour over the chicken salad and mix thoroughly.

Place the lettuce on a serving dish and spoon the chicken mixture into the centre. Serves 4 to 6.

COOKED CHICKEN: Place the 4 fillets in saucepan with half an onion, carrot, bay leaf, 1 teaspoon salt, 4 peppercorns and water to cover. Bring to simmer and cook 12 minutes. Cool in cooking liquid.

Avocado and chicken salad

2 avocados
2-3 teaspoons lemon juice
4 poached chicken breasts, cooled, cut into pieces
1 x 230g can water chestnuts, drained and sliced
6 tablespoons natural yogurt
½ teaspoon worcestershire sauce
Salt and pepper
6 tablespoons mayonnaise

Peel avocados and cut into cubes. Place half in a bowl, pour over the lemon juice and toss well; this will prevent the avocado discoloring. Add the chicken and water chestnuts and mix together.

Mash the remaining avocado with the yogurt, worcestershire sauce, and salt and pepper to taste. Blend until smooth, then add to the mayonnaise and mix thoroughly.

Spoon the dressing over the chicken mixture and toss well to combine. Spoon on to a shallow serving dish. Serves 6.

Right: Clockwise from top left — Tortellini Salad, Curried Chicken And Pineapple Salad, Zucchini Salad, Four-Bean Salad, Haricot And Tuna Salad and Avocado And Chicken Salad.

Haricot and tuna salad

250g haricot beans
Salt
6 small tomatoes, skinned
¼ cup black olives, halved and stoned
1 salad onion, thinly sliced
1 stick celery, sliced
2 tablespoons chopped parsley
1 x 200g can tuna in oil, drained
4 tablespoons vinaigrette

Soak the beans overnight in water. Drain the beans, place in a pan and cover with cold water. Bring to the boil, cover and simmer for 1 to 1½ hours, until tender, adding a little salt towards the end of cooking. Drain well and leave to cool.

Cut each tomato into 6 wedges and place in a bowl with the beans, olives, onion, celery and parsley.

Flake the tuna into large pieces and add to the salad. Pour over the dressing and toss well. Serves 6.

Zucchini salad

8 small zucchini, thinly sliced
6 tablespoons vinaigrette
4 small tomatoes, sliced
¼ cup black olives, halved and stoned
1 small salad onion, sliced
2 cloves garlic, finely chopped
1 tablespoon chopped basil
1 tablespoon chopped parsley

Place the zucchini in a bowl, pour over the dressing and leave to marinate several hours.

Add the remaining ingredients, toss thoroughly and turn into a salad bowl. Serves 6.

Cold green shallot soup

This soup is best when slightly chilled, and should be served on the day it is made.

1 large bunch green shallots including tops
1 tablespoon butter
1 onion, chopped
¾ teaspoon ground cumin
Pinch Mexican-style chili powder
4 cups chicken stock
2 potatoes, peeled and sliced
1 teaspoon sugar
Salt and freshly ground black pepper
¼ cup cream

Chop shallots, reserving 1 green top for garnish. Melt butter in a large, heavy saucepan, add onion and cook, covered, stirring once or twice, until it is soft.

Add cumin and chili powder and cook, stirring, 1 minute. Add stock and potatoes and stir until boiling, cover and cook gently 10 minutes. Add chopped shallots and sugar and simmer, partly covered, for 15 minutes.

Puree the soup in batches in a blender or food processor, transferring it as it is pureed to a bowl, and season with salt and pepper. Cool, whisk in cream, cover and refrigerate just until lightly chilled, not too cold. Garnish with finely chopped green shallot tops to serve. Serves 4.

Tortellini salad

1 packet frozen tortellini
3 tablespoons vinaigrette
½ cup mayonnaise
2 tablespoons tomato sauce
4-5 sun dried tomatoes, sliced (optional)
1 tablespoon chopped parsley
1 tablespoon chopped basil (optional)

Cook tortellini in boiling salted water about 13-15 minutes, or follow instructions on packet. Drain.

Toss tortellini in vinaigrette in a bowl and allow to cool. Combine mayonnaise and sauce and fold through tortellini, adding dried tomatoes, if using, and top with chopped parsley and basil. Serve in a bowl, lined if liked with lettuce.

Beetroot soup

1kg beetroot
6 cups chicken stock
1 cup dry red wine
1 teaspoon sugar
1 carrot
1 Spanish or mild white onion
2 tablespoons snipped fresh dill
1 tablespoon red wine vinegar
Salt and freshly ground black pepper
Sour cream

Trim tops from beetroot, leaving about 2.5cm of stem attached. Wash beetroot but leave whole and do not peel. Place in a saucepan with chicken stock, wine and sugar and simmer, covered, for 30-40 minutes or until beetroot is tender. Remove beetroot with a slotted spoon and, when cool enough to handle, slip off the skins.

Strain cooking liquid through a fine sieve lined with a dampered paper towel into a large bowl. Chill, covered, at least 4 hours or overnight.

Cut carrot and beetroot into match-stick strips. Slice onion very thin lengthwise and separate into strips. Drop carrot into boiling salted water, boil 30 seconds, add onion and boil 30 seconds longer. Drain into a colander and refresh under cold water. Chill these vegetables and the beetroot separately, covered.

Skim any fat from the chilled cooking liquid, add vegetables, dill, vinegar and salt and pepper to taste. Stir until well mixed, ladle soup into chilled bowls and serve, passing sour cream separately. Serves 6.

Avocado lime soup

Two avocados serve 6 people when made into this inviting soup.

2 ripe avocados
3 cups chicken stock
1 tablespoon fresh lime or lemon juice (to taste)
1 cup cream
Salt
Cayenne pepper
6 very thin lime or lemon slices

Peel and stone avocados. Reserve a wedge for garnish, brush it with lime or lemon juice, wrap in plastic film and chill.

Chop remaining avocado and puree it with the chicken stock in batches in a blender or food processor. Transfer to a large bowl and stir in lime or lemon juice, cream and salt and cayenne to taste.

Cover and chill 1-2 hours, no longer, or soup will darken. Slice reserved avocado and serve soup garnished with lime or lemon and avocado slices. Serves 6.

Minted cucumber soup

4 cucumbers
1 cup buttermilk
½ cup plain yogurt
Salt and pepper
1 tablespoon finely chopped mint
250g cooked prawns, shelled and deveined (optional)

Peel, seed and chop 3 of the cucumbers, place in a blender or food processor with buttermilk and yogurt and process until smooth. Strain the puree through a fine sieve into a bowl, pressing hard on the solids, and add salt and pepper to taste.

Peel the remaining cucumber very thinly to leave some of the green under the skin. Halve, scoop out seeds and chop flesh fine. Add to the soup with the chopped mint, cover and chill. If including prawns add at this time, reserving for garnish.

Serve in chilled bowls, garnishing each with a cucumber slice and a prawn or mint sprig. Serves 4.

Right: Clockwise from bottom — Avocado Lime Soup, Cold Green Shallot Soup, Beetroot Soup and Minted Cucumber Soup.

● *For vinaigrette and mayonnaise recipes, see page 12.*

December

Baking for Christmas

Baking for Christmas is one of those reassuring rituals we all seem to enjoy. It is mostly a family affair with the children taking their turn in stirring the pudding, chopping fruits and nuts for the cake, creating pretty boxes for gifts or wrapping sweetmeats in plastic wrap. It is a happy time.

In my family we all have our jobs. One sister makes the mincemeat and the pudding or cake, another sister is a dab hand at shortbread. Suzanne, my daughter, gets her children to help with special biscuits and sweetmeats — they make lovely marzipan fruits. One thing for sure, our pantries are filled to the brim with all the delectable, rich, fruity and spicy treats that come out at the festive season, for all our friends. The recipes are basically the same with little changes introduced to see if there can be any improvements.

Here are all the lovely things we make for Christmas.

Christmas spice cookies

You can cut this spicy dough into any Christmas shapes — stars, reindeers, hearts or animals — and decorate them with icing and cherries, silver cachous; they make great gifts for visiting children.

60g butter, softened
½ cup brown sugar, firmly packed
½ cup golden syrup
3½ cups plain flour
1 teaspoon bicarbonate of soda
1 teaspoon ground cinnamon
1 teaspoon ground cardamom
½ teaspoon salt
About ⅓ cup water
Currants, cherries, silver cachous, icing etc, to decorate

Cream the butter and sugar well, then mix in the golden syrup. Sift the flour with the soda, spices and salt and add to the creamed mixture in three lots, alternately with the water, add just enough water to make a firm, pliable dough.

Roll the dough out thinly on a floured surface and cut out the shapes. You can make a pattern out of stiff cardboard and cut around it with a sharp knife.

Decorate before baking with currants for eyes, a piece of cherry for a mouth, silver cachous for buttons, etc, other decorations may be added later with icing. Bake on greased trays in a preheated oven 180C (350F) for about 8 minutes, depending on thickness. Test to see if they are cooked by pressing with a finger — the dough should spring back. Remove and cool on a wire rack.

Use a toothpick or fine pipe to make details on shapes and finish with extra pieces of cherry, angelica, silver cachous etc.

ICING: Beat half an egg white until just frothy and gradually beat in ¾-1 cup sifted icing sugar until thick and smooth.

Eccles cakes

A very old-fashioned recipe that has stood the test of time. So easy with frozen puff pastry.

30g butter, melted
2 tablespoons brown sugar
2 tablespoons chopped mixed peel
¾ cup currants
¼ teaspoon mixed spice
1 packet frozen puff pastry, thawed
Milk and castor sugar to glaze

Stir the butter, sugar, fruit and spice together. Cool.

Place an oven shelf in the second top position and set the oven to hot, 220C (425F). Roll out the pastry about 3mm thick and cut 9-10cm rounds, using a floured cutter.

Place a scant tablespoon of filling

Right: A wonderful array of seasonal baking — Christmas Cake, Rich Christmas Pudding, Mince Pies and Christmas Spice Cookies in a variety of shapes.

in the centre of each round. Dampen the edges of the pastry with water, then draw them up to meet in the centre and seal by pressing together. Turn them over, and roll gently with a rolling pin to make circles 8-9 cm across.

Place the cakes on dampened baking trays and chill for 15 minutes. Brush the tops with milk and sprinkle with castor sugar. Cut 3 slits across the top of each cake and bake for 15-20 minutes in a hot oven until golden brown. Makes 16.

Christmas cake

Christmas cake means a large, rich fruit cake which is best made well before Christmas so it will age and develop a rich luscious flavor.

125g candied peel, finely chopped
250g sultanas
250g currants
250g raisins
125g glace cherries, cut in half
60g angelica, finely chopped
2½ cups plain flour
½ teaspoon baking powder
½ teaspoon salt
250g butter
1½ cups soft brown sugar
125g chopped almonds
5 eggs
3 tablespoons rum or brandy

Place the fruits in a bowl and sprinkle with 3 tablespoons of the flour, tossing them to coat the pieces evenly. Set aside and sift the remaining flour with the baking powder and salt.

Cream the butter and then add the sugar gradually, beating until the mixture is light and fluffy. Add the chopped almonds. Add the eggs one by one, beating in between each addition.

Fold in the flour (about 6 tablespoons at a time) and mix carefully until thoroughly incorporated.

Mix the fruit into the cake batter and then stir in the rum.

Spoon the cake batter into a 20cm lined tin and smooth the top, making a slight depression in the centre so that the top of the cake will be level when baked. Place on the centre rack in a preheated oven at 150C (300F) for about 2 hours, then lower the oven temperature to 140C (290F) and bake for a further 1½ hours until a fine skewer inserted in the centre of the cake comes out clean. If the cake tends to brown too much during baking, place a double sheet of dampened brown paper over it.

Remove the cake from the oven and allow to cool in its tin for 30 minutes, then remove to a cake rack and allow to cool completely. Wrap securely in aluminium foil and store in a dark, cool place until ready to ice.

Note: If liked, top the cake with split almonds before baking.

LINING THE TIN: Cut a strip of double thickness greaseproof or baking paper 8cm higher than the cake tin and cut two circles of paper to fit the base of the tin — one in greaseproof paper, one in brown paper. Grease the tin well and fit the paper strip and then the greaseproof paper circle in the base. Brush with melted butter.

Cut a strip of brown paper or kitchen paper 10cm higher than the tin and make a 1cm hem. Nick the hem with a pair of scissors at 2.5cm intervals and fit this strip into the tin, making sure the hem lies flat on the base.

Place second disc of paper into the tin giving a neat finish to the lining and then brush the whole paper lining with melted butter.

Note: Instead of fitting a brown paper strip inside the tin it may be tied around the outside, giving the same protection.

Rich Christmas pudding

This is a rich Christmas pudding steamed in a basin rather than a pudding cloth. This pudding improves with keeping and is particularly good served with a brandied butter, a custard sauce or a sabayon sauce.

750g mixed dried fruit
60g candied peel
3 tablespoons overproof rum or brandy
250g butter
250g brown sugar
Grated rind of 1 orange and 1 lemon
4 eggs
60g blanched almonds, chopped
1 cup plain flour
½ teaspoon each salt, mixed spice, nutmeg, ginger, cinnamon and bicarbonate of soda
125g soft breadcrumbs

Mix the fruit and peel, sprinkle with rum and leave overnight.

The next day, cream the butter and add the sugar gradually with the fruit rinds. Add the eggs which have been lightly beaten, a little at a time to prevent the mixture from curdling, then stir in the fruit and blanched chopped nuts alternately with sifted dry ingredients and breadcrumbs.

Put into a large well-buttered pudding basin lined with a circle of greased greaseproof paper cut to fit the base. Cover with another circle of greased greaseproof paper (to fit the top of the pudding basin) then with a pudding cloth which has been scalded, wrung out and floured lightly. Tie firmly with string.

Steam covered in a saucepan with boiling water to come half-way up the sides of the pudding basin for 6 hours. Add more boiling water if necessary. Remove from the water and when cold cover with fresh greaseproof paper and tie up once more.

On Christmas Day put the pudding into a saucepan of boiling water as described above and steam for 2½ hours, or the pudding may be resteamed overnight in a crockpot on low.

Turn the hot pudding on to a heated serving plate. Warm a little rum or brandy in a soup ladle or small saucepan, set alight and pour over the pudding at the table. Serve immediately.

Scottish black bun

Black Bun is the New Year cake of the Scots — a rich fruit cake perfumed with spices and encased in pastry. All Scots will make it now for the New Year.

PASTRY
3 cups self-raising flour
Pinch salt
125g butter
Cold water
Beaten egg to glaze

FILLING
4 cups plain flour
1 teaspoon freshly ground black pepper
1 teaspoon each ground allspice and cinnamon
1 teaspoon ground ginger
1 teaspoon bicarbonate of soda
2 teaspoons cream of tartar
185g almonds
125g mixed peel
1kg raisins
1kg currants
1⅓ cups firmly packed brown sugar
1 to 1¼ cups milk

PASTRY: Sift the flour and salt into a bowl. Rub in the butter until the mixture resembles fine breadcrumbs. Add enough cold water (about 3 tablespoons) to make a firm dough. Knead lightly until smooth, then form into a ball, wrap in wax paper and chill.

Grease a deep, round 25 or 30cm cake tin and set oven temperature at moderate 180C (350F). Roll two-thirds of the pastry dough thinly and line the bottom and sides of the tin, allowing pastry to overlap the sides a little

Spoon the filling into the pastry-lined tin and pack down well, so that it is 1cm below the rim. Fold edge of pastry over the fruit filling and brush with lightly beaten egg. Roll out remaining pastry and place on top, pinching the edges together to seal.

With a skewer make a few holes right through the bun. Prick the top of the pastry with a fork and brush with beaten egg. Bake in moderate oven for at least three hours. If the top browns too quickly, cover with damp brown paper. Remove from oven and allow to cool in tin before turning out.

FILLING: Sift the flour, pepper, spices, ginger, bicarbonate of soda and cream of tartar into a large bowl. Chop the almonds, peel and raisins and add to the bowl with the currants and brown sugar. Combine all the ingredients and mix to a stiff consistency with milk.

Boiled plum pudding

Everyone has a favorite recipe for plum pudding. For those who like to boil their pudding in a cloth, this is not as heavy as the usual pudding and has no spices, but develops a marvellous flavor after two weeks' maturation. You need a very large saucepan for this pudding, otherwise make it in a basin and steam it.

185g raisins, roughly chopped
125g dates, roughly chopped
185g sultanas
125g currants
90g mixed peel
¼ cup brandy
60g chopped almonds
4 cups self-raising flour
1 teaspoon salt
250g suet, grated
1 cup castor sugar
½ cup treacle
1½ cups water

Sprinkle the fruit with brandy and let stand overnight. Next day add the almonds.

Sift the flour and salt into a large mixing bowl. Grate the suet and add to the bowl.

Rub the grated suet into the flour until it resembles breadcrumbs. Stir in the sugar, fruit and then the treacle mixed with the water. Mix thoroughly to a firm batter.

Put a large pudding cloth in boiling water, remove (using rubber gloves) and wring out well. Sprinkle with sifted flour and shake off any excess. (This makes the skin that everyone loves and seals in the pudding.)

Turn pudding mixture into the centre of the cloth and gather the cloth firmly around the pudding. Secure the cloth firmly with string.

Tie the ends of the pudding cloth around a wooden spoon and rest the wooden spoon on the edges of the boiler preventing the pudding touching the bottom of the pot. Cook in boiling water to cover and place a lid over the top. Steam for 1 hour and by this time the pudding will have taken shape and the wooden spoon may be removed. Steam for a further 2½ hours.

Hang the pudding for at least 2 weeks to mature in a dark, dry place.

On Christmas Day, steam the pudding for a further 1 to 1½ hours. Turn on to a heated platter, heat some brandy, set alight and pour flaming over the pudding, taking it immediately to the table.

Serve with vanilla ice cream, Rum Butter or just whipped cream.

Note: Do not remove the pudding cloth before resteaming, even if a mould forms on the cloth. Just wipe it off — the boiling water will sterilise any mould.

Fruit malt loaf

Every visitor to England seems to fall in love with the dark, moist, fruit loaf flavored with malt. Here's the recipe that will bring back memories! It's perfect during Christmas because it keeps fresh for days wrapped in plastic in an airtight tin. In very hot, humid weather, store in the refrigerator.

2 cups wholemeal bread flour
½ teaspoon salt
¾ cup sultanas
60g butter
3 tablespoons malt extract
1½ tablespoons molasses
30g fresh yeast, or 2½ teaspoons dried yeast
⅓ cup lukewarm water
1 tablespoon honey, to glaze

Place the flour, salt and sultanas in a warmed bowl and mix together. Place the butter, malt and molasses in a small saucepan and heat gently until the butter melts. Allow to cool for 5 minutes.

Blend the yeast with a little of the water, stir in the remaining water, then add to the dry ingredients with the butter-malt mixture. Stir with a wooden spoon until the dry ingredients are moistened and the mixture forms a soft dough.

Turn out on to a lightly floured surface and knead for 10 minutes until smooth and elastic. Place the dough in a warmed, greased bowl, turning it to grease all surfaces, and cover with greased plastic wrap. Leave in a warm place for 1 hour until doubled in size.

Punch down to knock out air bubbles, turn out on to a floured surface, and knead again for 5 minutes. Pat the dough into a rectangle, fold into three, and fit into a warm greased, 500g bread tin, shaping it into the corners. Cover with plastic and leave in a warm place for 30 minutes, until the dough has risen to the top of the tin. Bake in a preheated hot oven 200C (400F) for 45 minutes. Turn out on to a wire rack, brush the top with honey, and allow to cool. Makes one 500g loaf.

Note: Bread flour, molasses, malt and yeast are all available from your health-food shop.

Marzipan sweetmeats

Christmas wouldn't be the same without these little marzipan sweetmeats. In many countries, the marzipan is moulded into little fruits and vegetables.

500g marzipan — an excellent Danish commercial brand called Odense is readily available in 227g rolls
TO FLAVOR AND COLOR
Sherry or rum and green coloring
Rum and pink coloring

Divide marzipan into two portions. Flavor one portion with sherry or rum and color it pale green and second portion with rum and pink coloring. Knead flavoring and color into marzipan until perfectly distributed, adding the color discreetly — a few drops at a time — a little more can always be added if the color is not distinct. At this stage, the marzipan may be wrapped in waxed paper or foil and stored in the refrigerator.

MARZIPAN PECANS: Roll small pieces of marzipan into balls about the size of a small pecan. Press a perfect pecan half into each side and roll in castor sugar. Place in paper cups and store in a box in the refrigerator if the weather is warm.

Stuffed figs

185g dried figs
1 cup coarsely chopped, lightly toasted almonds
⅓ cup finely chopped peel
Icing sugar

Place figs in a saucepan with sufficient water to cover, bring slowly to the boil, reduce heat and simmer 5 minutes. Drain and cool. Make a lengthwise slit in figs, shape around the rounded side of a teaspoon to make a cavity for the stuffing.

Combine almonds and peel and fill each fig with a good teaspoon of the mixture and press figs to close. Dust with icing sugar.

Store in refrigerator until required, or gift wrap.

Scottish shortbread

250g butter
½ cup castor sugar
500g plain flour

Cream the butter until it resembles whipped cream and then add the sugar gradually, beating it until it is light and fluffy. Work in the flour gradually and then knead the dough for about 5 minutes until the mixture is very smooth.

Divide the dough into three pieces and press into 20cm circles or flan rings standing on baking sheets or sandwich tins.

With the heel of the hand push the dough out until the mixture is very smooth, then smooth over surface with a palette knife.

Remove the flan ring, is using, and crimp the edges by pressing the edge of the pastry with the finger and then pinching the edge together. If using a sandwich tin, fork the edge for decoration.

Prick the surface of the shortbread with a fork and bake in the centre of a moderate oven 180C (350F) for 20 minutes and then reduce the temperature to 150C (300F) and bake for a further 25 minutes.

Note: The surface of the shortbread is pricked with a fork to release the moisture as it cooks, making the shortbread crisp.

When shortbread is gift-wrapped for any length of time it may soften a little. This can be remedied by placing it in a moderate 180C (350F) oven for 15 minutes.

Boiled whisky fruit cake

Some people prefer a not-so-rich Christmas cake. This one has the added bonus that it's economical and extra-quick to mix.

750g mixed dried fruit
185g butter or margarine
¾ cup water
1¼ cups brown sugar, firmly packed
¼ cup whisky
3 large eggs
1 cup plain flour
1½ cups self-raising flour
1½ teaspoons mixed spice
¼ teaspoon salt
½ teaspoon bicarbonate of soda

Grease a deep, 20cm cake tin and line with greased brown paper or baking paper. Set the oven at moderate, 180C (350F).

Place the dried fruit in a large saucepan with the butter, water and brown sugar. Bring slowly to the boil, then simmer for 5 minutes. Remove from the heat and cool until lukewarm.

Stir in the whisky and add the eggs to the mixture one at a time, beating well each time with a wooden spoon. Sift the flours with the spice, salt and bicarbonate and stir into the mixture, combining thoroughly.

Spoon into the prepared tin and bake for 45 minutes. Reduce the heat to moderately slow 160C (325F) and cook a further 45 minutes, or until a skewer inserted in the centre of the cake comes out clean. Leave the cake for a minute or two in the tin, then turn out on to a wire cake rack and allow to cool before removing the paper.

Note: For Christmas, the top of the cake can be decorated with almonds before baking, or it can be iced afterwards.

Fruit Mincemeat

This is an excellent fruit mince, best stored in the refrigerator when the weather is very hot.

375g seedless raisins
250g mixed candied peel
185g sultanas
3 medium apples, peeled and cored
60g glace cherries
125g blanched almonds
100g dried apricots
185g currants
2 cups firmly packed brown sugar
Grated rind and juice 1 lemon
Graded rind 1 orange
2 teaspoons mixed spice
½ teaspoon nutmeg
125-185g finely grated suet
⅓ cup brandy or rum

Finely chop or mince raisins, mixed peel, half the sultanas, the apples, cherries, almonds and apricots. Add remaining sultanas and currants. Stir in brown sugar, lemon rind and juice, orange rind, spice, suet and brandy or rum. Mix well and put into a large jar. Cover and chill. Stir every day for a week. Mincemeat can be kept for a few weeks in the refrigerator. Makes about 6 cups.

Mince pies

Mince pies can be made ahead, frozen and reheated when required. Use small individual tart cases or tiny petits-fours pans for baking pies. You can dust the cooled pies with sifted icing sugar or leave them plain. Either way, the taste of crisp pastry and tangy fruit mincemeat is magnificent.

90g butter
¼ cup castor sugar
1 egg
1½ cups flour
½ teaspoon baking powder
Beaten egg to glaze
1 cup Fruit Mincemeat
Sifted icing sugar

Cream butter with sugar. Add egg and beat well. Sift flour and baking powder and stir into creamed mixture. Knead lightly on floured board. Wrap dough in plastic wrap and chill for 1 hour. Roll out thin and cut into rounds to fit lightly greased patty tins.

Cut same number of smaller circles to fit tops of pies. Moisten edges with beaten egg and put 1 heaped teaspoon Fruit Mincemeat into each. Make a small slit in each pastry lid or cut with a small star cutter. Top each filled pie with lid and press edges of pastry well to seal. Glaze with beaten egg. Bake in a preheated moderate oven 180C (350F) for 20-30 minutes or until pale golden-brown. Remove from oven and dust with icing sugar. Makes about 12 individual pies or 24 petits-fours size.

Rum butter

The combination of a chilled hard sauce flavored with the spirit of your choice and a piping hot rich fruit pudding is particularly enticing. These flavored butters may be made at the same time as the pudding and stored successfully in the refrigerator or freezer.

250g unsalted butter
125g brown sugar
1 tablespoon grated lemon rind
½ teaspoon lemon juice
Freshly grated nutmeg
2 tablespoons overproof rum

Cream the butter until soft and white. This may take a little time but it's well worth the effort. Beat in the sugar gradually until the mixture is light and fluffy, then beat in the lemon rind, juice and nutmeg.

Lastly, add the rum, a little at a time, beating constantly so the mixture does not curdle. Pack the rum butter into a container with a firm fitting lid, first covering the top with plastic wrap or foil. Store in the refrigerator or freezer until Christmas Day.

Dundee cake

This is for those who prefer a lighter cake for Christmas. Like all fruit cakes this Dundee Cake improves with keeping and is best made at least 2 weeks before serving.

250g butter
1 cup castor sugar
2 oranges
5 eggs
2½ cups of plain flour
¼ teaspoon baking powder
½ teaspoon salt
½ cup blanched almonds, chopped
1 cup sultanas
1 cup glace cherries

¼ cup mixed peel
1 cup currants
Extra almonds

Grease a 20cm round tin and line with one thickness of brown and one thickness of greaseproof paper. Grease the paper. Set the oven temperature at 150C (300F).

Cream the butter and the sugar with the grated rind of the oranges. Beat in the eggs, one at a time. Sift the flour with the baking powder and salt. Mix into the fruit and chopped almonds. Stir into the creamed mixture with 1 tablespoon of orange juice. Turn into the prepared tin. Smooth the top and arrange the extra blanched almonds around the top. Bake in a slow oven for about 2½ hours or until a skewer placed in the centre comes out clean. Cool in the tin.

Note: Fruit cakes will keep for weeks, even months. So care must be taken to prevent them from drying out after they have been baked.

There is a correct way to cut fruit cakes. Cut a 1cm slice from one side of the cake and continue slicing as needed. The cut surface is then covered with greaseproof paper or it stands on its end (the cut end) depending on the cake tin. It keeps freshest this way.

An old trick is to put a wedge of apple in the tin to help keep the cake moist.

Bishop's cake

Mostly fruit and nuts and known also as American candied fruit cake, this gets its name from the lovely stained glass appearance when cut in thin slices. Keep refrigerated and slice as needed. Serve with coffee or a glass of sherry or gift wrap for some lucky person.

2 cups plain flour
2 teaspoons baking powder
½ teaspoon salt
500g glace pineapple, coarsely diced
500g glace pears, apricots, peaches or a mixture of these, coarsely diced
500g mixed dried fruit
250g glace cherries, red and green, halved
4 eggs
1 cup sugar
1kg shelled pecans, walnuts, brazil nuts, blanched almonds or a mixture of these
½ cup Grand Marnier, Cointreau or curacao.

Grease two 23 x 13 x 8cm loaf pans or 3-4 smaller pans and line with greased brown paper. Sift flour, baking powder and salt into a large bowl. Add fruits and mix well with hands to coat each piece of fruit with flour. Beat eggs until frothy and gradually beat in sugar. Add to fruit and mix well. With hands, mix in nuts.

Turn mixture into pans and press down firmly with fingers. Bake in a very slow oven 140C (275F) for about 1½ hours. Leave cakes in pans and, while still hot, pour liqueur over a little at a time. Leave until quite cold, then remove from tins and take off paper. Wrap well and store in refrigerator. Serve straight from refrigerator, cut into very thin slices.

Above: Fruit and nuts galore in a Bishop's Cake, and what Christmas is complete without Mince Pies? Also shown are delectable Stuffed Figs.

Christmas dinner

Christmas dinner is one of the big family meals of the year, it is a time for feasting and rejoicing. Thanks to the general feeling of goodwill, it is a time when the family is eager to join in and help with the preparations, for, tackled alone, Christmas dinner can be an almost overwhelming job.
I am lucky, for in my family there are three good cooks. We rotate the venue each year and we each prepare a course. This gives us a chance to do our own thing with table settings and decorations which we always keep as a surprise.
What shall we have for Christmas dinner this year? — every year we discuss the merits of turkey, goose, duckling, turkey buffe, tiny whole chickens.
Picture us sitting around the table planning our Christmas dinner as you plan your own special dinner — the most joyous meal of the year.

Turkey Tips

BUYING: If buying a large bird make sure beforehand that your oven is large enough to hold it. There's a turkey just the right size for every occasion.

WHAT SIZE TURKEY TO BUY? A size 27 turkey weighs 2.7kg and will serve 4 people; sizes 31-34 weigh 3.1-3.4kg and serve up to 6; sizes 36-38 weigh 3.6-3.8kg and serve up to 8; sizes 45-54 weigh 4.5-5.4kg and will serve between 12 and 16 people.

THAWING: Frozen turkey must be completely thawed before cooking. The best way to thaw a frozen turkey is in the refrigerator, in its wrapping, on a dish to catch the juices. This will take two or three days. Thawing may be hastened by leaving the bird at room temperature in its wrapping. The giblets and neck should be removed as soon as the cavity is thawed. This will take 15 to 24 hours. If you must thaw it very quickly, leave it in its wrapper and submerge it in cold water in the sink. Change the water frequently.

WIPE DRY: The bird should be washed and then dried inside and out with a paper kitchen towel before using.

STUFFING: Stuff turkey just before cooking, never ahead of time. Stuff the crop first. Fold over the skin of the neck and secure with a poultry pin. Then stuff the inside cavity. Never overstuff the turkey as the stuffing expands and may cause the skin to burst during cooking.

TO TRUSS: Place the turkey on its back, legs towards you. Take a piece of string and place the middle of the string below the breast at the neck end, bring the ends down over the wings and then down underneath the bird. Cross the string underneath then bring it forward and up to tie the ends of the drumsticks and the parson's nose together.

Wipe bird with a paper towel and spread butter over, being sure to cover the breast and legs well. Grind a little pepper over.

HOW TO COOK A TURKEY: In aluminium foil: stuff and truss the turkey. Brush with 30g melted butter. Wrap in heavy-duty aluminium foil enclosing the bird completely. Fold edges of foil together on top.

Alternatively, the turkey may be placed in a baking dish and covered with aluminium foil. The width of most packages of foil is not usually large enough to cover a whole turkey. Two sheets can be joined by folding edges together. Place over turkey and seal foil to edges of baking dish. Roast in a moderate oven 180C (350F) using the following times as a guide: 3-4kg — 3 hours; 4-5kg — 3½ to 4 hours; 6-8kg — 4 hours.

About 1 hour before the end of cooking, unwrap the turkey, baste regularly with melted butter and pan juices and cook, uncovered, until tender and golden brown. Allow to stand 15-20 minutes before carving.

COOKING A TURKEY IN AN OVEN BAG: Turkey size oven bags can be purchased from most stores. They are easy to use and simple instructions come with every pack of bags.

Using this method turkeys will cook faster. The bag will retain all the moisture in the meat and leave your oven clean afterwards. Cooking times using the bag method are as follows: size 27 — 1 hour, 20 minutes; size 45 — 1 hour, 50 minutes; size 72 — 3 hours, 10 minutes.

WHEN IS THE TURKEY COOKED? The turkey is cooked if a meat thermometer pushed into the thickest part of the thigh registers 90C (190F). If you don't own a meat thermometer pierce the thickest part of the thigh with a fork. If it is easily pierced and the juice which is released is clear, the turkey is cooked.

Never hurry the cooking of a bird at a high heat, as the outside skin will scorch before the heat has penetrated inside.

HOW TO CARVE THE TURKEY: Remove the trussing string and poultry pins. Place a long-bladed sharp knife between the thigh and the body of the bird and cut through the joint. Remove the leg by pressing it outward with the knife and bending it back with the fork. Separate the thigh and drumsticks and slice off dark meat. Repeat with other leg.

Left: A magnificently cooked turkey takes pride of place on the Christmas dinner table, surrounded by gravy, the stuffing, cranberry sauce and a selection of tempting vegetables.

Remove wings. Carve the breast with straight, even strokes. Carve the stuffing in the crop into thin slices and remove stuffing from the body with a spoon.

STORE LEFTOVERS CAREFULLY: After any meal store leftovers promptly. If stuffing is involved, remove from bird and store separately.

Stuffing the festive bird

Some say the stuffing is almost the favorite part of a festive roast bird or meat. As well as adding an interesting flavor, a stuffing can help the cook by holding the food in shape, keeping it moist and making it go further.

Mix and handle stuffings lightly so as not to compact them, and to leave room for the stuffings to expand during cooking and stay light. If some stuffing is left over after filling food, cook it separately in a greased baking dish.

It is best to cook onion and garlic lightly before adding them to stuffing, as this improves the flavor and aids digestion. You should also precook pork or sausage mince until it changes color, to make sure that it will be cooked through. Always stuff poultry just before cooking; this is a safety measure.

Make fresh breadcrumbs for stuffings, using bread 2-4 days old, by pulling it apart very lightly with your fingers or with two forks. Do not put bread through a mincer, as the stuffing will be too compact.

Of course, if you have a blender or food processor, beautiful crumbs can be made in a trice.

Roast stuffed turkey

I like to use two different stuffings for a turkey. A meat stuffing for the breast gives a beautiful shape and keeps the meat moist, a bread stuffing for the cavity has the traditional flavoring. Form leftover stuffing into balls and bake to serve with turkey.

Size 55 (5.5kg) turkey
1 quantity Sausage Stuffing
1 quantity Herb Stuffing
60g softened butter
Freshly ground pepper

Wipe cavity of turkey with damp paper towels. Spoon Sausage Stuffing into the crop, being careful not to pack it too tightly, and press the outside of the breast to mould the stuffing to a good shape.

Bring the neck flap over the stuffing to the back and secure it with a poultry pin or small skewer. Spoon Herb Stuffing into the cavity. Shape the bird nicely with both hands.

Dot bird with butter and sprinkle with pepper. Follow directions for roasting.

Turkey gravy

2 tablespoons plain flour
30g butter
3 cups turkey giblet stock
1 turkey liver

Skim about 2 tablespoons of fat from the pan juices and blend with the flour to a smooth paste. Pour off excess turkey drippings, leaving about 3 tablespoons. Place the roasting pan on the heat, stir in the butter and flour, allow to brown lightly. Stir in 3 cups of stock, scraping up all the crusty pan residue. Bring to the boil. Simmer 2 minutes. Strain.

Fry the turkey liver separately in a little butter until well browned all over, but still a pale rosy pink inside — about 2 minutes. Remove from heat, dice and add to the strained gravy just before serving. Adjust seasoning if necessary, skim excess fat from top. Serve piping hot.

TURKEY STOCK: Gently simmer turkey giblets and neck with 1 halved onion, 1 bay leaf, 1 stick celery, and 7 cups water until reduced to 5 cups. Strain and use to make gravy.

Note: Chicken, duckling or goose gravy is made in exactly the same way as Turkey Gravy, substituting chicken backs and wings for the basic stock and any giblets or trimmings of the bird being cooked.

Oyster stuffing

Sufficient for a small turkey or use to stuff breast or cavity.

180g butter
1 large onion, finely chopped
3 cups fresh breadcrumbs
3 sticks celery, chopped
1 teaspoon mixed dried herbs
1 tablespoon chopped parsley
Salt and pepper to taste
1 egg lightly beaten
2 small or 1 large bottle(s) of oysters, about 12 oysters.
Little milk or water to bind

Melt butter in a saucepan, add onion and cook until soft. Add 1 cup crumbs, cook over low heat until butter is absorbed. Place mixture in a bowl, add remaining crumbs, celery, herbs, egg, salt and pepper. Drain, lightly chop oysters. Add to crumb mixture. If necessary, bind with a little milk or water.

Sausage stuffing

½ cup milk
4 slices white bread, cubed
500g pork sausage meat
2 stalks celery, finely sliced
1 small onion, chopped
1 tablespoon parsley, chopped
2 teaspoons chopped thyme
1 beaten egg
Salt and pepper

Pour milk over bread cubes and let stand for 30 minutes. Mix together sausage meat, celery, onion, herbs and soaked bread, blend well together with beaten egg, season with salt and pepper. If pork sausage meat or mince is unobtainable buy pork sausage, split the skin and hold the sausage under the cold tap, the meat will separate easily from skins.

Herb stuffing

1 small onion, finely chopped
30g butter
2 cups fresh breadcrumbs
1 tablespoon chopped fresh herbs
2 tablespoons chopped parsley
2 teaspoons grated lemon rind
1 egg, beaten
Salt and pepper to taste
Lemon juice or stock

Combine onion, butter, breadcrumbs, herbs and lemon rind and store in the refrigerator in a covered bowl until ready to use.

Add beaten egg, salt and pepper and a little lemon juice or stock. Toss with a fork, don't overmix.

Turkey buffe

Everyone gets the choice breast meat in this superb turkey cut. The complete bone-in breast (the drumsticks, thighs and wings to the first joint have been removed) has been one of the glamor meats found at many grand banquets and parties over recent years. Now you can order it from major supermarkets and poultry shops. The average weight is 5kg. It is snap frozen, so simply thaw and roast as required.

1 turkey buffe
2 tablespoons oil or butter
Salt and freshly ground pepper
1 quantity sausage or oyster stuffing

Thaw turkey buffe in bag in refrigerator for 24 hours or at room temperature overnight. Smear butter over breast, season with salt and freshly ground pepper. Place in baking dish and cover loosely with foil, roast 30 minutes per kg in a moderate oven 180C (350F) about 2½ hours, remove foil from top for last 30 minutes of cooking.

Prepare stuffing which may be cooked separately in a small oven-proof container and bake, covered with foil, about 45 minutes or rolled into small balls and baked 20 minutes.

Roast potatoes and other vegetables may also be cooked with turkey, if so add about ½ cup oil or other fat to roasting pan, boil potatoes first, about 10 minutes and score with a fork before baking.

Serve with gravy and green vegetables. Turkey buffe is also delicious served cold.

Duck and pawpaw salad

One of the new-fashioned salads is warm duckling with chilled fruit and greens. You can roast a duckling and allow it to come to room temperature and serve this salad for a new-style Christmas dinner.

750g cooked duck
Jellied turkey or duck juices (if available)
1 good-sized ripe pawpaw, peeled, seeded and finely sliced
Juice ½ lemon
½ cup walnut pieces
Curly endive or mignonette lettuce
DRESSING
2 tablespoons walnut oil
2 tablespoons safflower oil
2 tablespoons finely snipped chives
Salt
Freshly ground black pepper

Carve duck breast into thin slices and cut leg into joints. Moisten meat with any jellied meat juices. Sprinkle pawpaw slices with lemon juice. Stand 10 minutes, then drain, reserving juice. Toast walnuts lightly in a preheated moderate oven 180C (350F).

Line a salad bowl or dish with endive or lettuce and arrange duck breast slices, leg joints and pawpaw on it or arrange on separate plates. Spoon over dressing and garnish with walnut pieces.

DRESSING: Combine 2 tablespoons of the reserved pawpaw juice with oil, chives, salt and pepper. Shake well to combine. Serves 6.

Sweet and sour red cabbage

When fresh red cabbage is unavailable use a large can of red cabbage. Excellent with roast pork, duck, venison or any game.

1 small red cabbage, shredded
90g butter
1 large onion, finely chopped
2 large cooking apples, cored and thinly sliced
Pinch caraway seeds
2 tablespoons honey
2 tablespoons vinegar
Salt
Freshly ground black pepper

Soak cabbage in cold water to cover for 15 minutes or drain and rinse canned red cabbage. Heat butter in a wide, heavy saucepan or deep frying pan and fry onion gently until soft. Lift cabbage from water with hands, leaving it moist, and add to pan with remaining ingredients. Stir to combine, then cover and simmer very gently for 1½ hours — canned cabbage should take only 45 minutes. By this time, cabbage should be very tender and all liquid absorbed. (If necessary, add a little boiling water during cooking to prevent cabbage from sticking.) Adjust seasoning, and spoon into a heated serving dish. Serves 4.

Puree of pumpkin or carrot

Make full use of your microwave oven and food processor at Christmas time. These purees can be made ahead early in the day, and placed in their serving dishes ready to be reheated.

1kg pumpkin or carrots
Salt and pepper
30g butter
Snipped chives or parsley (optional)

Remove skin from pumpkin, discard seeds and cut into medium-size pieces. If using carrots scrub and

trim. Cover vegetables with boiling salted water, use very little salt, and let them cook till tender. Drain and puree in blender or food processor. Season with pepper and butter. Turn into serving dish and, just before serving, sprinkle with snipped chives. Serves 6.

Frozen plum pudding

Very easy, but full of Christmas flavors.

2 cups mixed, dried fruit
2 slices glace pineapple, chopped
½ cup brandy
2 litres best-quality chocolate ice cream
125g dark chocolate, grated
Whipped cream to serve

Soak the fruit and pineapple overnight in the brandy. Leave the ice cream at room temperature until softened, turn into a bowl, and quickly stir in the soaked fruit and grated chocolate. Pack into a pudding basin, cover tightly, and freeze until firm. Serve cut in slices with whipped cream. Serves 8 to 10.

Eggnog pie

CRUMB CRUST
1¾ cups semisweet biscuit crumbs
⅓ cup castor sugar
125g butter, melted
FILLING
1½ tablespoons gelatine
⅓ cup cold water
1 cup milk
4 large eggs, separated
¾ cup sugar
Pinch of salt
¼ teaspoon freshly grated nutmeg
3 tablespoons rum, whisky or brandy
1 teaspoon vanilla
¾ cup cream, whipped
Extra whipped cream and nutmeg to decorate

CRUST: Combine crumbs, sugar and butter and press firmly against the sides and base of a 25cm flan ring with a removable bottom. Bake in a preheated hot oven 200C (400F) for 5 minutes. Cool in the ring, placed on a wire rack.

FILLING: Soften gelatine in water and set aside. Heat milk until bubbles appear around the edge, and remove from heat. Place egg yolks, half the sugar, salt and nutmeg in a bowl and beat until thick. Add a little hot milk and stir well, then stir this mixture back into milk in saucepan. Return to low heat and continue stirring until mixture coats the back of a spoon. Dip bottom of saucepan in cold water to stop further cooking.

Stir gelatine in a basin placed over hot water until melted, then stir into custard. Strain into a clean bowl, add rum and vanilla, and allow to cool. Chill until the consistency of unbeaten egg white.

Beat egg whites until foamy, then gradually beat in remaining sugar until stiff peaks form. Fold into custard mixture with whipped cream. Spoon into crumb crust, chill until firm, and decorate with whipped cream and a sprinkle of nutmeg. Serves 8.

Note: This may be made the day before and kept covered in the refrigerator — but add whipped cream decoration just before serving.

Above: This Duck And Papaw Salad is just right for a warm Christmas Day.

Holiday party food

Planning a New Year's party? Perhaps you prefer to have a few friends or family over on New Year's Day? Certainly that is a time of the year when we are all in a holiday mood, with time to spare relaxing, drinking and nibbling on little savory treats with not a care in the world. To be perfectly relaxed over this happy time it is advisable to think and plan ahead. Have some treats made and frozen to be used when friends drop in or for a big party. Enter into the spirit of farewelling the Old Year and welcoming the New Year with some special treats you've made yourself. Use modern cooking equipment to the full — microwave, freezer and food processor — and enjoy the preparations for your own next party.

Frankfurters in blankets

These savory hors d'oeuvre may be prepared, but not baked, several days in advance, covered and stored in the freezer. Thaw at least 30 minutes before baking.

1⅓ cups plain flour
½ teaspoon salt
125g unsalted butter, cut into bits
1 large egg, beaten lightly
1 tablespoon sour cream
2 tablespoons dijon-style mustard
8 beef frankfurters
An egg wash made by beating 1 egg with 1 teaspoon water
2 teaspoons caraway seeds

Into a bowl sift together the flour and the salt and blend in the butter until the mixture resembles coarse meal. In another bowl beat together the egg and the sour cream, add the mixture to the flour mixture, and stir the mixture with a fork until it forms a dough. Form the dough into a ball, dust it with flour, and flatten it slightly. Chill the dough, wrapped in wax paper, for at least 1 hour or overnight.

Roll the dough into a rectangle 3mm thick and trim it into a strip whose width is equal to the length of a frankfurter. Spread the strip with a thin layer of the mustard and arrange one frankfurter lengthwise along a short side. Roll the dough around the frankfurter to just enclose it, leaving a 1.2cm overlap at the seam, and cut off the dough-enclosed frankfurter from the rest of the rectangle. Seal the seam on the frankfurter, cut the frankfurter crosswise into thirds and arrange the pieces on an ungreased baking tray. Roll up the remaining frankfurters in the remaining dough in the same manner, rerolling the dough scraps and spreading the dough with the mustard when necessary, and cut them into thirds. Brush the dough with the egg wash, sprinkle it with the caraway seeds, and bake in a preheated moderately hot 190C (375F) oven for 20 minutes, or until the dough is golden and flaky. Serve warm or at room temperature. Makes 24 hors d'oeuvres.

Stuffed egg platter

A lovely platter of stuffed eggs is a popular dish at any celebration. Finely shredded lettuce or parsley sprigs can be the base then arrange an assortment of eggs on the platter, replacing the eggs as they are eaten. Keep boiled egg whites in water and toppings in separate bowls until required. Choose 3 or 4 of following fillings.

8 eggs
4 tablespoons mayonnaise
1 teaspoon french mustard
Salt
Cayenne or seasoned pepper
Slivered, canned pimiento

Boil the eggs in simmering water for 11 minutes, stirring for the first 6 minutes so that yolks are centred. Plunge into cold water, lightly cracking the shells. Shell and cut in halves with a stainless-steel knife. Cut a tiny slice from the bottom of each half to make it sit on the plate.

Remove yolks and put whites into cold water to prevent drying out. Rub yolks through a sieve and mix with mayonnaise and seasonings. Remove egg whites from water and dry. Pile or pipe yolks back into whites and garnish with pimiento. Makes 12.

CRAB EGGS: Fill the egg whites with finely flaked crab meat. Mix egg yolks with mayonnaise and seasonings, pile or pipe over crab meat and decorate with a caper or tiny sprig parsley.

PATE EGGS: Fill the egg whites with a good liver pate. Mix egg yolks with mayonnaise and seasonings and pile or pipe over liver pate and finish with chopped parsley.

ROQUEFORT EGGS: Mash some roquefort cheese and beat until creamy, use to fill egg whites. Mix egg yolks with mayonnaise and seasonings and pipe or fill whites over cheese, decorate with a tiny piece of roquefort or chopped parsley.

HERBED EGGS: Stir 1 tablespoon finely chopped fresh herbs or 1 tablespoon parsley and ¼ teaspoon

Left: Greet the New Year with old favorites — with a new twist. Clockwise from the upper left are: Guacamole (recipe on page 8) with raw and lightly cooked vegetables: Gingered Chicken Wings (use recipe on page 32 and sprinkle with sesame seeds before grilling); Franfurters In Blankets and a tempting Stuffed Egg Platter.

dried herbs into yolks. Garnish with chopped parsley or snipped chives.

HAM AND CHEESE EGGS: Stir 1 tablespoon finely chopped ham and 1 tablespoon grated cheddar or blue cheese into yolks. Garnish with slivers of ham.

ANCHOVY EGGS: Mash 3 anchovy fillets and stir into yolks. Garnish with slivers of anchovy and capers.

CURRIED EGGS: Stir 1-2 teaspoons of curry powder or curry paste and 2 finely chopped shallots into the yolks. Garnish with shredded green shallots.

Devils on horseback

You can cook these in your microwave on crumpled paper for 3-4 minutes.

30g butter
1 onion, finely chopped
1 teaspoon dried sage
1 cup fresh breadcrumbs
20 large prunes, stoned
10 rashers streaky bacon, rind removed

Melt the butter in a pan, add the onion and fry gently until soft. Stir in the sage and breadcrumbs. Stuff the prunes with this mixture.

Stretch the bacon with the back of a knife, then cut each rasher in half. Wrap each prune in a piece of bacon and secure with a wooden cocktail stick. Grill for 4 to 5 minutes on each side, until the bacon is crisp. Makes 20.

Terrine of three meats

Here's something special to have on hand for New Year's Day. Serve sliced with crusty bread or hot toast and a platter of crisp raw vegetables.

500g minced veal
250g minced beef
250g lean minced pork
60g butter, softened
2 teaspoons finely chopped oregano or ½ teaspoon dried
2 teaspoons finely chopped parsley
¼ teaspoon cumin seed
Pinch of nutmeg
1 clove garlic, crushed
1½ teaspoons salt
Good grinding black pepper
¼ cup brandy
1 bay leaf
½ cup flour

Mix meats in a large bowl and beat in butter, herbs, cumin, nutmeg, garlic, salt, pepper and brandy. Pack into a terrine, level surface and place bay leaf on top. Mix ½ cup flour with enough water to make a thin paste. Place lid on terrine and seal the crack with flour paste. Stand terrine in a pan of water and bake in a moderate oven 180C (350F) for 4-5 hours, replenishing water as needed.

Remove baked flour and water crust and lid. Place a plate or small board on the meat and weigh with two tins of food. Allow to cool, then chill overnight, still weighted. Turn out on to a platter to serve. Serves 8-10.

Blue cheese mousse

From Denmark, a super-easy mousse to serve with drinks. Unmould it on a pretty platter, surround with sliced french bread and crisp crackers, and let guests help themselves. It keeps beautifully in the refrigerator, so can be made well beforehand.

185g butter
250g blue cheese
2 tablespoons brandy
1 tablespoon finely chopped parsley
Dash cayenne pepper
Oil to grease mould

Have the butter and cheese at room temperature. Beat the butter until light and creamy, then beat in the cheese little by little. Continue beating until the mixture is very fluffy (an electric mixer takes the hard work out of this). Add brandy, parsley and cayenne pepper and combine well.

Brush a 3-cup mould or basin with oil and turn the mixture into it. Cover and chill overnight to blend the flavors. At serving time, run a knife around the edge of the mould to loosen the mousse, and invert on to a platter. Makes 8 to 10 servings.

Plantation fruit compote

Fresh fruits are always welcome after rich party food and this pretty compote is particularly good when served well chilled on a summery night.

½ large watermelon
1 pineapple
1 fresh coconut
1 large can lychees

SYRUP
½ cup castor sugar
½ cup lychee syrup
3 tablespons light rum
1 tablespoon lemon juice or 1 small can coconut syrup

Cut watermelon into thick slices, remove white rind and skin and cut pink flesh into chunks, removing any seeds. Cut skin from pineapple, cut in two lengthwise, then into thin wedges. Split coconut (best done by first making a hole in the eyes, draining coconut milk, then throwing coconut on stone surface) and cut thin strips of coconut from the shell. Drain lychees, reserving syrup.

Arrange watermelon, pineapple, fresh coconut and lychees in large bowl, cover with foil and chill well. When ready to serve combine castor sugar, lychee syrup, rum and lemon juice and drizzle over fruit. If using coconut syrup, simply drizzle this over the fruit. Serves 8-10.

Note: Coconut syrup from Samoa is available in cans at many health food shops. It goes well with fresh tropical fruits or simply spooned over ice cream.

Tomato and cucumber salad

2 cucumbers
1kg tomatoes
250g feta cheese, crumbled or cubed
3 tablespoons chopped mint or parsley
DRESSING
⅓ cup olive oil
3 tablespoons white wine vinegar
1 teaspoons castor sugar
1 teaspoon dry mustard
2 cloves garlic, crushed
Salt and pepper

Thinly slice the cucumbers and tomatoes into a large salad bowl. Sprinkle with the cheese and herbs.

Put all the dressing ingredients, with salt and pepper to taste, in a screw-top jar and shake well. Pour over the salad just before serving, tossing lightly. Serves 20.

Gingered melon

A lovely light melon compote, perfect for a hot summery day; use gin for the grown-ups, orange juice for the young diners.

1 large melon, cubed (or choice of 2 different melons)
2 tablespoons honey
¼ cup crystallised ginger, finely chopped
2 tablespoons gin or orange juice
Mint sprigs to decorate

Combine the melon, honey, ginger and gin or orange juice. Place in the freezer compartment for 5-10 minutes then spoon into a large glass bowl or 6 individual bowls decorated with sprigs of mint. Serves 6.

Prawn Salad With Greens

Use a combination of greens for this salad — choose from cos, mignonette or iceberg lettuce and spinach or silverbeet and, if you can get it, peppery watercress.

½ bunch spinach or silverbeet, 1 bunch watercress and/or ½ lettuce
24 medium-large prawns, cooked, shelled and deveined
⅓ cup oil
1 teaspoon dijon mustard
3 tablespoons lemon juice
1 clove garlic, chopped
1 tablespoon chopped dill pickles
Salt and freshly ground black pepper to taste

Wash the greens in several changes of cold water. Drain and dry well. Tear the spinach and lettuce leaves in half if desired or leave whole. Trim the stems from the watercress if using. Arrange the greens on a platter.

Combine the oil, mustard, lemon juice, garlic, dill pickles and salt and pepper. Whip with a fork until well blended. Toss prawns in the dressing and arrange the prawns down the centre of the platter on the salad greens. Serves 4-6.

Summer wine punch

A good light and refreshing punch, very easy to make.

1 4-litre cask riesling
1 bottle dry sherry
1 x 1.25-litre bottle sparkling mineral water
Ice cubes
2 mint sprigs
½ punnet strawberries, optional

Mix the wine and sherry and divide between jugs. Top up with mineral water and ice cubes. Top with mint, and sliced strawberries if using. Makes about 20 cups.
Note: Any dry white wine may be used in place of riesling.

Smoked haddock scramble

My Scottish mother used to make this for New Year's Eve 'high tea' to see us through until supper at midnight. It's a good savory dish to serve for a late breakfast the morning after, too.

500g smoked haddock or other smoked fish
1 cup milk
8 eggs
Salt and pepper
60g butter
2 extra tablespoons milk
½ cup cream
1 teaspoon worcestershire sauce
8 slices hot buttered toast

Poach the fish in milk for 5-10 minutes. Drain and flake, removing bones.

Beat eggs together and season well. Melt butter in a saucepan on low heat, add the 2 tablespoons milk and eggs and stir gently until beginning to set. Stir in cream then flaked fish and worcestershire sauce. As soon as eggs are soft and creamy, turn into a heated serving dish and serve with toast. Serves 4-6.

Atholl brose

Just a wee dram to fortify you and help you welcome in the New Year.

⅓ cup medium oatmeal
About ⅓ cup water
1 tablespoon honey
About 2 cups Scotch whisky

Mix oatmeal with water in a bowl, stirring until it is a thick paste. Allow to stand for 30 minutes, then drain off liquid, pressing down well with a spoon so that oatmeal is quite dry. Discard oatmeal. Combine liquid and honey, stirring until well blended. Pour into a 750ml (3-cup) bottle and fill up with whisky. Cork well. Shake before using. Serves 8.

Coffee cream

This dessert seems luxurious but is brilliantly easy.

1½ tablespoons instant coffee
3 cups hot water
48 marshmallows
3 cups cream
Extra cream and grated chocolate to decorate

Mix instant coffee with hot water in a large saucepan, add marshmallows and bring to the boil, stirring. Simmer until mixture becomes clear. Cool, then whip cream and fold in. Pour into serving bowl. Cover and chill. Serve decorated with extra whipped cream and grated chocolate. Serves 12.

Turkish chicken

This festive chicken dish — flavored with ground and crispy fried nuts — is an adaptation of an ancient recipe.

8 whole chicken breasts
3 carrots, sliced
5 onions, quartered
1 bouquet garni
Salt and pepper
¾ cup hazelnuts
1 cup walnut pieces
90g butter
250g onions, sliced
1 cup ground almonds
500g plain yogurt
1 teaspoon paprika
Watercress sprigs to garnish

Place chicken breasts in a large heavy pan with the carrot, onion and bouquet garni and salt and pepper to taste. Cover with cold water, bring to the boil, then simmer for 20 minutes. Leave in the cooking liquid until cool, then remove the skin and remove flesh from the bones and cut each breast in 3, set aside. Reserve 1 cup of the cooking liquid.

Grind the hazelnuts and half the walnuts; set aside.

Melt the butter in a large pan, add the remaining walnut pieces and fry until gold brown. Remove and set aside for garnish. Add the sliced onions to the pan and fry until soft but not brown.

Add the ground hazelnuts and walnuts to the pan with the ground almonds, yogurt, paprika and reserved stock. Add the chicken meat and heat through gently, stirring.

Transfer to a warmed serving dish, sprinkle with the walnuts and serve, garnished with watercress and a big dish of steamed rice or Pilaff. Serves 20.

Note: If liked, heat the chicken pieces gently in stock and, when sauce is made, place chicken on serving dish and coat with sauce, then top with fried walnuts. If sauce thickens too much, adjust with a little more stock.

Above: Prawn Salad With Greens and Gingered Melon are appetising for a summer party.

● *For other large party recipes, see 'Crowds' in index.*

Index

Design by Michael Davey
Photography by Ray Jarratt
and Norman Nicholls
Front cover: Norman Nicholls
Back cover: Ray Jarratt